BREWING BATTLES

A HISTORY OF AMERICAN BEER

BREWING BATTLES
A HISTORY OF AMERICAN BEER

AMY MITTELMAN

Algora Publishing
New York

Library of Congress Cataloging-in-Publication Data —

Mittelman, Amy.
    Brewing battles : a history of American beer / Amy Mittelman.
        p. cm.
    Includes bibliographical references and index.
    ISBN-13: 978-0-87586-572-0 (trade paper: alk. paper)
    ISBN-13: 978-0-87586-573-7 (hard cover: alk. paper)
    ISBN-13: 978-0-87586-574-4 (ebook)
    1. Beer—United States--History. 2. Beer industry—United States—History. 3.
Beer—Taxation—United States—History. I. Title.
    TP573.U6M58 2007
    641.2'309—dc22
                        2007036283

Front Cover:
        Top: Bub's BBQ, Sunderland, MA. by Alan Berman
        Bottom: Smiling woman with beer glass © Emely/zefa/Corbis
Back Cover: Author photo by Andrea Burns.

Printed in the United States

This book is dedicated to the memory of my parents,
Beatrice and Louis Mittelman

TABLE OF CONTENTS

Introduction

Beer is one of humankind's oldest drinks. There is evidence that humans have been drinking beer since the beginning of civilization. In early modern Europe people considered beer essential for good health. The *Mayflower* landed at Plymouth Rock in part because they were running out of beer.

Taxes on beer have at times provided over fifty percent of this country's internal revenue and the industry today has a gross national product of $144 billion. Some 84 million Americans drink beer. This is more people than drink milk, according to some estimates. The marketing and drinking of beer are facts of daily American life.

I like to drink beer; I have done so since the age of eleven. In 1965 my father lost his job. My sister was fifteen, my brother eighteen. My mother, an eternal optimist, looked at this as an opportunity for our family to take an extended vacation, while we were all still "home" and able to travel together. The five of us flew to Denver and proceeded to drive across the western part of the United States. Each night at dinner, my father would order a beer, and I would ask for a taste.

Researching this book, I discovered that alcohol and tobacco taxes played a large role in supporting the financial activities of the federal government from 1862 to 1913 and that, in self defense, beer brewers formed the United States Brewers Association (USBA). It turns out to have been the country's oldest trade association, and it lasted 124 years. The relationship between the federal government and the liquor industry is an important part of the story, but it is the enjoyment beer provides that led me to focus on beer and brewing in the first place. Thus I highlight the German brewers who founded the USBA to ameliorate federal taxation. Those brewers were first generation German immigrants who came to America and transformed the brewing industry. The story of beer brewing in America is a classic immigrant story. Steeped in the long brewing traditions of their homeland, Germans came to this country determined to make lager beer the nation's premier beverage. They labored hard, persevered through a devastating Prohibition, rose again, and achieved their goal. Yet, as happened to so many immigrants and their descendants, at the very moment of their triumph a challenge arose. Micro-brewers and craft brewers claimed the German immigrant brewers' descendants had lost their soul on the way to the top. This morality play of beer, its evolution into a multimillion dollar business with a pervasive influence throughout American society, and the determination of micro-brewers not to let the craft and traditional aspects of brewing be lost forever are the latest chapters in beer's long history in America.

The German ethnicity of the early brewing entrepreneurs gave a distinctly modern cast to the American industry. The brewers accepted government regulation and organized themselves to facilitate their relationship with the federal government. The USBA was formed in 1862. Most American industries did not develop such cohesiveness until the 1930s or later.

In our current consumer society where extremely large businesses dominate most industries, it is tempting to see each industry as nothing more than those businesses. Almost all industries began with many small firms competing for their share of the market. All these businesses faced the rules and regulations of the national government as well as local municipalities. The sense that they would fare better if combined occurred to the brewers very early on. Thus the USBA was born. Other industries also saw the need for such unity; by the 1930s, most industries had some form of industry-wide association. For brewers, the association could provide a public face that would present and promote the industry in a favorable light, something that was very important to an industry that was illegal for fourteen years. As the brewing industry grew and consolidated, there became fewer and fewer breweries. The need for unity within the industry, however, did not disappear. This book looks at how these needs changed over time as the industry changed.

Industry does not operate in a vacuum. The United States brewing industry has been the object of federal taxation since 1862. Further, brewing, along with manufacturers of distilled spirits and wine, is one of only two economic activities which legislation has ever prohibited. The other, slavery, has obviously not returned while the cessation of liquor manufacture was only temporary.

Brewing in America has always proceeded under the watchful eye of the federal government. This book will discuss the relationship between the federal government and the brewing industry, as well as specific breweries. This relationship goes back to the origins of the brewing industry and the origins of this country; milestones include the initiation of federal taxation and the brewers' response, the growth of the industry under the system of federal taxation, the cessation of taxation with the advent of Prohibition, and the resumption of taxation with Repeal.

When liquor manufacture first resumed in 1933, the federal government expected brewers to play their historic role of providing revenue via excise taxes. The country had had an income tax since 1913, and the country's financial structure further diversified during the Depression and World War II. Although beer, liquor, and wine all helped finance World War II and the Korean War, the country's revenue no longer depended so heavily on liquor taxes. This, however, did not mean that the government would not play a role in regulating the liquor industry. This book looks at the growth and consolidation of the brewing industry in the forty year period of 1951–1991, during which taxes remained stationary. Taxes did not rise, but breweries were required to place a warning label on beer bottles, create returnable cans, and not sell liquor to people under the age of twenty-one.

The Federal Minimum Age Act, 1984, set twenty-one as the legal drinking age; brewers, large and small, once again faced the reality that the federal government possessed the power to regulate the industry as much or as little as it pleased. The federal presence in the brewing industry originated with the need for revenue. This need has persisted; much of federal intervention correlates with how much revenue the government needs. The book examines the ebb and flow of federal regulation of the brewing industry with Prohibition as its peak.

An industry is not just corporate executives or consumers. It is also people whose innovations, decisions, and actions contribute to the development and evolution of the product and the business that purveys the product. Brewers, brewmasters, workers, and drinkers all contributed to the growth of the industry. The book looks at these different elements from the early colonial period to the present.

In examining society from a historical perspective, one cannot simply take the reality of the present and read it backwards. Anheuser–Busch leads the brewing industry and controls over fifty percent of the United States market. Investigating that one fact can tell us much about society today. Yet one cannot assume Anheuser–Busch's dominance in the past. In fact, Anheuser–Busch did not even begin to achieve its current supremacy until the 1940s. This book will tell the story of that journey and will focus on all the players — even if they are not household names today.

The story of American industry since the Great Depression is one of consolidation and concentration. While the brewing industry fits this pattern, another development has been niche markets within large, highly concentrated industries. Luckily, for the consumer, the brewing industry is no exception to this phenomenon. The past thirty years has witnessed the birth of craft brewing; America now has over one thousand brewers. The new brewers who use old methods to produce their beers also operate under the aegis of federal taxation and regulation. What new issues have craft brewers faced as they built their segment of the brewing industry?

The history of the American brewing industry is a history of a battle between control and individual freedom. The federal government sought to control the industry by taxation while brewers sought the freedom to pursue their economic livelihood. Next, a battle developed over the right of society to determine healthy behavior, which led to Prohibition. Brewers and others fought for the freedom of individuals to determine their own behavior. In the late twentieth century the battle became one over choice: the desire of beer drinkers to have a variety of options in alcoholic beverages.

The story of America in many ways began with the Pilgrims and the landing of the *Mayflower* at Plymouth Rock. Beer was present at that time. The two hundred year history of the brewing industry is about to unfold. Enjoy a beer while you read it.

Chapter 1. Every Man His Own Brewer: Brewing in the United States during the Colonial, Early National, and Antebellum Periods

Beer brewing dates back to the beginning of human existence. Almost all civilizations have some record of consuming fermented beverages. Yet some countries, as they developed, turned more to wine, some to sprits. The United States is a beer drinking country. Americans drink an average of twenty-two gallons of beer a year.[1] How did beer become America's national beverage? To answer that, let us start with the making of beer.

The brewer begins with malted barley or another grain cereal. Malted barley is dried, sprouted, or germinated barley which the brewer grinds and then heats with warm water, which converts the starches to sugars. The brewer filters this "mash" to remove solids, and then boils the resulting wort after adding hops. When the wort has cooled, the brewer adds the yeast which will ferment and ultimately produce beer.[2] Hops give beer its distinctive bitter flavor; before the Dutch introduction of hops brewers used a variety of spices for flavoring.[3] Malt is an ingredient in beer, whiskey, vinegar, and malted milkshakes. Both heating and cooling are essential parts of the brewing process. Prior to the devel-

---

1 Nathan Littlefield, "Holiday Cheer: The World's Most Bibulous Countries," *The Atlantic Monthly* 294.5 (Dec 2004): 57.

2 "Post-Fordism and the Development of the Full Sail Brewery as a Quality Craft Brewer," http://www.lclark.edu/-soan221/99wlc/fullsailonline.htm (accessed March 3, 2006).

3 Gregg Smith, *Beer in America: The Early Years 1587–1840* (Boulder, CO: Siris Books, 1998), 16.

opment of artificial refrigeration, both European and American brewers required a steady source of ice to keep beer production consistent.[4]

Beer appears to have been the most common beverage in sixteenth-century Europe. The early settlers of the New World brought beer along as part of their provisions for the sea trip. Europeans routinely drank more beer than water. Most people thought water was not safe to drink, and a moderate amount of alcohol including beer also provided nutrition. During the 1520s adults in Coventry, England apparently drank seventeen pints of ale a week.[5]

The first English and Dutch settlers in Massachusetts, Virginia, and New Amsterdam all came from societies that regularly brewed and drank beer. Before the fifteenth century, English brewers brewed ale; this did not contain hops. The Dutch had more advanced brewing techniques and were the first to use hops. All the beer brewed in the seventeenth century used top fermenting yeast. There were different types of beer depending on its alcoholic content.[6]

All European ships to the New World had beer provisions for both passengers and crew. Once ashore, the emigrants were often left without anything potable to drink. This was the case in Jamestown, and the London Company, owners of the new colony, attempted to send trained brewers to Virginia to remedy the situation. There is no record of them succeeding. The settlement, however, had the minimum raw ingredients necessary to brew beer — barley and water. Like their English ancestors, in the absence of hops, they substituted other flavorings.[7]

The Pilgrim passengers of the Mayflower and subsequent settlers of New England had similar experiences. The Mayflower crews' desire to return to England with a sufficient supply of beer played a significant part in the landing at Plymouth Rock. Although the ship's original destination was the Hudson River, unfavorable winds and poor navigation forced them to land near Cape Cod. The crew feared going any further and risking depletion of their meager supply of beer. They put the passengers ashore and did not leave them any beer at all.[8]

Despite this dire situation, the colonists had come prepared with the tools, such as kettles, and some of the ingredients — hops — to produce their own beer in their new home. English ships often had a cooper aboard to protect the beer stock; the Mayflower had John Alden, a signer of the Mayflower Compact

4 William L. Downard, *Dictionary of the History of the American Brewing and Distilling Industries* (Westport, CT: Greenwood Press, 1980), 19, 157-158; Smith, *Beer in America*, 16.

5 A. Lynn Martin, "How Much Did They Drink? The Consumption of Alcohol in Traditional Europe," Research Centre for the History of Food and Drink, University of Adelaide, http://www.arts.adelaide.edu.au/centrefooddrink/ (accessed July 21, 2006).

6 Stanley Baron, *Brewed in America: A History of Beer and Ale in the United States* (Boston: Little, Brown and Company, 1962), 15-18.

7 Baron, *Brewed In America*, 4.

8 Ibid., 7.

and a figure in Longfellow's poem *The Courtship of Myles Standish*.[9] By the first Thanksgiving in 1621, the Pilgrims had learned from Samoset and his fellow Native Americans to use corn to produce a drinkable brew.[10]

Henry Adams, the great-great grandfather of both John Adams, the second president, and Samuel Adams, noted patriot, emigrated from Somerset County, England with his wife Edith to Mount Wollaston, now Braintree, in the Puritan colony of Massachusetts, around 1636. Henry's arrival in the New World was twenty-seven years after the *Mayflower* and seven years after the founding of the Massachusetts Bay Company. He was a farmer.[11]

Henry Adams immigrated to the Massachusetts Bay Colony with his wife, eight sons, and a daughter. The youngest son, Joseph, was born in 1626. As an adult, Joseph pursued his economic livelihood by farming and malting, preparing barley for its use in fermentation and brewing.[12]

The first few generations of colonists had planted barley, built malt kilns, and by 1635, were able to brew their own beer. English brewing had been women's work until the early sixteenth century. Gradually it became more skilled; eventually male artisans produced beer under the aegis of guilds. Colonists hoped to follow this model in the New World.[13]

The lack of a road system, the perishable nature of beer, and the limited number of people available to transport the final product made centralized production of beer in the new colony impossible. The colonists still wanted beer, however, and home production became the norm. Brewing took place in the kitchen, usually in the same large pot or kettle used for preparing the family's meals. Women did the brewing as part of their overall responsibility for food.

Some of the households that produced beer for their own consumption evolved into rudimentary drinking establishments or "ordinaries." Colonial ordinaries did not sell food and served only a few people at one time. When a family committed to producing beer on a regular basis for clientele, they needed a reliable source of raw materials and dedicated equipment. Even a basic establish-

9 James E. McWilliams, "Brewing Beer in Massachusetts Bay, 1640-1690" *The New England Quarterly*, 71, no. 4 (December 1998): 543-569; "John Alden," *Dictionary of American Biography* Base Set. American Council of Learned Societies, 1928-1936, Biography Resource Center. Farmington Hills, Mich.: Thomson Gale, 2006, http://galenet.galegroup.com/servlet/BioRC (accessed March 3, 2006).

10 Smith, *Beer in America*, 14.

11 "John Adams," *Dictionary of American Biography* Base Set. American Council of Learned Societies, 1928-1936. Reproduced in *Biography Resource Center*, Farmington Hills, Michigan: Thomson Gale, 2006, 6-9, 15. http://galenet.galegroup.com/servlet/BioRC (accessed March 3, 2006); Benjamin H. Irwin, Samuel Adams, Son of Liberty, Father of Revolution (New York: Oxford University Press, USA, 2002), 6-9, 15.

12 James Grant, *John Adams, Party of One* (New York: Farrar, Strauss and Giroux, 2005), 18.

13 McWilliams, "Brewing Beer in Massachusetts Bay," 543-569.

ment would have had tables, cups, brass kettles, measuring equipment, and a cask.

By the 1670s colonial drinking tastes were changing, and ordinaries evolved as well. Ordinaries encompassed both production and retail sales, since the operation was home based. As colonists were open to drinking something new in alcoholic beverages, some proprietors retreated to home brewing. Others expanded and became true brew houses. These new establishments not only sold beer to individuals for personal use, but sold larger quantities of beer to ship captains as provisions for their crew.[14]

Joseph Adams' malting operations seem to have passed down to Deacon Samuel Adams, father of his namesake, the patriot Sam Adams who was born in 1722. At the time of his birth, settlement in the New World was over one hundred years old and the production and consumption of alcoholic beverages, including beer, was thriving. His father's malt house generated enough income to provide the family with a house, orchard, garden, and a few slaves.[15]

In the seventeenth century the colonies imported rum from the West Indies; the price varied from twenty-seven cents to over $1.00 a gallon. Rum was wildly popular, even ubiquitous. Colonialists produced it entirely from imported materials. In the early eighteenth century, the Northern colonies became more directly involved in the triangular shipping trade, importing molasses from the Caribbean and erecting distilleries to manufacture rum in New England, which was cheaper than importing the finished product. The center of rum production in British America was Rhode Island and Massachusetts.[16]

Fermented beverages, however, remained popular in the Middle Atlantic Colonies, particularly New York and Pennsylvania. In both regions, farmers could take their grains — barley and hops — to a local malt house for brewing and barreling. When New York was still New Amsterdam, it had four ale houses as well as six wine taverns. Although New Yorkers became British subjects, brewing continued, and home and commercial brewing coexisted. A typical Pennsylvania brewery had a malt cellar, a storehouse, a horse-powered malt mill, and a cooper for barrel making. Also on the premises were workers' and slave quarters, barns, stables, and other out-buildings. Brewing was the product of unskilled hand labor. The beer was for local and immediate consumption since methods of refrigeration and pasteurization did not exist.[17]

---

14 Ibid.

15 Irwin, *Samuel Adams*, 17.

16 Victor Clark, *History of Manufactures in the United States*, 3 vols. (New York: P. Smith, 1929), vol. I, 139; Downard, *Dictionary*, 161; Waverly Root and Richard de Rochemont, *Eating in America A History* (New York: William Morrow and Company, 1976), 363.

17 Root and de Rochemont, *Eating in* America, 361; Clark, *History of Manufactures*, 166–167.

By 1750, most New Englanders drank apple cider as well as other fruit liquors. Producing alcoholic cider from apple juice requires no real labor; this may explain the rural shift from beer to cider at this time. Although rum became the preeminent colonial drink, the colonialists kept on drinking cider, which was relatively low in alcoholic content (about eight percent). People drank both beer and cider more as a part of their meals and less for any intoxicating properties.[18]

Alcohol production of some sort existed throughout the colonies, primarily as an agricultural adjunct; because the Southern colonies specialized in tobacco production for the market they imported rum and cider from New England. Beer was never as popular in the Southern colonies or states because of its propensity to spoil in warm weather.[19] Those colonists (North and South) who could afford it drank Madeira, a heavy sweet wine fortified with brandy. Madeira, like West Indian rum, was imported. Agriculture, shipping, and trade shaped much of the colonial liquor industry. Rum distilleries represented the only consistent and significant commercial production.[20]

Colonial Americans' drinking patterns were typical of rural, pre-industrial societies. People drank at home, at work, and in public. All celebrations and festivities mandated the drinking of rum; funerals were no exception. Few members of colonial society completely abstained from alcohol. Although society frowned on excessive drinking, the concept of alcoholism — either as disease or addiction — did not exist.[21]

On the eve of the Revolution, both rum and the tavern were ubiquitous. The colonial town tavern, the ordinary, and the frontier tavern were multifunctional institutions in a society that offered limited social services or resources. Usually centrally located, the tavern provided much-needed meeting space. Virginia held trials of interest to the general public in a tavern. Taverns also served as distribution centers where people purchased their individual supplies of liquor and "wholesalers" bought large amounts to sell throughout the countryside. Townspeople frequented taverns to read newspapers and receive information about official notices and meetings. In colonial Connecticut, "probably no . . . man was more than three miles from one, and most were far closer." In 1776 Hartford had twenty-four of them.[22]

---

18 Root and de Rochemont, *Eating in America*, 108, 362, 367.

19 Smith, *Beer in America*, 55.

20 Root and de Rochemont, *Eating in America*, 363-364.

21 Jack S. Blocker, *American Temperance Movements: Cycles of Reform* (Boston: Twayne Publications, 1989), 3-6.

22 John Allen Krout, *The Origins of Prohibition* (New York: A.A. Knopf, 1925), 40-41; Ian R. Tyrrell, *Sobering Up: From Temperance to Prohibition in Antebellum America, 1800–1860* (Westport, CT: Greenwood Press., 1979), 22-23; Bruce C. Daniels, *The Connecticut Town: Growth and Development, 1635-1790* (Middletown, CT: Wesleyan University Press, 1979), 157-158.

Although people habituated taverns to drink, colonial officials defined the social purpose of taverns as providing comfort and aid to travelers. Society tolerated heavy drinking, but the sale and consumption of alcohol did not go unregulated. Officials limited the number of licenses available to liquor dealers and generally prohibited unlicensed sales, as well as setting limits on tippling or excessive drinking. Legally recognized drinking usually took place at establishments that provided lodgings and food; colonial governments frowned on institutions purveying only alcohol. The issue of whether serving food with alcohol in retail establishments is desirable is still debated today.[23]

Figure 1: Late 18th century. Wood, paint, base metal: wrought iron. American. Photo courtesy of Historic Deerfield. Penny Leveritt Photo.

Larger cities such as New York and Philadelphia experienced different patterns of public consumption and distribution of alcohol. Anticipating the nineteenth-century drinking culture, a myriad of institutions, including restaurants and oyster bars, met the alcoholic needs of this larger and more diverse population. By 1775 taverns in urban towns in Connecticut catered to specific groups of drinkers. At the end of the eighteenth century, Philadelphia had about thirty-five taverns and "brewers' alley," a street full of breweries.[24]

Both New York City and Philadelphia were major brewing centers; this explains the large number of taverns each had at the time of the Revolution. Brewing in New York began with the Dutch when the city was still New Amsterdam. In 1613 Adrian Bloch and Hans Christiansen turned a log house into a brewery at the southern tip of Manhattan. Between 1695 and 1786 the city had over twenty

---

23 Tyrrell, *Sobering Up*, 21-23.
24 Daniels, *Connecticut Town*, 69, 150; Tyrrell, *Sobering Up*, 22; Downard, *Dictionary*, 144-145.

breweries. The owners of these establishments were English and Dutch with names such as Rutgers, Davis and Oothout. Eighteenth century breweries rarely lasted into the nineteenth.[25]

Philadelphia, which had an active tavern life, illustrates the close connection between brewers and tavern owners at this time. It was common for brewers to sell beer on credit to tavern licensees as well as receiving services such as meals in exchange for beer. This reciprocity was a forerunner of brewer ownership of saloons in the late nineteenth century.[26]

One Philadelphia concern that had a longer life was Francis Perot's Sons. Anthony Morris II started a brewery near Walnut Street, Philadelphia, in 1687. Morris was a Quaker and the second mayor of the city. In 1721, his son Anthony Morris III became the owner. Francis Perot worked in the brewery in the early nineteenth century and married into the family in 1823. He ran the business and renamed it Francis and William S. Perot. In 1850 it became solely a malt house. The company incorporated in 1887; Francis Perot's Sons Malting Company survived Prohibition but disbanded in the 1960s or 1970s. While it existed it held the title as oldest continuing business in America.[27]

Alcohol was ubiquitous and many women were involved in producing, selling, and drinking alcoholic beverages. In Philadelphia women were licensed tavern keepers, and, in the Chesapeake, during the late seventeenth and early eighteenth century, women were the primary producers of liquor for the home market.[28]

Rum's popularity in the eighteenth century caused the entanglement of the industry in the growing political crisis. In 1733, the British Parliament passed the Molasses Act which placed a six cents per gallon excise tax on imported molasses. Colonial rum manufacturers often imported molasses from the French West Indies which had a larger supply. The Molasses Act was an attempt to force the colonies to trade exclusively with the British West Indies. Colonists protested the law because they feared that it would raise the price of rum. They openly evaded the law through bribes and smuggling; rum remained immensely popular.[29]

---

25 Downard, *Dictionary*, 132; Baron, *Brewed In America*, 68; Smith, *Beer in America*, 16.

26 Peter Thompson, *Rum, Punch and Revolution Taverngoing and Public Life in Eighteenth-Century Philadelphia* (Philadelphia: University of Pennsylvania Press, 1999), 64-66.

27 Baron, *Brewed in America*, 46; Downard, *Dictionary*, 124-125, 143-144.

28 Sarah Hand Meacham, "They Will Be Adjudged by Their Drink, What Kinde of Housewives They Are: Gender, Technology, and Household Cidering in England and the Chesapeake, 1690 to 1760," *Virginia Magazine of History & Biography*, 111, no.2.

29 Downard, *Dictionary*, 123, 161; Frederick H. Smith, *Caribbean Rum, A Social and Economic History* (Gainesville, FL: University Press of Florida, 2005), 64.

Figure 2: Samuel Adams. Painting (bust) by John S. Copley. Photo courtesy of the National Archives.

Thirty-one years later, the British government attempted to enforce the Molasses Act and improve the country's economic situation following the cessation
of the costly French and Indian War. Although the new Sugar Act tax was less
than that of the Molasses Act, more stringent enforcement meant that the colo-

nialists would have to pay. The Sugar Act brought Sam Adams to prominence as he wrote eloquently in opposition to the tax. Adams was concerned that the Sugar Act represented the first shot in a battle for a widespread taxation system. He argued for individual control over economic activity against the grasp of the British government. "If our trade may be taxed, why not our lands? Why not the produce of our lands and everything we possess or make use of?"[30]

Sam had inherited the malt house on Purchase Street in Boston from his father when he died in 1748. He had not shown any previous aptitude for business and had always been more interested in politics. By the 1760s Sam worked more often as a town tax collector than at the malt house. This position increased his political connections.[31]

Although the Sugar Act did not prompt widespread resistance, partly because it predominantly affected Boston merchants, Adams' argument about taxation and representation and the rights of Englishmen would reappear in the opposition to the Stamp Act. Sam Adams' family involvement in the brewing industry, and his frequent use of taverns to promote his political activity epitomized the importance of beer drinking and production in colonial life and society.[32]

Adams and his fellow patriots often planned their activities at taverns such as the Green Dragon. He and John Hancock met frequently at the Black Horse tavern in Winchester. Adams, Hancock, and other patriots organized the Sons of Liberty and planned the Boston Tea Party at various taverns. His patronage of drinking establishments led his enemies to nickname him Sam the Publican; Sam wore the label proudly — he was an unabashed advocate of the people and of public houses.[33]

Taverns played an important role in the Revolution and the beginning of the new nation. One of the most prominent was Fraunces Tavern, at 54 Pearl Street, located in lower Manhattan. Established in 1762 by Samuel Fraunces and originally called "Queen's Head," George Washington was present in the tavern several times. New York City was the nation's first capital from 1785 to 1790, and the tavern housed the Departments of State, Treasury, and War. Today Fraunces Tavern is a restaurant and a museum.[34]

In short, beer drinking and taverns had become an integral part of American life. Once the Revolution was underway, the Continental Congress legislated

---

30 Quoted in Irvin, *Samuel Adams*, 44-45, 47; Baron, *Brewed in America*, 74-75.

31 Irvin, *Samuel Adams*, 44-45, 47; Baron, *Brewed in America*, 74-75.

32 Irvin, *Samuel Adams*, 45-48.

33 Ibid., 54; Smith, *Beer in America*, 78; Richard Brown, "Adams, Samuel," in Eric Foner and John A. Garraty, *The Reader's Companion to American History* (Boston: Houghton Mifflin, 1991), 10-11.

34 "Tavern History," Fraunces Tavern, http://www.frauncestavern.com/index2.htm (accessed August 2, 2007).

that soldiers receive a beer ration of one quart a day. The beverage was often actually spruce beer or hard cider since the raw ingredients for malt beverages were in short supply. The scarcity of brewing resources predated the Revolution; colonists had trouble procuring barley and hops throughout the eighteenth century. Home brewers in particular, were very willing to use a variety of ingredients as substitutions, including spruce, birch, sassafras, and pumpkin. General Jeffrey Amherst was one of many colonials who home brewed spruce beer. His recipe for this includes the direction "take 7 pounds of good spruce and boil it well." Home brewers probably used spruce as an alternative to hops while ingredients such as pumpkin would take the place of malt. Commercial brewing obviously stuck to the tried and true recipe of hops and malted barley, yet these flavorings found their way into non-alcoholic drinks in the nineteenth and twentieth centuries. Today craft brewers often attempt to revive the old home brew recipes.[35]

The beer ration for revolutionary war soldiers reflected, in part, General George Washington's fondness for beer. As hostilities heated up between the colonies and Britain prior to the Revolution, patriots such as Sam Adams and others encouraged Americans to "buy American." Washington, who loved porter and often imported it from England, agreed wholeheartedly. In the 1790s Washington got his porter from Benjamin Morris, a member of the Morris and Perot brewing family.[36]

Brewing was still a home-based activity for many Americans who considered a daily ration of some form of alcoholic beverage a necessity. In 1796, Samuel Child published an American edition of *Every Man His Own Brewer*. Essentially a recipe book, Child wanted, to "induce the Tradesman, the Artisan, and the Mechanic to turn their attention to the profitability of supplying themselves and families with a beverage much cheaper, and more nutritive than Porter, and yet retaining all of its good qualities and excluding its noxious ones."[37]

The ingredients to make five barrels of porter included malt, hops, treacle, licorice root, red pepper, efeintia bina, color, Spanish licorice, ginger, lime water, cinnamon, and cocculus India berries. Some of these Child recommended for their laxative effect; the use of treacle and licorice were "the principal means of rendering Porter and Beer in general wholesome and healthy." The basic recipe involved malt, hops, yeast, and various forms of sugar. It is not clear whether this

35 Smith, *Beer in America*, 26-27, 59, 62, 99; Baron, *Brewed in America*, 98.

36 Baron, *Brewed in America*, 113-117.

37 Samuel, Child, *Every man his own brewer, a small treatise, explaining the art and mystery of brewing porter, ale, and table-beer; recommending and proving the ease and possibility of every man's brewing his own porter, ale and beer, in any quantity. From one peck to an hundred bushels of malt : Calculated to reduce the expence of a family, and lessen the destructive practice of public-house tippling, by exposing the deception in brewing* (Philadelphia: T. Condie, 1796), microform, Early American Imprints, 1st series, no. 30189, 6, 7, 13.

method would have produced a pleasing beverage, but Child's main point was the affordability of the brew.[38]

After the Revolution, a discriminatory tax on spirits distilled from foreign materials affected the use of West Indian molasses and sugar for the manufacture of rum, and patterns of consumption began to change. Alexander Hamilton, the first Secretary of The Treasury, initially sought to encourage whiskey production to help domestic agriculture and to reduce the consumption of rum. Although domestic producers rejected the notion of any taxation, the policy succeeded to some extent. Rum declined in popularity, but drinking did not.[39]

In 1790 Hamilton presented Congress with a far reaching financial program designed to create economic stability and progress for the young nation. A critical element of the government's assumption of state debts was taxes on distilled spirits. Colonial legislatures had had various approaches to the taxation of alcohol: Pennsylvania and New York had excise laws and New York collected import duties on rum and other items as well. Despite a colonial familiarity with excise taxes, it was not clear that Americans would look favorably on the Secretary's finance plan.[40]

Although the Secretary thought excise taxes on distilled spirits were feasible, Hamilton and others felt brewing was a small, vulnerable industry in need of protection. Brewing was not big business and was not economically concentrated as it is today. In the early nineteenth century most breweries produced and sold beer in a local area. Output did not reach one million barrels until 1860. The Excise Act of 1791 left malt beverages alone. Hamilton also hoped that increased production and consumption of beer would lead to a reduction in excessive drinking of distilled spirits. This was an early temperance position; the joining of revenue and social control would continue into the twenty-first century. Legislative protection had little economic effect on the brewing industry, which only began to experience growth in the 1840s.[41]

Hamilton sought to protect beer, but he had different plans for distilled spirits. High consumption and steady demand meant people would purchase alcohol even if the price rose. Officials did not take into account the effect of taxes on grain farmers, the main manufacturers of alcohol. This miscalculation resulted in the infamous Whiskey Rebellion of 1793 in western Pennsylvania and North Carolina. The federal government suppressed this insurrection, but officials col-

---

38 Ibid.

39 Tun-Yuan Hu, *The Liquor Tax in the United States 1791–1947* (New York: Graduate School of Business, Columbia University, 1950), 15-16.

40 Harold C. Syrett, ed., *The Papers of Alexander Hamilton* (New York: Columbia University Press, 1961-1987), 7: 99-102.

41 Downard, *Dictionary*, xvi-xvii; Hu, *The Liquor Tax in the United States 1791–1947*, passim.

lected little revenue. A wide geographic distribution of stills exacerbated the problem. The assumption of an inelastic demand for alcohol is at the center of the internal revenue policies of most western countries. When Thomas Jefferson took office in 1801 he abolished this troublesome system of internal revenue.[42]

Thomas Jefferson had a personal interest in brewing and beer. Both he and President Madison corresponded with Joseph Coppinger, author of *The American Brewer and Maltster's Assistant.* Coppinger had a plan to establish a national brewing company in Washington. The goal would be to "improve the quality of our malt liquors in every point of the Union." Jefferson felt this was not necessary since "the business of brewing is now so much introduced in every state, that it appears to me to need no other encouragement than to increase the numbers of customers."[43] Because of the sporadic nature of adequate brewing supplies and other issues, the quality of American beer was not always what it should have been. Throughout the colonial period many people had persisted in buying imported beer from England. Jefferson sought to ease this problem and generate more customers for American beer by inviting Bohemian brewers to America to train domestic producers. There was a small brewery on the grounds of Monticello, and Martha, his wife, brewed small (or low alcohol) beer at home.[44]

As early as 1811, government officials realized the nation was again facing war. The government sought to raise revenue via excise taxes; this became a much repeated pattern. Although liquor once again provided a prime source for such taxation in 1813, tensions similar to those of the 1790s did not develop and taxes on distilled spirits remained in force until 1817. These taxes also maintained the preferential treatment for malt beverages that Hamilton had established. The federal government did not tax beer during the War of 1812. Conceiving of the internal revenue measures as temporary, Congress abolished the collection bureaucracy when it rescinded the taxes. Thus no federal governmental agency existed to deal with taxation and revenue from 1817 until 1862.[45]

This limited experience with national taxation of liquor production took place in the context of changing patterns of liquor consumption. Society disapproved of excessive drinking, but deemed rum and fermented cider beneficial under almost all circumstances, including work. Consumption ranged from 3.5

---

42 Hu, *The Liquor Tax in the United States 1791–1947*, 1, 13-35, Baron, *Brewed In America*, 134-148.

43 Quoted in Baron, *Brewed in America*, 140-143.

44 Smith, *Beer in America*, 129-132.

45 Hu, *The Liquor Tax in the United States 1791–1947*, 13-35; U.S. Department, Internal Revenue Service, *History of the Internal Revenue Service 1791-1929, prepared under the direction of the Commissioner of Internal Revenue,* (Washington: U.S. Government Printing Office, 1930), 3; Dall W. Forsythe, *Taxation and Political Change in the Young Nation 1781-1833* (New York: Columbia University Press, 1977), 58-59.

gallons of alcohol per capita in 1770 to 5 gallons in 1825.[46] Americans consistently drank large amounts of liquor during this era.

Temperance agitation began in New England around 1813 and reached its ante-bellum heyday between 1846 and 1855. The War of 1812 and a trade embargo had caused economic and social problems. Reformers felt drinking was to blame. The second Great Awakening, a protestant evangelical movement lasting from 1800 to the 1830s, also contributed to increased temperance sentiment since evangelicals sought to create a more perfect world.[47]

The American economy was moving from an agricultural basis to one of commerce. Both work and drinking patterns changed. People no longer drank primarily at home; public drinking became an issue. Drinking had been a family activity with both men and women participating. As the home became more exclusively women's domain, drinking became a male pursuit. All of these societal changes combined to produce America's first temperance movement and first experience with prohibition.[48]

In Jacksonian America, the various states regulated the retail sale of alcohol, placing license fees on dealers as a minimal control on consumption. The growing temperance movement attacked the license system as inadequate and advocated new legislation. By 1850 reformers had moved from local control of liquor sales to statewide prohibition.[49] In every northern state except New Jersey and Pennsylvania legislators enacted or popular referenda passed "inclusive prohibitory or constitutional measures."[50]

In the 1850s, no state had the police capacity to enforce the provisions of this legislation, known as the Maine Law. As a result, advocates of the legislation created extra-legal groups, ostensibly to gather evidence and swear out complaints. Unfortunately, the "leagues" often overstepped these boundaries, generating violence. Both retailers and drinkers refused to accept the legitimacy of prohibition legislation. Liquor sellers organized to fight the Maine Law and the extra-legal enforcement "leagues," and German and Irish immigrants opposed the law for cultural and economic reasons. The working class as a whole also resisted state intrusion into customary behavior.[51]

---

46 Krout, *The Origins of Prohibition*, 26-50; Tyrrell, *Sobering Up*, 16-29; William J. Rorabaugh, *The Alcoholic Republic* (New York: Oxford University Press, USA, 1979), 5-21.

47 Tyrrell, *Sobering Up*, 34; Ruth Clifford Engs, *Clean Living Movements* (Westport, CT: Praeger, 2000), 36.

48 Blocker, *American Temperance Movements*, 8-10.

49 Tyrrell, *Sobering Up*, 226.

50 *The Cyclopaedia of Temperance and Prohibition* (New York, 1891), 275–361.

51 Tyrrell, *Sobering Up*, 290-307.

In 1855 Chicago was the site of a demonstration that revealed the ongoing clash between immigrants and American-born citizens around drinking. German and Irish immigrants became incensed about increases in liquor license fees and harsh enforcement of the Sunday blue laws. John Huck, founder of Chicago's first lager brewery, led the protest which newspapers called the "Lager Beer Riot." No one lost his life in the riot but a police officer received a leg wound. A Chicago sheriff then shot a young German man. Nativists had advocated the harsh legal measures; the violence reduced public support for such sentiments.[52]

Similar violence occurred in other cities including New York when legislation imposed Sunday closings, costly liquor licenses, or restrictive legislation. In July 1857 several thousand Germans fought with police over saloon closings in Little Germany, a neighborhood on the lower east side of Manhattan. The day after the riot ten thousand people, mostly Germans, marched up Broadway to commemorate a German worker who had died in the fight.[53]

This opposition, which included sizable portions of the population, limited enforcement. Prohibitionists had linked increased social order to enactment of sumptuary legislation. When the opposite occurred as sellers and drinkers openly flouted the law, the public ceased to support the extreme prohibitionists' position and by 1860 the first wave of prohibition had faded completely. Society had also shifted its focus from the ills of drinking to the slavery crisis.[54]

From the colonial period on, beer drinkers drank English or Dutch style beer. Brewers produced ale, porter, and beer the same way with top fermenting yeast. Albany, New York was the center of ale production in the United States throughout the nineteenth century. The country's most well-known ale-brewer was Matthew Vassar, founder of Vassar College. Vassar's father, James, had migrated with seven children from England in 1797. In 1798 he raised the first crop of barley in upstate New York; three years later, James built a brewery, which burnt down in 1811. In 1814 Matthew decided to rebuild in partnership with Thomas Purser of England. They founded the firm of M. Vassar & Co., which occupied a large brewery, The Eagle, and a malt house on Vassar Street in Poughkeepsie, New York. In 1866 the Vassar family sold its interest in the company to Oliver H. Booth and J. V. Harbattle. In 1889 the Eagle produced 60,000 barrels of ale, exporting much of it to the West Indies. The company closed in 1896.[55]

52 Richard C. Lindberg, *To Serve and Collect: Chicago Politics and Police Corruption from the Lager Beer Riot to the Summerdale Scandal* (New York: Praeger, 1991): 4-5; Downard, *Dictionary*, 20, 92.

53 Barnet Scheter, *The Devil's Own Work: The Civil War Riots and the Fight to Reconstruct America* (New York: Walker & Co, 2005), 66-67.

54 Clark Warburton, "Prohibition" in *The Encyclopedia of Social Sciences*, eds. Edwin R. Seligman and Alvin Johnson (New York: Macmillan, 1930), 500-501.

55 Downard, *Dictionary*, 6-7, 200; *Poughkeepsie Eagle*, Souvenir Edition, 1889, Vassar Library, Poughkeepsie, New York.

Another prominent ale brewer was William Massey. He was born in England, where his father was a brewer. In 1849, after working in Philadelphia and New Orleans, he formed a partnership with Charles W. Poultney and Frederick Collins. Collins and Massey became involved with trade issues following the imposition of taxes in 1862. The firm went through numerous partnership changes and in 1870 Massey became sole proprietor. By 1877 William Massey & Company was the eleventh largest brewery in the nation. The brewery closed in 1894, three years after the death of William Massey.[56]

One of the country's most long lived ale brewers also had its origins in the antebellum period. Peter Ballantine, an immigrant from Scotland founded Ballantine Ale in Newark, New Jersey in 1833. By 1877, it was the nation's fourth largest brewer and the only one that brewed ale exclusively.[57]

America's oldest brewery, Yuengling, began the trend of German brewing in the United States in 1829 in Pottsville, Pennsylvania. David G. Yuengling migrated from Wurttemberg, Germany. Originally called Eagle Brewery, the firm served mostly workers who moved to the area to work in the anthracite coal fields. The company was and is family run; in 1877 it was the country's eighteenth largest brewery.[58]

Yuengling was part of the first, smaller wave of German immigration and these early arrivals began to change the brewing industry. In the 1820s German immigrants made their way into Wisconsin and Missouri and began producing *alt* and *weiss* beers along with porter and ales. Ales are top fermented beers and usually have a higher alcoholic content than lager. Porter is a dark brown ale with a large amount of black or chocolate malt. *Alt* is the German word for old; alt beer is an ale which is aged cold. *Weis* means wheat in German and *weiss bier* is lower in alcoholic content than other beers. Another name for this style is white beer.[59]

One of the German families that immigrated to America in the 1820s was the Lauer family. George Lauer and his twelve-year-old son Frederick came from Gleisweiler, Germany. The father established a brewery in Pennsylvania and

56 Downard, *Dictionary*, 117.

57 "Ballantine Ale," Falstaff Brewing Corporation, http://www.falstaffbrewing.com/index.htm (accessed January 13, 2006).

58 "History," http://www.yuengling.com/history.htm (accessed August 27, 2007); Knut Oyagen, review of *Yuengling A History of America's Oldest Brewery*, by Mark A. Noon, *The Social History of Alcohol and Drugs* 20 (2005); Downard, *Dictionary*, 221-22, 240.

59 Smith, The Early Years, 141; Klein, Bob, *The Beer Lover's Rating Guide* (New York: Workman Publishing, 1995), 6-12.

eventually settled in Reading. This journey would have particular significance for the brewing industry in the coming years.[60]

Between 1840 and 1860 over 1,350,000 Germans immigrated to the United States, primarily to the Midwest and large urban areas throughout the country. They transformed the malt beverage industry. Seeking both entrepreneurial and political freedom, many Germans sought to reestablish themselves in the trades they had pursued in the old country. They also hoped to drink and eat familiar foods. Americans, when they drank beer, usually drank ale; until the nineteenth century this term was used to describe all fermented liquor. The Germans brought lager, a different product — lighter, effervescent, and much more pleasing to the American palate. Per capita consumption of beer tripled between 1840 and 1860.[61]

Historians generally recognize John Wagner as the nation's first lager brewer. Wagner was a brewmaster from Bavaria who immigrated in 1840 and began a small home brewing concern in Philadelphia. Brewing in Philadelphia dated from the 1600s and originated with William Penn. By 1790, the city had an area known as "Brewers Alley" and over thirty-five taverns. Prior to Wagner's arrival, the city's brewers brewed ale exclusively.[62]

Bergner & Engel was another of the Philadelphia lager brewers which began in the 1840s when Charles Engel and Charles Wolf obtained some yeast from John Wagner. The firm was the country's third largest brewer in 1875, but had dropped to fifteenth by 1895. The company did survive Prohibition but was unable to compete following Repeal in 1933. It closed shortly after it had reopened. The Philadelphia beer industry suffered a similar fate. In 1879 the city had ninety-four breweries; in 1935 it had fifteen.[63]

60 Andrew T. Kuhn, "Frederick Lauer Reading's Philanthropic Brewer," *Historical Review of Berks County*, Fall 1992, The Historical Society of Berks County.

61 Will Anderson, *The Breweries of Brooklyn: An Informal History of a Great Industry in a Great City* (New York: Anderson, 1976), 17; Eric Foner, *Free Soil, Free Labor, Free Men* (New York: Oxford University Press, 1995), 246. From 1815 to 1866, thirty-nine states were part of the German Confederation, primarily a union for mutual defense. As part of a larger European phenomenon, German liberals revolted in 1848. Conservatism triumphed however and the country did not become a unified state until the 1870s. See "Germany." *The Columbia Encyclopedia*, 6th ed. (New York: Columbia University Press, 2001–04). www.bartleby.com/65/ (accessed March 3, 2006).

62 Downard, *Dictionary*, 145; Greg, Kitsock, "A Short History of Lager Beer," *German Life*. 7, no. 2 (September 2000).

63 Greg Smith, "Bergner & Engel Brewing, Philadelphia PA," http://www.americanbreweriana. org/history/bergeng.htm (accessed December 12, 2004); Downard, *Dictionary*, 20, 144-145.

Figure 3: Bergner and Engel Brewery, circa 1895. Photo courtesy of American Breweriana Association.

Although the ante-bellum prohibition movement failed to extinguish drinking, by 1860 liquor consumption had diminished from its early national high. The influx of Germans in the 1840s contributed to changing consumption and industrial patterns. The liquor industry in 1860 was not a monolith; it had several distinct and independent branches. The major product categories were distilled spirits (corn and rye whiskey), malt beverages including ale, porter, stout, and lager, rectified alcohol, and wine. Over $4 million worth of industrial non-drinkable alcohol was also produced in 1860. More than a simple and profitable way to transport surplus goods, the production of alcohol in 1860 remained primarily local and small scale. Kentucky had 216 distilled spirits establishments, more than any other state, but with a value of only $1.5 million. Economic historians often characterize liquor as a food related industry. Another such industry, flour and meal, had a value of $248,580,365, nearly four times the value of alcohol.[64]

On the eve of the Civil War there were 1,269 brewers producing over one million barrels of beer. Their product had a value of $21,310,933. The liquor industry had only a small economic significance in 1860, and according to the Census, alcoholic beverages accounted for approximately three percent of the nation's

---

64 Paul Gates, *The Farmer's Age: Agriculture, 1815-1860*, (New York: Harper & Row, 1960), 162.

total manufacturing output. Malt beverage made up less than half of this $56 million; lager accounted for only one quarter.[65]

The leader in malt beverage production was New York State with a product valued at $6,320,724. The state also had the most establishments in the country: 220. There were seven states which had production worth over one million dollars. The 951 establishments in New York, Pennsylvania, Ohio, Illinois, New Jersey, Missouri, and California obviously were the majority of the total number of 1,269 establishments throughout the country. These states also had large immigrant populations.[66]

Per capita consumption of beer tripled between 1840 and 1860.[67] Despite this remarkable growth, brewing remained predominantly a village and family operation. Brewing was not big business. The events of the Civil War and its aftermath would serve to shape and consolidate the nascent industry in a unique manner.

65 Figures computed from *American Industry and Manufacture in the 19th Century; a basic source collection* vol. 6 (Elmsford, N.Y.: Maxwell Reprint Co., 1971); Kenneth Elzinga, "The Beer Industry," in *The Structure of American Industry*, ed. Walter Adams (New York: Macmillan, 1971), 191; John P. Arnold and Frank Penman, *History of the Brewing Industry and Brewing Science in America* (Chicago: United States Brewers Association, 1933), 57.

66 *American Industry and Manufactures in the Nineteenth Century*, passim.

67 Downard, *Dictionary*, 225.

CHAPTER 2. MORALITY FOLLOWS IN THE WAKE OF MALT LIQUOR: THE BREWING INDUSTRY AND THE FEDERAL GOVERNMENT 1862–1898

From the moment Southern troops fired on Fort Sumter the federal government required large sums of money to finance the Civil War. A Special Session of the Thirty-Seventh Congress (July–August 1861) attempted to meet this need by increasing certain customs duties, imposing a direct tax of $20 million on the States, and instituting an income tax.[68]

It soon became clear that these measures alone could not relieve the country's financial burdens. Secretary of the Treasury Salmon P. Chase was hoping to raise $85 million and sent a bill to the Thirty-Seventh Congress. Congress, which reconvened on December 2, 1861, reviewed his request for a small increase in the income tax and excise taxes on manufactured goods. Distilled spirits, malt liquors, cotton, tobacco, carriages, yachts, billiard tables, gross receipts of railroads, steam boats and ferries, and playing cards all became taxable items. Signed by President Lincoln July 1, 1862, the measure became effective the following month.[69] By the 1870s Congress had repealed most of the excise taxes;

---

68 U.S. Department, Internal Revenue Service, *History of the Internal Revenue Service 1791-1929*, *prepared under the direction of the Commissioner of Internal Revenue* (Washington, D.C.: U. S. Government Printing Office, 1930), 2.

69 Ibid., 3; Charles A. Jellison, *Fessenden of Maine: Civil War Senator* (Syracuse, N.Y.: Syracuse University Press, 1962), 149; Leonard P. Curry, *Blueprint for Modern America: Non-Military Legislation of the First Civil War Congress* (Nashville: Vanderbilt University Press, 1968), 149–181; Bray Hammond, *Sovereignty and an Empty Purse: Banks and Politics in the Civil War* (Princeton: Princeton University Press, 1970), 52; Charles Estee, *The Excise Tax Law* (New York: Fitch, Estee, 1863), passim.

the liquor tax, however, has remained in effect until today. The Internal Revenue Act of 1862 marked the entrance of the federal government into the affairs of the liquor industry; it has never left.

The federal government did not regard the liquor industry as an ordinary business. Alcohol was more than a manufactured item — officials saw drinking as a luxurious, even evil, habit that deserved a heavy tax. Ignoring the mixed history of ante-bellum attempts at taxation, collection, and sumptuary legislation, Civil War legislators assumed that an excise on distilled and fermented beverages would raise a large amount of much needed revenue.

Civil War legislation of 1862 established the federal system of taxation of alcoholic beverages. At that time, the government instituted excise taxes on liquor, tobacco, and other items as well as imposing an income tax. Most of these Civil War taxes were short lived; the liquor and tobacco taxes were permanent. Until the imposition of the federal income tax in 1913, liquor taxes generated a significant portion of the nation's internal revenue and played an important part in maintaining the economic health of the country.

Taxation provided the context for an explicit relationship between the state and industry, a pattern that would become more common later in the century. For the liquor industry as a whole the relationship did not develop smoothly. Throughout the nineteenth century, mismanagement and politicization of the Bureau of Internal Revenue led to fraud and corruption. The government did not seek and could not maintain regulatory power over the liquor industry. Although several individuals devoted themselves to reform efforts, officials failed to develop or maintain long range plans for efficient tax collection. Within this context, the brewing industry developed a good working relationship with the Bureau of Internal Revenue and was able to hold the line on tax increases.

Many early temperance advocates had endorsed malt beverages as a moderate alternative to whiskey. In 1862, when Congress began debate on liquor taxation, an increasing number of Americans were drinking German lager. This style of beer was lower in alcoholic content than the usual American beer or whiskey. Despite these changes in consumption, Civil War legislators, holding the same assumptions about inelastic demand that had motivated Alexander Hamilton to tax liquor heavily in the 1790s, believed that drinkers would pay any price to continue drinking. As Justin S. Morrill (R., VT), a member of the House Committee on Ways and Means, pointed out, "England taxes spirits enormously, but has her drunkards still." At the same time that many representatives saw drinking and smoking as indulgent habits, they also believed that liquor and tobacco were "articles that were considered by all to be luxuries. . . ."[70] Although luxury and habit describe two different kinds of behavior, legislators saw alcohol consumption as a combination of the two. They did not question whether the principle of inelastic demand applied to luxuries, or the possibility that people will give up habits if they become exorbitantly expensive. Presumably luxuries are extras that people can do without if prices are too high while people with a habit will sacrifice anything to satisfy it.

Believing that liquor taxation was a "sure thing," Congressmen discussed alcohol in an almost flippant manner when they formulated the tax policy. Legislators spent several weeks debating those sections of the bill which applied to liquor, but the final law did not differ much from the original bill. The debate on alcohol taxation served more as a means to place on record the views of various members regarding liquor as a manufactured item and temperance as a moral choice, than it succeeded in the creation of a well formulated program for raising revenue via spirits and fermented beverages. Most legislators remained comfortable in characterizing liquor as a commercial item suitable for taxation.

Both the manufacture of whiskey and beer require fermentation and use similar ingredients; they are, however, distinct branches of the liquor industry. Beer generally has a lower alcohol content than whiskey; society has usually perceived of malt beverages as lighter and less harmful. Congress, as a result, placed a lower tax on beer than they did on distilled spirits. Beer was obviously neither the habit nor the luxury that whiskey was. German brewers often described their product as special and different, not only from whiskey, but from other malt beverages as well. Several members of the House also saw lager beer in this light and sought to have the tax reduced. John B. Steele (D., NY) desired to "reduce the tax on those fermented liquors that have not the intoxicating effect which strong liquors have. Of all of them, lager beer is the least intoxicating."[71]

The discussion of lager beer provoked frivolity among representatives. Some Congressmen claimed that lager had little or no effect while Samuel C. Fessenden (R., ME) believed that it did more damage than whiskey or brandy. Francis P. Blair, Jr. (R., MO) responded, saying, "I have drank a great deal of it, and never felt any effect from it." Thaddeus Stevens contributed an account of his own experiences with lager beer.

> Mr. Stevens. It would appear from this debate . . ., contrary to the general theory, that lager beer is rather intoxicating. (Laughter.) I think it is my duty to say a word . . . as I own a lager beer establishment myself. (Renewed laughter). . . . I must say that its effects are sometimes eccentric and amusing. The tavern which sells it, and which I also own, is next to my own

---

70 *Congressional Globe,* 37th Cong., 2d sess., 1861–1862: 1194, 1404.
71 Ibid., 1312–1313.

house, and . . . I have many a night looked out and seen the honest men who go there to drink beer stumble up against the fence. Once they knocked the fence entirely down (laughter). I should, therefore, designate the effect of lager beer not as intoxicating but rather as exhilarating.

A Member. It has the effects of exaltation. (Laughter.)

Mr. Stevens. Yes, sir, exaltation. . . . I drank one or two glasses once, and I must say that its influence upon me was high. (Laughter.) A constituent of mine, Othinger by name, came to see me on New Year's Day. "How are you?" "Vare goot. I have trank my twenty-seven glasses lager."(Great laughter.) . . .[72]

Perceiving alcohol as a luxury and a habit, officials discussed it as a folk custom and not an economic entity. Legislators expected both whiskey and beer to provide significant amounts of revenue, but they did not regard either branch of the liquor industry seriously. Fiscal policy reflected this light-heartedness.

Legislators found it hard to determine a tax rate that would deter drinking yet produce sufficient revenue. Aware that Britain taxed liquor at a high rate, several members of Congress wished to do the same in America. Those Senators and Congressmen who advocated temperance found a high tax particularly appealing. Fessenden stated that, "So far as ale, porter and lager beer are concerned . . . if such a duty should be imposed upon them as should result in an absolute prohibition, the revenue of the Government would rather be increased than diminished thereby." Most temperance advocates believed that removing alcohol from society would bring economic prosperity. Many representatives viewed revenue raised from liquor favorably and looked forward to a tax that eliminated drinking. Yet was this really a temperance position? Few legislators seemed aware that a tax on liquor bestowed on it legitimacy and stability the industry was unlikely to achieve on its own. Senator Henry Wilson (R., MA) did seek to eliminate license fees for retail dealers because "the Federal Government ought not to derive a revenue from the retail of intoxicating drinks. . . . It will lift into a kind of responsibility the retail traffic in liquors." The majority of the Senate did not agree with Wilson that it was putting a seal of approval on the liquor traffic. Wilson's amendment applied a standard of morality to internal revenue which contradicted the philosophy of "taxing the luxuries and vices of the community as the most proper subjects of taxation."[73]

This contradiction was just one of many that the internal revenue bill did not resolve. Congress never determined what the economic status of alcohol was or how the different branches of the business related to each other. The law, signed by President Lincoln on July 1, 1862, placed a heavy tax burden on the liquor

---

72 Ibid.

73 *Congressional Globe*, 37th Cong., 2d sess., 1861–1862: 1312, 2376.

industry but did not make explicit what the responsibility of the government would be as a result. Bureau of Internal Revenue officials were also enforcement officers, yet neither legislators nor administrators anticipated that taxation of alcohol could lead to significant illegal activity by manufacturers, consumers, and even government officials. There was far more discussion of what effect taxation would have on intemperance than of problems that could arise in the administration of the law. The economic nature of alcohol in American society was far from the minds of most legislators.

The law required distillers and brewers to pay fifty dollars for a yearly license, a tax of twenty cents per gallon on spirits, and one dollar for every thirty-one gallon barrel of lager, ale, porter, and beer. The President appointed the Commissioner of Internal Revenue to head the Office of Internal Revenue, usually known as the Bureau of Internal Revenue. The Secretary of Treasury was his immediate supervisor. The Internal Revenue Act conferred all powers and duties on the Commissioner. All other authority for the organization derived from him. Dividing the country into collection districts, the President designated, with Senate approval, an assessor and collector for each area. Collectors and assessors were the primary work force of the Bureau, having powers of seizure and prosecution to aid in enforcement.[74]

On July 22, 1862, President Lincoln appointed George Boutwell to be the first Commissioner of Internal Revenue. A two-time Governor of Massachusetts, Boutwell had been a Whig and a moderate anti-slavery man. This work plus political alliances with the Governor of Massachusetts, John A. Andrew, and Senator Charles Sumner led Secretary of the Treasury Salmon P. Chase to give Boutwell the job.[75]

Staffing and organizing the Bureau preoccupied Boutwell, who had almost four thousand jobs at his disposal. The size of the federal government expanded tremendously during the Civil War; the Treasury Department was no exception. The endless patronage possibilities caused both Boutwell and Secretary Chase to devote the first year of Internal Revenue's existence to staffing. They paid little attention to other administrative or regulatory concerns. On August 7, 1862 Chase complained that he had "very little accomplished as yet, though much, I

74 Estee, *Excise Tax*, 31, 35, 37, 42-44, 105; *History of the Internal Revenue Service*, 4-5; United States Treasury Department, *The United States Treasury* (Washington, D.C: Treasury Department, Office of Information, 1961), 15.
75 Thomas H. Brown, "George Sewall Boutwell: Public Servant 1818-1905" (Ph.D. diss., New York University, 1979), 53, 56, 59, 110.

hope, in the train of accomplishment. Engaged nearly all day on selections for recommendation of Collectors and Assessors."[76]

Six months after Boutwell took office, he had the department organized, at least nominally. The majority of employees were in the field. There were 366 collectors and assessors, 898 deputy collectors, and 2,558 assistant assessors. The Washington office consisted of the Commissioner, fifty-one male clerks, and eight female clerks. The law authorized the establishment of collection districts which corresponded roughly to congressional districts. There were 185 districts in the loyal states.[77]

In response to the initiation of federal taxation, a group of New York brewers, all German immigrants, founded the United States Brewers Association (USBA). This organization, the nation's first trade association, existed until 1986 and distinguished brewing from other branches of the liquor industry in the nineteenth century. During the 1850s wave of sumptuary and temperance legislation, many immigrants, including Germans, had participated in violence directed against local authorities. The Civil War and draft legislation had also precipitated immigrant violence. The nature of the brewing industry at this time meant that little separated brewery workers, brewery owners, and beer drinkers — socially or economically. Yet the brewery owners decided not to fight tax legislation in the streets but to organize themselves to deal peacefully and, it turns out, effectively with federal authorities.

After the Civil War, Congress repealed most taxes, yet retained those on alcohol and tobacco. As a result, the liquor industry and the state became intimately and almost uniquely connected. Long before the creation of modern day regulatory agencies, the Bureau of Internal Revenue oversaw the manufacture of beverage alcohol in this country. Because the brewers had an effective national lobby they had considerable impact on the specific ways in which the federal government regulated their industry. Although the USBA by no means represented all brewers in the United States, they did present a unified front to officials and the public. Their ideology shaped how they dealt with the government and their expectations for the future.

On August 21, 1862, three weeks after the new tax legislation became effective, John Katzenmeyer, a bookkeeper for the brewery of A. Schmid & Co. organized a meeting of area brewers in New York. Representatives from thirty-seven breweries attended. Katzenmeyer was a German banker who had fled political per-

---

76 Salmon P. Chase, *Inside Lincoln's Cabinet: The Civil War Diaries of Salmon P. Chase*, ed. David Donald (New York, 1954), 110-111.

77 *History of Internal Revenue*, 4; Schmeckebier and Eble, *Bureau of Internal Revenue* 8; Estee, *Excise Tax Law*, 310.

secution and lived in Switzerland before coming to America. Augustus Schmid, Katzenmeyer's employer, and Schmid's frequent partner, Emanuel Bernheimer, along with Katzenmeyer, helped found the new organization. Schmid and Bernheimer operated the Constantz Brewery, as well as others. A successor to this brewery, The Lion Brewery, run by their sons and nephews, was the sixth largest brewery in the United States in 1895. A fourth key organizer was James Speyers, owner of Speyers Brothers and later a partner with Emanuel Bernheimer.[78] The brewers realized that to protect their nascent industry they had to organize.

The New York brewers met more or less informally a few times, calling a national meeting of all interested brewers in New York for November 12th. Thirty-four eastern brewers attended this meeting — the first convention of the United States Brewers Association although the organization had not yet chosen an official name. James Speyers presiding, the association elected Frederick Lauer, of Pennsylvania, president of the national organization and Katzenmeyer secretary. At this convention brewers appointed a committee to propose relevant modifications of the recent tax legislation.[79]

Figure 4: Frederick Lauer, statue. Photo courtesy of Historical Society of Berks County, Reading Pennsylvania.

A brewer from Reading, Pennsylvania, Frederick Lauer actively participated in the USBA from the first national convention to his death in 1883. Lauer's father, George, owned considerable property in Bavaria but left the country for political reasons in 1823. In 1826 he erected a brewery on the site of an Indian log cabin in Reading. Frederick eventually became the owner of this brewery, one of Reading's most prominent citizens, and a well-known lobbyist for the USBA in Washington.

---

78 John Arnold and Frank Penman, *History of the Brewing Industry and Brewing Science in America* (Chicago: United States Brewers Association, 1933), 231; Gallus Thomann, *Documentary History of the United States Brewing Association* (New York: United States Brewers Association, 1896-1898), 100; *One Hundred Years of Brewing* (Chicago and New York: Rich & Co., 1903), 246-247, 540; Stanley Baron, *Brewed in America: A History of Beer and Ale in the United States* (Boston: Little, Brown and Company, 1962), 214-215; William Downard, *Dictionary of the History of the American Brewing and Distilling Industries* (Westport, CT: Greenwood Press., 1980), 21.

79 Arnold, *History of the Brewing Industry*, 233; Baron, *Brewed in America*, 214-215.

After his death the USBA erected a statue in his honor in City Park, Reading, Pennsylvania. At the unveiling ceremony, Henry H. Reuter, former president of the USBA, said, "Frederick Lauer stands there, for us, as the exemplar of true temperance, as the champion of personal liberty, as the exponent of the just claims of our time-honored trade, as its ever-ready defender and untiring promoter. Frederick Lauer felt and understood his social mission as a brewer...."[80]

The brewers met again in February of 1863 and appointed a committee "to attend to the interests of the General Association at Washington." Frederick Lauer chaired this body and before leaving for the capital he consulted with Frederic Collins of Philadelphia and Matthew Read of Read, Price & Ferguson of New York, both ale-brewers. Lauer aimed "to enlist the cooperation of the various interests connected with the business, . . ." There had been no ale-brewers at the first national meeting although numerically they still represented a majority of the industry. By the second convention of the USBA Frederick Lauer and others had recognized the importance of involving Americans in their organization. Collins and Read, along with William Massey, a partner of Collins, remained involved with the USBA through the 1860s. By 1865 all three belonged to the Association of Ale and Porter and Lager Beer Brewers, located in Philadelphia. Since the federal tax laws applied equally to all fermented beverages, both the USBA and the ale-brewers were extremely sensible to join hands. The organization remained firmly and undeniably German, yet Frederick Collins and the other Americans occupied positions as honored and respected advisors and observers.[81]

Given the new involvement of the federal government in the liquor industry Katzenmeyer and the other German-American brewers created the USBA to ameliorate the effects of taxation. Trade, price, and competition did not significantly interest the founding members of the USBA. Temperance, according to them, was not the biggest threat they faced. They functioned as an industrial group to the extent of assessing every member twenty cents per one hundred barrels of beer sold. This system of fees and income for association work continued until the USBA disbanded in 1986.[82]

The brewers' most pressing concern was a request to the federal government for a refund of tax paid on beer brewed before September 1, 1862. Many members of the USBA, including Frederick Lauer, had paid taxes on their stock on hand

---

80 *New York Times*, September 7, 1883, 4; *One Hundred Years of Brewing*, 194-195, 541, 558.

81 USBA, *Proceedings of Third Convention* (Cincinnati, OH: USBA), 1863, 6-8; Downard, *Dictionary*, 144-145, 117; *One Hundred Years of Brewing*, 237-238.

82 USBA, *Proceedings of Third Convention*, 4-5; "The History of Brewing in St. Louis," schafly.com, (accessed August 16, 2007).

on September 1, 1862, the date the Internal Revenue Act of July 1, 1862 became effective. The law dictated that manufacturers had to remove all goods before September 1; the government would tax all remaining stock. The brewers admitted that the beer had remained on the premises, making taxation appropriate within the technical letter of the law. They based their argument on an interpretation of "the spirit of the Act."[83]

The USBA claimed that they could not have removed beer brewed before September 1 without destroying it. To substantiate this, the brewers continually explained, to anyone who would listen, the manufacturing process of lager beer. Brewers made lager in the winter; they stored this "stock" beer in underground vaults, preferably directly below the brewery, attempting to maintain as cold a temperature as possible throughout the summer season. St. Louis had natural limestone caves; brewers used ice from the Mississippi River to keep the lager cold. Despite these precautions the temperature of the vaults did rise. If it rose beyond a certain point the lager fermented prematurely, disrupting the process irreparably. To the brewers, these specific, perhaps unique, conditions made it "perfectly obvious" that once they closed the vaults in April they could not remove the beer without rendering it undrinkable. Because the facts were so clear, "in most districts no tax was claimed or collected upon old beer."[84]

The German brewers also produced another beer called winter beer, which they brewed in September and tapped in October. Although both were lager beer, they asserted that winter beer differed completely from stock beer and that no substitutions could take place. Contending the above to justify a refund of the tax, the USBA built a case for the special nature of lager beer. "It might have been possible, at some risk and expense to remove ale and porter brewed prior to September 1, 1862, yet it was utterly impossible to remove lager beer prior to that date without destroying the article." Lager uses different yeast from ale and other beers. The yeast generates bottom fermentation. The yeast settles in the bottom of the vat and fermentation takes place at forty-five to sixty degrees Fahrenheit within six to ten days. This type of fermentation produces a distinctly carbonated beverage. Top fermentation which has a shorter fermentation period of five to seven days, at a higher temperature of fifty degrees to seventy-five degrees Fahrenheit produces ale, porter, and stout. Ale, porter, and stout are similar to each other but differ in degree of malt and hop content, resulting in differences of color and flavor.[85]

---

83 USBA, *Proceedings of the Fourth Convention* (Milwaukee, WI: USBA, 1864), 11.
84 Ibid., 11-13.
85 Ibid., 12; Downard, *Dictionary*, 29, 67, 106, 149, 184, 194.

Although the bottom fermentation process produced a distinctive beer, the USBA argument for special treatment ultimately rested on another aspect of lager beer production. After fermentation, as the brewers explained, they stored the beer in casks for several weeks. This storage, combined with bottom fermentation, gave German lager beer its distinctive flavor as well as its name. Lager means storage in German but storage is not necessary to produce a drinkable beer. Thus the emphatic assurances of the brewers that no fraud against the government could occur without also irreparably damaging their product were somewhat exaggerated. Yet the Germans maintained there was an important distinction between beer and lager. The German brewers felt their case was perfectly clear and obvious; government officials saw the matter differently. In December of 1862, the Bureau of Internal Revenue decided that brewers had to pay taxes on the beer they had brewed before the first of September and kept on hand. The government stated that "beer which was stored in vaults in the months of February and March, 1862, was not then, and could not become, lager beer until after September 1, 1862, and to have removed (it) from the vaults prior to that date would have prevented it from ripening and ruined it." Using the careful explanations of the USBA, officials had drawn an opposite conclusion.[86]

In February 1863, the House Committee on Ways and Means informed Lauer and his associates that they had prepared a bill refunding the tax. The final law, however, contained no such provisions. According to Lauer, the Senate had defeated the bill because, "the States, in which malt liquors are comparatively little used, have the majority." Lauer persisted but Congress did not pass legislation refunding the taxes. Although continuing to pursue the matter with the Bureau of Internal Revenue, at the sixth annual USBA convention, the Washington Committee, which had hired legal counsel, recommended that members file power of attorney with Frederick Lauer. Filing suit against the government, the lawyers eventually succeeded in convincing the Court of Claims to refund the taxes.[87]

Frederick Lauer had originally become involved in the USBA to retrieve the money he had paid in taxes and was largely responsible for this victory. Because of his personal stake in the matter, he expressed impatience with his fellow brewers who appeared to lack his sense of cooperation and had "commenced acting on their own responsibility, and the result was, that instead of a speedy and satisfactory refunding of all such erroneously paid taxes, the delay caused by want of united action has brought all these claims within the provision of limita-

86 U.S. Office of Internal Revenue, *Decisions T.D.* (Washington, D.C., Dec. 8, 1862), 45.
87 *Proceedings of the Third Convention*, 12; USBA, *Proceedings of the Sixth Convention* (St. Louis Missouri, 1866), 12; *Proceedings of the Eighth Convention* (Buffalo, New York, 1868), 12.

tion and they must prove a total loss and the innocent have to suffer with those upon whom rests the blame and guilt in this matter."[88]

Despite this apparent weakness in the USBA, Lauer and many other brewers received their refunds in 1869, seven years after they had paid the taxes. This first issue of the USBA reflects their aims in founding the organization. Lauer realized that through a unified appeal he would satisfy his own interests. Strengthening the brewing industry concerned Katzenmeyer. Both men held the same view of what was necessary for the brewing industry to survive under a system of federal taxation. The tactics Lauer and other brewers used in resolving the stock on hand issue formed the cornerstone of the new organization.[89]

The United States Brewers Association was a modern response to government regulation. In the eighteenth century distillers had responded to taxation by promulgating the Whiskey Rebellion. In the twentieth century the federal government in its attempts to cope with the Great Depression would require all industries to have trade associations. The brewers drew upon their German heritage to establish a new way for industry and government to coexist.

Although the brewers cooperated from the beginning with the government, the first few years of liquor taxation did not generate as much revenue as had been expected, particularly from distilled spirits. In 1864, the first complete fiscal year under the 1862 law, the federal government collected $30,329,149 from distilled spirits. Legislators and government officials conceived of liquor as a luxury with a static demand. The failure of the government to see beyond this simple analysis meant reduced revenue despite frequent increases in the rate. By January 1, 1865 the rate was $2.00 a gallon, ten times the rate of 1862 and eight to twelve times the average cost of production.[90]

The high rate led inevitably to tax evasion, illicit distillation, and speculation, and deeply damaged the production of alcohol for industrial purposes. Many officials hoped that the high taxes would have a sumptuary effect as well as generating income. Yet high taxes increased the consumption of adulterated liquor and did not decrease drinking.[91]

In response to the endemic problems with the liquor tax and collection of revenue, Secretary of the Treasury Hugh McCulloch, under authority granted him by the Internal Revenue Act of March 3, 1865, created a three-person Rev-

---

88 *Proceedings of the Eighth Convention*, 12, 15.
89 Delano to Boutwell, December 4, 1869, Letters from Executive Officers, 1869, vol. 4, Record Group 56, National Archives, Washington, D.C.
90 Hu, *The Liquor Tax*, 41–43.
91 Ibid.

enue Commission. The chair of the commission was David Ames Wells, author of *Our Burden and Our Strength*, an influential pamphlet about wartime finances.[92]

When a meeting of the Association of Ale and Porter and Lager Beer Brewers learned that Secretary of the Treasury McCulloch had created the Revenue Commission, the organization resolved to create its own two man commission to "obtain full and accurate information of the Excise Laws of Europe appertaining to malt liquors, . . ." Secretary McCulloch approved the brewers' proposal, and the USBA added a representative to the panel. Frederick Collins and Matthew Read traveled through Great Britain for two weeks; Frederick Lauer joined them in visiting Belgium, France, the German States, and Switzerland.[93]

Once again, the brewers behaved in an unusual and modern manner. No other branch of the liquor industry had a sufficient degree of organization to participate in determining the course of tax legislation. By joining the fact-finding mission, the brewers were able to determine their own fate.

A topic of tremendous interest for the brewers was the rate of taxation on malt liquors in the countries they visited. Everywhere they went the rate was lower than in the United States. The only exception was Austria. "Even in France, where the increase of consumption of malt liquors is comparatively of recent date and the necessities of the Government demand a large revenue, the tax is but two-thirds of that of the United States." England was a good example of the serious consequences, at least for brewers, of high taxes since "the consumption has fallen or risen with the increase or decrease of duty with the sensitiveness of a thermometer, . . ." That country had found that "ninety-four cents a barrel secures the greatest consumption and the greatest revenue."[94]

The respect and dignity European governments, especially the German states, accorded the malt liquor industry impressed the travelers even more than the low to moderate tax rates. The brewers found the situation in Bavaria particularly appealing; there, beer was "truly a national beverage, used by the people at their meals, at their places of public amusements and at their festivals, and is largely substituted by the poorer classes for coffee. . . . Malt liquor, . . . is regarded by the people of Bavaria as essential to their health and enjoyment." In Bavaria, light taxation kept the prices low and encouraged consumption. By describing

92 Herbert Ronald Ferleger, *David A. Wells and the Revenue System 1865-1870* (New York, 1942), 19-21.

93 USBA, *Report of the Commissioners Appointed by the United States Brewers Association to the United States Revenue Commission on The Taxation and Manufacture of Malt Liquors in Great Britain and on The Continent of Europe* (Philadelphia: s.n., 1866), preface. For a detailed discussion of the Revenue Commission see Amy Mittelman, "The Politics of Alcohol Production: The Liquor Industry and the Federal Government, 1862–1900." (Ph.D. diss., Columbia University, 1986), 12-102.

94 Ibid., 44, 15.

the commitment of European governments to low taxes and widespread drink-ing, the USBA hoped to inspire the American government to pursue a similar policy. If the state chose to make this commitment, lager would eventually be the national beverage.[95]

The brewers acknowledged that the use of stimulants such as liquor, tobacco, coffee, and tea, was a universal habit. However different products affected peo-ple differently; use of distilled spirits had some "fearful consequences" for society. Although beer also contained alcohol, its sale and manufacture in no way harmed the public. Doubting the efficacy of the temperance movement, the brewers as-serted that society would nonetheless become more temperate as long as "the manufacture and sale of (lager) is extended . . . Malt liquor had the advantage of being a non-Intoxicating, non-addictive stimulant. Many Europeans, including women and children, drank beer regularly and were never drunk."[96]

Although the Revenue Commission had intended to present a separate es-say on brewing in its final report, David Wells used the USBA paper verbatim. Thus the brewers' involvement had been well-advised. The final report of the United States Revenue Commission was a general overview of taxation in Amer-ica, a discussion of the tariff, and thirteen separate reports on various industries. Wells stressed that reduction of taxes was the most important task, superseding even the reduction of the debt. The Commission recognized that the most equi-table tax laws required "efficient and judicious administration."[97]

At the same time that Wells grappled with what the right rate was for dis-tilled spirits, he continued to seek the advice of the brewing industry. In October of 1865, Wells met with nineteen delegates from the fifth convention of the USBA to discuss various options for improving tax collection. The USBA commission had observed the various methods used by European governments. Most either taxed the malt used in beer manufacture or the wort while Frankfort taxed the barley. Taxing malt or barley places the excise on the raw materials necessary for beer production. The wort results when grains have been boiled, strained and rinsed. The brewmaster adds yeast to the wort, beginning fermentation. Taxing the wort makes ongoing inspection a necessity.[98]

While Wells and the committee discussed these three options, they chose to continue to collect the tax on the final product, focusing their energies on better enforcement methods. Ultimately the USBA and Wells resolved on a stamp to be

---

95 Ibid., 29, 43-44.
96 Ibid. 46-48.
97 United States and David Ames Wells, *Report of the United States Revenue Commission on Distilled Spirits As a Source of National Revenue* (Washington: Treasury Department, 1866), 44.
98 Thomann, *Documentary History*, 155-157; Downard, *Dictionary*, 219.

attached to the spigot of every barrel removed from a brewery. This system went into effect on September 1, 1866.[99]

The goal of the founders of the USBA had been to ensure the survival of the young lager beer industry against the perceived onslaught of federal taxation. The supportive attitude of European governments toward the brewing industry may have encouraged German-American brewers, unlike distillers, to cooperate with the federal government. Seeking to develop an amicable working relationship with government officials and legislators, the brewers were unlikely to engage in open tax evasion. In accomplishing this, the USBA also played a major role in shaping the country's tax system. The stamp method of collection remained the same until Prohibition. Of all the options available, this required the least government involvement in the day-to-day affairs of brewers. Regarding themselves as craftsmen, the USBA, reluctant to change time-honored traditions simply to conform to government regulations, treasured such non-interference.

One reason the brewers sought autonomy from officials was the fragile and vulnerable nature of beer production. A crop failure of either hops or barley could be devastating; transportation problems and climatic uncertainties also affected the final brew. Many industries suffer from similar problems, yet the USBA asserted that, "in scarcely any other branch of manufacturing are there so many obstacles . . . as in that of malt liquors." Storing lager for several weeks after fermentation increased the brewer's sense of both the special and difficult nature of their product. In their dealings with the government the USBA often explained, in a detailed manner, the specific aspects of lager brewing which necessitated special consideration by officials. Brewers manufactured according to tradition: those not involved in the process had difficulty understanding it.[100]

The USBA patterned their strategy for dealing with officials and legislators on "friendly advice. . . . by members of Congress not to send an attorney to represent them, but to personally present their claims, wishes and objections to the proper committees." The USBA Agitation Committee, chaired by Frederick Lauer, fulfilled this function for many years. In the 1880s, Louis Schade, an influential member of the German-American community and publisher of the *Washington Sentinel* also represented the brewers in Washington. Congressional supporters of the USBA usually came from large beer producing states or the South and included, at various times, Senator George Vest (D., MO), Representative Henry L. Dawes (R., MA), and Senator Zebulon B. Vance (D., NC).[101]

---

99 Thomann, *Documentary History*, 155-157.

100 USBA, *Report to the Revenue Commission*, 43.

101 Thomann, *Documentary History*, 100, 292, 359; USBA, *Proceedings of the 23rd Convention* (Detroit, 1883), 32-33; *The National Cyclopaedia of American Biography* (New York: J.T. White, 1892), 313-314.

The USBA also got along well with top officials of the Bureau of Internal Revenue, who encouraged their cooperation. The Commissioner often sent representatives to USBA conventions. Louis Schade first appeared in this capacity in 1871. Brewers usually limited their criticism of the Bureau to subordinates, believing "experiences have taught the brewers to expect the smallest measure of favor or justice from these subordinate officers who during many years of official routine acquire a habit of clinging to technicalities and construing any law in the strictest literal sense, regardless of its spirit or the manifest intention of its framer." Excellent at articulating issues and drafting legislation, manufacturers preferred negotiating with the Commissioner of Internal Revenue and his aides to conducting their daily business under the watchful eyes of revenue agents and collectors in Milwaukee or Chicago.[102]

The brewers' attitude towards their industry and the government significantly impeded a good relationship with local officials. The brewers claimed they were willing to pay taxes and that they had founded their organization, in part, to prevent fraud and non-compliance. Compliance meant the brewers would obey the law, but they felt that cooperation gave them the right to conduct their business without interference. The USBA always maintained that their industrial practices could not be easily explained or understood by those not directly involved in the manufacture of beer. As a result, they felt that local revenue officials should treat them with a degree of respect and understanding that might not always correspond to the letter of the law. Instead, "revenue officers often abused their official functions and power, needlessly harassing the brewers by arbitrary interpretations of the regulations and by an utter disregard of the part which unavoidable accidents and mishaps played in the management of the trade." The brewers never committed criminal acts; the exigencies of brewing explained all lapses. From the brewers' point of view it was incomprehensible why local officials persisted in persecuting model tax-payers.[103]

The USBA defined its relationship with the government as one of reciprocal duties and obligations. The obligation of the brewers was to be law abiding tax-paying producers, while it was the duty of the government to "foster, encourage and protect the interests of brewers." From 1880 to 1890, when almost $1.5 billion dollars in internal revenue primarily came from spirits, beer, and tobacco, brewers paid over $250 million in taxes. The brewers were financial supporters of the federal government; they hoped no harm would come from the connection. Thus they maintained that "the laws of the United States relating to fermented liquors need revision in such a way that without relaxing in any respect their necessary

102 Thomann, *Documentary History*, 265-267, 269, 290, 359-361, 385-387.
103 Ibid, 265.

rigor as to the due collection of the tax, they may impose no useless restrictions, create no needless obstructions to the freedom of trade, and require no vexatious and annoying interruptions to business that can safely be avoided, . . ."[104]

The brewers' identity came from the federal excise tax. Their relationship with the federal government, which made them unique, also kept their focus on the federal level rather than confronting regulation and legislation on the state level. Most large industries, such as the railroads, did not have an ongoing relationship with the federal government until later in the nineteenth century. The first federal regulation of railroads did not occur until 1887; twenty-five years after the creation of the Bureau of Internal Revenue, legislation established the Interstate Commerce Commission.[105]

Figure 5: George Ehret. Photo courtesy of Beer-history.com

The brewing industry had to expand and succeed within the context of the federal excise tax. During the late nineteenth century brewers did very well, overall, as output went from over 6.6 million barrels in 1870 to more than 39 million in 1900.[106] Per capita consumption, based on a drinking population of 15 years or older, increased from 5.9 gallons to over 23 gallons.[107] The brewers contributed over $73 million in taxes to the federal government in 1900. By the turn of the century brewing was almost a billion dollar industry.[108] Immigration, the growth of large national shipping breweries such as Anheuser-Busch and

104 Davis Dewey, *Financial History of the United States* (New York: Longmans, Green, and Co., 1903), 420; Thomann, *Documentary History*, 265-267.

105 Glenn Porter, *The Rise of Big Business, 1860-1910* (Arlington Heights, IL: AHM Pub. Corp., 1973), 38-39.

106 *Historical Statistics of the United States, Colonial Times to 1970* (Washington, DC: Government Printing Office, 1975), 689-91.

107 Downard, *Dictionary*, 225.

108 United States Brewers Association, *Brewers Almanac*, 1940, 26.

Pabst, increased leisure time for male workers, and the relative low price of beer all contributed to the industry's growth.[109]

Despite this growth most brewers in the Gilded Age did not differ substantially from the original members of the USBA. Until the 1880s most brewers distributed locally because of a lack of refrigeration and the perishable nature of their product. The nation's largest brewery in 1877, George Ehret, produced 138,449 barrels of beer, which he sold only in New York State.[110]

Ehret migrated from Germany in 1857 and founded the Hell Gate Brewery in 1866 which was located on the East River in Upper Manhattan. As an officer and trustee, Ehret was a participant in the USBA. Although Ehret added an up-to-date refrigeration system to his plant following a fire in 1870, he did not maintain the lead in brewing for long.[111]

Because of the diversity of the brewing industry and the preponderance of small and medium breweries, the USBA did not represent "big" business. Many of its leaders, however, were also industry leaders. In 1877, six of the thirteen officers and trustees of the newly incorporated USBA came from the ranks of the nation's top twenty brewers, who produced from 59,000 to 125,000 barrels. Frank Jones, a Congressman from New Hampshire, an ale brewer, and the nation's fourteenth largest brewer also belonged to the USBA.[112]

Another prominent ale brewer was Ballantine Ale; in 1877, the company brewed 107,592 barrels of ale exclusively and was the fourth largest brewer in the country. Two years later, the firm bowed to the ever growing popularity of lager and began brewing that as well. By the 1880s, this expansion helped them hold their position among the nation's top ten brewers. Ballantine consolidated all of its production at the lager brewery site in 1912 and persisted as a family owned business through Prohibition.[113]

German brewers were dependent on ice to cool their beer; brewing became the first industry to use mechanical means of refrigeration. In 1870 S. Liebmann's Sons Brewing Company, Brooklyn, New York, used an absorption machine to keep its beer cold. By 1891 almost all American breweries had refrigeration machines. The development of pasteurization, refrigerated freight cars, and advances in bottling led several breweries to distribute nationally in the 1880s and 90s.

---

109 Roy Rosenzweig, *Eight Hours for What We Will: Workers and Leisure in an Industrial City, 1870-1920* (Cambridge: Cambridge University Press, 1983), 40; Martin Stack, "Local and Regional Breweries in America's Brewing Industry, 1865 to 1920," *The Business History Review*, vol. 74, no. 3. (Autumn, 2000): 435-463.

110 Downard, *Dictionary*, 68.

111 Ibid., 68-69.

112 *One Hundred Years of Brewing.* 554, 566-567.

113 Downard, *Dictionary*, 240; *One Hundred Years of Brewing*; "Ballantine Ale," Falstaff Beer Fan Site http://www.falstaffbrewing.com/index.htm (accessed January 1, 2006).

Pabst, shipping nationwide, sold one million barrels in 1892. By 1895 Pabst led the country's brewers and Ehret's had fallen to fourth place.[114]

Philip Best and his brothers had all been brewers in Mettenheim, Germany. They immigrated to the United States in the 1840s and established various breweries in Milwaukee. In 1863, Philip Best became partners with Captain Frederick Pabst in Best & Company. In 1865, Pabst and his brother-in-law Emil Schandein bought out Best. Pabst devoted a considerable amount of energy to expanding his business and, in 1888, renamed it the Pabst Brewery. Pabst Blue Ribbon, created in 1895, was the company's signature brand.[115]

Pabst embraced technological advancements, including pasteurization and artificial refrigeration. Frederick Pabst's greatest contribution to both his own business and the overall brewing industry was in the area of bottled beer. The 1862 legislation taxed kegged beer. Before brewers could bottle beer, they had to keg it, pay the tax, and then transfer the beer to bottles. Congress passed legislation in 1890 that enabled brewers to directly bottle beer at the site of production. Pabst had heavily promoted this bill. His company doubled its bottled beer production following this change.[116]

Although the number of breweries in the United States decreased from a high of 4,131 in 1873 to less than two thousand in 1900, many companies survived comfortably producing less than 90,000 barrels of beer.[117] Ehret's continued to do well, relying solely on the large New York market, and persisted throughout Prohibition. George Ehret died in 1927, his estate valued at $40 million.[118] His heirs sold Hell Gate Brewery to Jacob Ruppert in 1935.[119]

Increased competition was one factor in the declining number of breweries. The cost of raw materials, as well as labor, rose while beer prices remained stable or declined. One way brewers attempted to deal with this competitive landscape was to use cheaper raw materials.[120]

This caused problems because brewers had promoted beer as the nation's safe and healthy alternative to liquor. When German-Americans began manufacturing lager in the 1840s, they used only malted barley and hops. In the late 1870s,

114 Barbara Krasner-Khait, "Impact of Refrigeration," *History Magazine*, March 2000, http://www. history-magazine.com/refrig.html (accessed August 16, 2007); Downard, *Dictionary*, 240.

115 William H. Mulligan, "Pabst Brewing Company," in Jack S. Blocker, David M. Fahey, and Ian R. Tyrrell, eds., *Alcohol and Temperance in Modern History: An International Encyclopedia* (Santa Barbara, CA: ABC-CLIO, 2003). 2, 471-472.

116 Stack, "Local and Regional Breweries," 440.

117 Arnold, *History of the Brewing Industry*, 74, 78.

118 *New York Times*, January 27, 1927, E11.

119 Downard, *Dictionary*, 68-69.

120 Kihm Winship, "The Evolution of North American Beer," Faithful Readers, Writing by Kihm Winship, http://home.earthlink.net/~ggghostie/faith.html#anchor601116 (accessed May 2, 2005).

brewers began adding corn, rice, and other carbohydrates as supplements. These "adjuncts" gave the beer more stability and reduced costs. With these supplements brewers created a lighter beer; flavored soda water was also becoming more popular at this time. Colonial brewers had brewed beer with whatever was on hand. Lager first found favor with the public because of its lightness. The use of adjuncts continued this trend.[121]

The brewers changed their manufacturing process at a time of heightened consumer concern about the purity of products. Investigations into adulterated whiskey raised questions about malt beverages. Several newspapers investigated the quality of beer and found it to be adulterated. The *Milwaukee News* came to this conclusion after seeing revenue collectors' books which recorded a large amount of corn in place at breweries. After commenting on the impropriety of such an investigation, the *Western Brewer* dismissed the *News* report, saying "The man who wrote the . . . articles . . . showed at the start that he did not know a malt house from a brewery, and for the life of him could not tell a kernel of malt, from a kernel of barley. . . . His article betrayed gross ignorance of the entire subject of brewing."[122]

Lager beer remained lager; brewers never advertised it as anything else. From 1862 on, the USBA presented their product as pure and unique, different even from other beers. The use of corn, rice, and other materials left brewers open to attack. Brewers claimed that "there is no adulteration of beer in . . . any . . . breweries in this country, that the trade has ever heard of . . ." Yet consumers were no longer purchasing what they had come to regard as beer. The brewers responded that they only used "pure" additives to manufacture a "pure" beer. Finally they maintained that there were many ways to manufacture beer from many different grains. "There is no more sense in talking of a normal beer than there would be in talking of a normal apple or of a normal pear, and it is just as desirable to have different kinds of beer, as it is to have different wines or different fruits. Any kind of grain, fit for human consumption, is equally so for the manufacture of beer, . . ." Lager beer was no longer an "utterly distinct" product. The practical realities of beer manufacture contradicted the main theme of the brewer's public approach.[123]

Whatever other problems the brewing industry faced throughout the latter half of the nineteenth century, it succeeded admirably in its original goal of controlling taxes. From 1864 to 1898 Congress increased the tax on distilled spirits

---

121 Downard, *Dictionary*, 5; Thomas J. Schlereth, *Victorian America: Transformations in Everyday Life 1876-1915* (New York: Harper Collins, 1991), 229.

122 *Western Brewer* 3 (Nov. 15, 1878): 751.

123 *Western Brewer* 3 (Nov. 15, 1878): 751; 6 (August 15, 1881): passim; 3 (May 15, 1878): 281; 12 (November 15, 1887): 2415; 12 (March 15, 1887): 544.

three times while keeping that on malt beverages the same. The distilled spirits industry had a completely different history with the Bureau of Internal Revenue. Despite reform efforts by David A. Wells and others, the combined forces of speculators and government spoils men dominated the federal tax policy and its administration. In the generally lax atmosphere of the Grant presidency corruption reached new heights. Using the need for funds for Grant's reelection as a pretext, mid-level revenue officials in St. Louis and other Midwestern cities set up a collection ring that cost the federal government millions in revenue from St. Louis alone.[124]

The fraud and tax evasion throughout the late nineteenth century represent not only the behavior of immoral individuals but the failure of officials to understand the implications of their policies. The modernization and bureaucratization of the liquor industry was not a conscious effort on the part of Congress and the Bureau of Internal Revenue. The Whiskey Rings that operated from 1865–1875 were one response. Officials formulated tax rates from the perspective of maximum revenue. They did not think about the indirect consequences of setting disproportionately high rates and were not concerned with controlling consumption of alcohol. As a result, fraud and speculation became irresistible. The entanglement of the administration of the Bureau with the politics and patronage of the era provided further inducements to illegal activity. An administrative, political, and legal breakdown culminated in the national whiskey frauds of 1872–1875.

In 1875, in the midst of the Whiskey Ring scandal which had lost the government millions of dollars, Congress determined to raise revenue by increasing liquor and beer taxes. Officials sought to tax malt liquors an additional dollar a barrel, bringing the rate to $2.00. Because of this threat the USBA Agitation Committee refrained from opposing increased tariffs on hops and seeking decreased duties on malt. Congress did not increase the beer tax that session, but did increase the liquor excise to ninety cents a gallon.[125]

Almost twenty years later, the USBA faced a more serious attempt to increase the tax on beer. In 1893, David A. Wells, in a report to Secretary of the Treasury John G. Carlisle, recommended raising the beer tax. Wells felt the government could not collect any greater tax on whiskey while it was not collecting as much as it might on malt beverages and tobacco. The brewers protested such an analysis and succeeded, once again, in preventing a tax increase.[126]

124 Mittelman, "The Politics of Alcohol Production," 12-102.

125 Thomann, *Documentary History*, 389-390.

126 USBA, *Proceeding of the Thirty-Fourth Convention* (Syracuse, New York, 1894), 22.

Yet the long arm of the federal government eventually touched even the relatively upright, law-abiding brewing industry. In 1898 America went to war again and once more turned to the liquor industry to help ease the financial burden. Congress decided to increase the tax on beer and leave whiskey alone. The government had recently raised the tax on distilled spirits; legislators refused to increase it any further. The brewers experienced the policy as a rude awakening from the pleasant existence they had led for over thirty years.

When not actually faced with an increase, the organization always maintained they were proud to pay their tax. In 1882 they declared that "The brewers desire to contribute their moiety towards the support of the Government, always and ever. They pride themselves upon being good tax payers and law abiding citizens; and however unusual it may appear, this class of citizens are satisfied with their tax, and do not desire to be relieved of it."[127]

Despite such strong expressions of good-natured compliance, when the brewers actually faced a rise in taxes they were less than pleased. Because so much of the public image of the USBA rested on cooperation and compliance with the government, they could do little except pay the tax. The brewers sought reassurance that they would "share the burdens of necessary taxation equitably with other citizens and other industries and should not expect to shoulder their unequal proportions. . . ."[128]

When prudent, the brewers began to agitate for a repeal of the war tax. They pointed out that they had for many years cheerfully and willingly paid the tax; they had no problem continuing this behavior. Yet, the additional $1 per barrel was a "full third of all the income derived from the last war tax." In the long run, the USBA maintained its influence with the federal government; in 1902, only three years after they had imposed it, Congress abolished the extra war tax and restored the rate to $1 a barrel.[129]

The brewers hoped their compliance with government would strengthen and perpetuate government support, leading to an increase in the consumption of lager. Such an increase would obviously strengthen the beer industry's economic position, but the USBA had a larger goal. In 1875 the *Western Brewer* proclaimed that the new journal would "preach the gospel of BEER, against the Gospel of Puritanism, of Prohibition, of Personal Thralldom." Changes in the pattern of alcohol consumption in the late nineteenth century helped confirm this ideological stance.[130]

---

127 *Western Brewer* 7 (December 15, 1882): 1951.
128 *Western Brewer* 23 (April 15, 1898): 684.
129 *Western Brewer* 23 (December 15, 1898): 2175.
130 *Western Brewer* 1 (August 15, 1875): 13.

From the end of the Civil War to the onset of Prohibition, whiskey consumption declined significantly and drinking of lager increased. In 1887, according to the *Western Brewer*, from 1881 to 1886, government receipts from beer increased $6 million and liquor receipts increased only $2 million. Concluding that, "at this rate the next decade will reduce the business of distillers down to just about the amount of alcohol required in the mechanic arts and for scientific purposes," the journal maintained that the decline in consumption of distilled spirits meant lager was well on its way to being the national beverage. The consequences of beer replacing whiskey were only positive; the brewers wished that prohibitionists would understand this. "The temperance people should be able to see . . . that beer is doing more to drive out strong drink than all their preachments and all their agitation. When the increasing power of beer drives out the potent spirits of the still, then will the era of true temperance have dawned. The old-fashioned days of King Alcohol will never return. A more benignant, temperate and healthful monarch is fast usurping his kingdom — the invincible Gambrinus."[131]

The USBA had cultivated its relationship with the federal government as the best way to protect their young industry from excessive taxation and government involvement. The association's leaders recognized the need for unity and strength to pursue their goal of ensuring economic success by preventing oppressive government involvement. An increase in the consumption of lager was essential for the economic well-being the brewers avidly desired. Thus it is not surprising that the USBA actively promoted widespread drinking of beer. The early members of the USBA were independent producers who held a strong faith in the benefits of beer to society and a perception of malt liquors as a "cheap, common, wholesale and nutritious beverage for the masses of the people."[132]

The laissez-faire ideology of the Gilded Age implied that business and the government had little to do with each other's affairs. Reality differed from this ideal; industry often called on the state for assistance with labor unrest, foreign competition, and the need for capital. The brewing industry was the first of many to seek special treatment from the federal government. In return for being "good tax payers and law abiding citizens," brewers insisted that the Bureau of Internal Revenue exert minimal regulatory impact. The brewers declared their autonomy from officials, yet they hoped that the government would protect them against the temperance movement. The USBA believed that their large annual contribution to the country's financial well-being made federal participation in the dismantling of their industry unlikely. The brewers unfortunately found themselves in a unique position since federal involvement in the liquor business

---

131 *Western Brewer* 12 (March 15, 1887): 567.
132 USBA, *Proceedings of the Fourth Convention*, 9.

ultimately mandated moral and social positions that regulation of other large industries did not require.[133]

At the turn of the century, however, Prohibition still awaited the brewing industry; the USBA continued to hold the same intertwined goals for their relationship with the federal government that had motivated the New York brewers to found the organization. Cooperation with the state would guarantee brewers the freedom to pursue economic success and a firm basis for widespread distribution of beer. By the 1890s brewers remained optimistic that beer would be the national beverage and they retained their original belief that "morality follows in the wake of malt liquors."[134]

133 *Western Brewer* 7 (December 15, 1882): 1951; 6 (May 15, 1881): 575.
134 USBA, *Proceedings of the Sixth Convention*, 6-8.

Chapter 3. Do As the Romans Do: Drinkers, Saloons, and Brewers, 1880–1898

The brewing industry had shaped itself within the context of federal taxes. Consumption of alcoholic beverages had risen since the Civil War. Although the first wave of temperance had subsided in the face of sectional conflict, animus towards liquor did not disappear. Thus, towards the end of the nineteenth century, brewers faced an ever-growing threat: the prohibition movement.

As the nineteenth century unfolded much of the temperance movement's energy was focused on the saloon. The prototypical saloon, a gleaming wooden bar populated solely by men, evolved from the 1800s on. The colonial tavern, ordinaries, and kitchen bars coexisted for several decades. As new immigrant groups poured into the cities in successive waves, they began anew in developing drinking establishments. The first stages were usually rudimentary home brewing and sparse service at a kitchen table for a few patrons. Women were always involved in these actives. In Irish neighborhoods in Worcester, Massachusetts and other similar places, men and women sat together at kitchen tables and drank beer.[135]

Saloons, pre-Prohibition drinking establishments, were similar to today's bars in that they supplied a variety of alcoholic beverages. Although we generally think of the nineteenth-century saloon as a working class, male establishment, in reality people of all different classes drank in a variety of settings ranging from the saloon to the home. Saloons were the primary retail outlet for the distribution of liquor, but people were able to purchase liquor from grocers, drug stores,

---

135 Rosenzweig, *Eight Hours for What We Will: Workers and Leisure in an Industrial City 1870-1920*, 42.

and other retail establishments. On-premises sales accounted for the majority of alcohol consumption.

The quintessential saloon, as a distribution outlet, seemed to occur most often in two situations, the frontier town and industrial city. In Chicago there were more saloons than groceries, butchers, or dry goods stores. Unlicensed establishments such as "blind pigs" and the ever present kitchen bar provided an additional 50,000 places for people to drink. The term blind pig described illegal establishments which charged admission for viewing an attraction such as a sightless animal, and then provided the customer with a free drink. In 1897, there were more than 215,000 licensed liquor dealers throughout the country.[136]

Wholesale and retail liquor and malt beverage dealers all paid "special taxes" to the federal government; fees ranged from $25 to $100.[137] The states also supplied licenses to both dealers and drinking establishments, including saloons. Prior to the 1880s, this fee was nominal, sometimes as low as $10. Beginning in 1881, states began legislating high licensing fees, starting at $500 and going up to $1,000. Some states differentiated the fees by the size of the city; others allowed saloons which only served malt liquor to pay a lesser amount. Thus the states were determined to regulate the liquor industry in a way the federal government did not. High license fees also served to intensify competition in the brewing industry: by raising the cost of a saloon doing business it furthered brewing ownership of drinking establishments.[138]

The first connection between a brewery and a saloon was usually through advertising or the distribution of free products such as glasses, trays, and wall hangings all bearing the company's name and a reduced price for the beer. In return, the saloonkeeper promised to sell only that brewers' beer. Saloonkeepers regularly violated these agreements, setting off price wars between the various brewers operating in any particular market.[139]

---

136 Jon Kingsdale, "The Poor Men's Club: Social Functions of the Urban Working-Class Saloon," *American Quarterly* 25 (October 1973): 472. At the turn of the century the United States was both urban and rural. California, Connecticut, Illinois, New York, Rhode Island, for example, were all more than fifty percent urban. However Wisconsin, which was a large brewing center, was only thirty-eight percent urban. America's population in 1900 was almost 76,000,000. See U.S. Congress, Department of Commerce, Bureau of the Census, *Twelfth Census of the United States, 1900* (Washington, D.C.) 1901.

137 United States, Internal Revenue Service, Annual Report of the Commissioner of Internal Revenue, 57th Cong. 1st Sess., House Document, 11 (Washington, D.C.: U.S. Internal Revenue Service, 1901), 4.

138 *Standard Encyclopedia of the Alcohol Problem*, ed. Ernest Cherrington (Westerville, Ohio: American Issue Publishing Company, 1924-30), vol. 4, 1541; Nuala McGann Drescher, "The Opposition to Prohibition, 1900-1919: A Social and Institutional Study"(Ph.D. diss., University of Delaware, 1964), 13.

139 Carl Miller, "The Brewer And The Saloonkeeper," under "saloons," http://www.beerhistory. com/library/holdings/saloon.shtml, (accessed October 20, 2006).

The brewers next moved to financing saloons. Most saloons operated in ethnic urban neighborhoods; the owner came from the same milieu. Lacking funds to open a saloon, the would-be owner paid a brewery $200; the brewer paid for the lease and license fees and furnished the bar. The saloonkeeper had to sell only the brewer's beer and paid a surcharge on each barrel of beer. In 1907, at least eighty percent of New York City's saloons operated under such an arrangement.[140]

Figure 6: Photo courtesy of beerhistory.com.

The glasses, trays, and other ephemera that brewers distributed to saloons in the late nineteenth century were all part of the evolving advertising and marketing of beer. Most often, promotional materials such as large pictures adorned brewery-owned saloons.[141] Anheuser–Busch was particularly innovative in this arena, associating Budweiser with a picture — *Custer's Last Fight* by Cassilly Adams. Anheuser–Busch eventually distributed over one million copies, all imprinted with the company's name.[142] Anheuser–Busch was emphasizing the masculine values of courage and capitalizing on the appeal of the West to male drinkers.

140 Kingsdale, "The Poor Man's Club," 474; Ron Rothbart, "The Ethnic Saloon as a Function of the Immigrant Experience," *Internal Migration Review*, 27, no. 2 (Summer, 1993):346.

141 Madelon Powers, *Faces Along the Bar: Lore and Order in the Workingman's Saloon, 1870-1920* (Chicago: The University of Chicago Press, 1998), 65.

142 Amy Mittelman, "Anheuser–Busch " in Blocker, et al., *Encyclopedia*, vol. 1, 43-45.

Figure 7: *Custer's Last Fight. Photo courtesy of Buffalo Bill Historical Center, Cody, Wyoming; Gift of The Coe Foundation.*

Saloons were retail distribution sites for beverage alcohol, an aspect of the industry which received minimal attention from the federal government; the national system of liquor taxation concentrated on production. Both wholesale and retail dealers had to pay nominal federal license fees. The regulation of the distribution and sale of alcohol took place on the state and local levels. From 1862 on, the federal government saw production and distribution as separate functions. No law mandated that they continue to be separate. During the last quarter of the nineteenth century, the growth of the saloon inextricably linked producers and distributors, particularly brewers. On the local level, the retail seller of liquor — the saloonkeeper — found himself in an ambivalent relation-ship with the federal government, quite similar to the position of the brewers since 1862.[143]

Municipal and local laws governed opening, closing and hours of operations for saloons. Many areas also limited the number of retail liquor establishments; municipalities received an economic benefit from liquor licenses. Sunday blue laws had prompted riots in the ante-bellum period and persisted well into the

---

143 Perry Duis, *The Saloon: Public Drinking in Chicago and Boston, 1880-1920* (Urbana: University of Illinois Press, 1983), 115-116.

twentieth century. Massachusetts, for instance, did not allow the sale of alcoholic beverages on Sundays until the late 1990s.[144]

Drinking was part of the fabric of working class life; work breaks and alcohol went together. One observer had noted, "It was a common custom among the anthracite miners of Pennsylvania to take a day's supply of whiskey down into the mines at the start of each shift." Such work customs had been prevalent in the ante-bellum period and persisted after the Civil War. Most working class and middle class men probably consumed the bulk of their alcohol off the job. The late nineteenth century saloon served as the focal point of male social life, a refuge from a "heartless" world. Providing free meals as a lure and a meeting space for unions and political groups when nothing else was available, the saloon became a community center, at least for men. A Denver worker described the saloon in the following way, "The saloon exists in our town because it supplies a want — a need. It offers [a] common meeting place. It dispenses good cheer. It ministers to the craving for fellowship. To the exhausted, worn out body, to the strained nerves — the relaxation brings rest."[145]

Although saloon culture was male dominated, it did not preclude female drinking. Most saloons had a side entrance for women who bought beer to take home. The ladies' entrance led to a back room where women could meet, eat, and drink.[146]

The male working class — primarily skilled and unskilled laborers, but not necessarily union members — expressed their identity by participating in recreational activities which revolved around drinking as a key ingredient. Beer gardens, July 4th celebrations, and dance halls all served as manifestations of both ethnic and class identities; they simultaneously facilitated the distribution of alcohol. These events were actually more public than the saloon with more women and families participating. Long before beer companies were sponsoring sporting events and underwriting cultural activities, Americans were integrating drinking with other recreational activities.

Because competition forced brewers into owning saloons, saloonkeepers gradually became employees. One exception to this was Consumers Park Brewing Co. of Brooklyn. In 1897, 1,000 saloonkeepers joined together to control the profits from both brewing and selling beer. The brewery produced 90,000 barrels in 1901. In 1913 Consumers Park merged with the New York and Brook-

---

144 Ibid., 50-52.
145 David Brundage, "The Producing Classes and the Saloon: Denver in the 1880s," unpublished manuscript, 1979, 13; Ronald Morris Benson, "American Workers and Temperance Reform, 1866-1933" (Ph.D. diss., University of Notre Dame, 1974), 18.
146 Powers, *Faces Along the Bar*, 32-33.

lyn Brewing Co., becoming Interboro Brewing Co. Interboro did not survive Prohibition.[147]

Saloons were local, neighborhood establishments; the bartender or saloon-keeper was usually of the same ethnic origins as the bar's clientele. In urban areas, particularly in brewer owned saloons, both the saloonkeeper and the saloon became political forces. Because brewers supplied the saloon with food, advertising, and attractive furnishings, many establishments became "reciprocity machines" in which favors, jobs, and votes, were all swapped for drinks.[148] Reformers disliked the connection between voting and drinking.

In the late nineteenth century, successive waves of immigrants began arriving in American cities. Many of them had come from wine drinking countries but the American taste for beer and whiskey was so pervasive that most groups adapted. Saloons primarily served beer and whiskey; they cost less than other liquors or wine. Brewery ownership led to a greater identification of beer with the saloon.[149]

In the antebellum period drinking had been ubiquitous, and all classes joined in the activity. The growing division in industrial America between public and private spheres did not stop most people from drinking. Public drinking became an increasingly working class male activity. Middle class and elite men often drank at private clubs or at home. Women drank primarily at home. Public celebrations and other public leisure activities also involved drinking.

Their conversion to beer aside, most immigrants brought their eating and drinking customs to America. One custom of Germans was family style drinking in beer gardens. Particularly in the Midwest, German immigrants attempted to recreate these establishments. Open to the entire public, beer gardens fit with the brewers' determination to promote beer as a temperance beverage and a healthy alternative to spirits. Beer gardens drew their largest ethnic crowds on Sunday, which was not only a day of rest for workers but the Christian day of worship as well. Prohibitionists objected to both the choice of day and the composition of the crowd which often included women and children. Beer gardens encouraged a style of drinking and leisure activity that would have to wait for a more gender neutral social culture than that of the late nineteenth century.[150]

---

147 Will Anderson, *The Breweries of Brooklyn: An Informal History of a Great Industry in a Great City* (New York: Anderson, 1976), 36-38.
148 Powers, *Faces Along the Bar*, 59, 65-66, 69-70.
149 Ibid., 83-90.
150 Stephen R. Byers, "Saloons and Taverns (United States)" in Blocker, et al., *Encyclopedia*, 537-539.

In many ways, Milwaukee was the center of American brewing in the late nineteenth century. The city had a very large German population and many breweries including Pabst and Schlitz. At the turn of the century Schlitz had a hotel, beer garden, and bar in the city. The brewery did not run these establishments, but provided the buildings, furnishings, and refreshments. The Schlitz Palm Garden was a very elaborate example of beer gardens; the room had black oak wainscoting and incandescent electric lights. "Palm leaves are worked into the decorations and the large windows show figures representing wine and beer." The Palm Garden sponsored concerts. It closed in 1921.[151]

Figure 8: Schlitz Palm Garden. Photo courtesy of Wisconsin Historical Society.

Pabst Brewing, as part of its attempts to become a national brewery, sought to bring beer gardens to New York City. In 1890, Milwaukee had 3,500 drinking establishments; women, primarily widows, ran about 300. Pabst sought more markets and built beer gardens in Times Square, 58th Street, and in Harlem at 125th St. He manned the gardens with waiters from Milwaukee and advertised them by paying people to go to other saloons and drinking places and say "I'm buying beer for the house! Everybody have a mug of Pabst and drink to the health of Capt. Fred Pabst, Milwaukee's greatest beer brewer." Pabst's slogan at this time was "Milwaukee beer is famous — Pabst has made it so." Pabst's competi-

---

151 Schlitz Brewing Company, "Schlitz Palm Garden" (Milwaukee, Wis.: Schlitz Brewing Company, 1896), http://www.wisconsinhistory.org/turningpoints/search.asp?id=1185, (accessed November 3, 2006).

tor, August Uihlein, owner of Schlitz, used similar words to develop a much more memorable phrase: "Schlitz — the beer that made Milwaukee famous."[152]

Milwaukee was so heavily German that visitors from other parts of the United States often felt they were visiting a foreign country. In a 1946 autobiographical work for adolescents, Maud Lovelace described her 15-year-old heroine Betsy's visit to her friend Tib, who lived in Milwaukee in the early 1900s. Tib's heavily-accented German relatives suggest a theater excursion on Sunday. "Betsy was silent, astonished. Nobody Betsy knew ever went to the theater on Sunday. For a moment Betsy wondered wildly whether she should refuse to go. I'm almost sure, Betsy thought, that Papa would say, 'When in Rome do as the Romans do.'" Later on the relatives offer Betsy some beer. Betsy, a Protestant of Irish descent from a small town in Minnesota, declines, thinking "Going to the theater on Sunday ... was concession enough to the Romans." Such cultural differences between inhabitants of different states would have serious consequences as the country moved towards a constitutional amendment outlawing the manufacture and sale of alcohol.[153]

New York City had many beer gardens in the late nineteenth and early twentieth century, some supplied by Milwaukee brewers and others more homegrown. Some were as elaborate as the Palm Garden and had ponds, circus performers, and carousels. In 1919, just prior to Prohibition, the Czech-Slovak cultural society built Bohemia Hall on the lower East Side of Manhattan. It still stands today.[154]

Although Germans were the major force in the developing American brewing industry and the Czech immigrant population was much smaller, Czech beers heavily influenced the type of beer German-Americans ultimately produced. The Czechs were pioneers in the brewing of lager; in 1842 brewers in Bohemia created pilsner which is the basis of today's American standard beer as exemplified by Budweiser.[155]

American Pilsner is more carbonated but less flavorful than European varieties. Pilsner is the lightest in color of all of the lagers and is the most popular style of beer in the world. Originally Pilsner beers had a high hops content, and the

152 "When Beer, Milwaukee Style, Was Introduced to New York," *Milwaukee Journal*, May 30, 1930, http://www.wisconsinhistory.org/turningpoints/search.asp?id=1269 (accessed November 3, 2006).

153 Maud Hart Lovelace, *Betsy In Spite of Her Self* (New York: Crowell, 1946), 127, 129.

154 Timothy Jacobs, "Last Beer Garden in New York," *Columbia News Service*, (June 22, 2003), http://www.jrn.columbia.edu/studentwork/cns/2003-06-22/221.asp (accessed November 3, 2006).

155 Timothy M. Hall, "Pivo and Pohoda: The Social Conditions and Symbolism of Czech Beer Drinking," Anthropology of East Europe Review, 21, no. 1 (Spring 2003), http://condor.depaul.edu/-rrotenbe/aeer/ (accessed November 3, 2006).

brewmaster fermented it twice. This secondary fermentation or krausening produces a foamy head, something that is a hallmark of American standard beer.[156] Czechs and Americans apparently shared similar tastes.

Beer gardens were less profitable than male-centered saloons, primarily because drinkers consumed less beer. Despite the fact that beer gardens and family-style drinking in a recreational setting were more consistent with the brewer's worldview, the economics of the liquor industry won out. The saloon was ultimately an economic institution and the best choice for brewers to distribute their product with a reasonable expectation of large sales.[157]

The work force of the brewing industry was obviously working class. What meaning did beer, alcohol, and the saloon have to them? How did this change over the nineteenth century as the saloon became the face of drink and the drink business?

Both brewing and distilling require workers for the stages of grain handling, mashing, fermentation, storage, and delivery. After the Civil War, this labor was primarily unskilled and most likely ethnic. Like most industrial work sites, distilleries remained unorganized until the 1930s.[158]

In 1860 an average brewery in New York State employed eight people and paid a wage of about $347 a year. New York produced the most malt beverages and had higher wages than most of the country. Wages ranged from about $240 to $360 a year. Brewery workers spent at least fourteen hours a day, seven days a week in a brewery.

New York State had 220 breweries which employed 1,703 men and 2 women. The forty-six breweries of New York City produced beer worth over $2 million. The workforce at an average establishment was twelve people. In the United States as a whole there were 1,269 breweries which employed 6,443 people (twenty-one women). An average brewery employed five people. In 1860 the annual cost of labor for the country's 1,269 breweries was $2,305,970. In Georgia, where there was only one brewery, with four employees, the annual average wage was $240.[159]

How did these wages compare to those of other workers in other industries? Wages as well as conditions of employment fluctuated greatly both during and immediately after the war. In 1868, some mechanics in New York earned $25 a week; workers with similar jobs in the United States armory in Springfield, Mas-

---

156 Ibid.; Klein, *The Beer Lover's Rating Guide*, 10. Contemporary Czech pilsner has high barley content while American brewers use corn or rice to produce the much desired head.

157 Byers, "Saloons," 537-539.

158 William Downard, *Dictionary of the History of the American Brewing and Distilling Industries* (Westport, CT: Greenwood Press., 1980), 211, 34-35.

159 *American Industry and Manufactures in the Nineteenth Century*, vol. 6 (Washington, D.C., 1865, reprint New York, 1970), passim.

sachusetts received $2 to $3 a day. Menial laborers in New York earned no more than $15 a week. Highly skilled workers in Pittsburgh glass factories received $250 a month.[160] Workers in the liquor industry thus fell towards the bottom of the ladder; they possessed neither high wages nor many skills.

Although the wages of brewery workers were not the lowest, their working conditions were often arduous. Brewing involved both high and low temperatures. Workers spent fourteen to eighteen hours in a brewery; they often slept on the premises. "It might be said that they were always working except when they were asleep. . . . In many cases they worked until ten o'clock, and were awakened at one to start work again."[161]

The Civil War fostered economic expansion in the North, but some benefited more than others. From 1860 to 1868, wages rose between sixty and seventy percent while the cost of living rose seventy-eight percent. Military production had expanded the economy of the North tremendously but rapid demobilization caused an equally dramatic contraction. A million people were out of work immediately following the war; chronic under and unemployment plagued the country throughout the remainder of the century. For workers, the Civil War, which brought new job opportunities, also brought greenbacks, taxes, and ultimately unemployment. Yet the Civil War did usher in a period of great economic growth for America, and the brewing industry shared in that growth.[162]

In the 1870s, the number of breweries in America reached a record 4,131 and by 1890, output had risen to over 227 million barrels from 3 million at the end of the war. Although there were breweries throughout the country, the business concentrated in urban areas. Lack of appropriate refrigeration made far flung distribution of beer impossible. Demographics also played an important role. Urban areas, with their large ethnic populations, particularly German, were the perfect marketplace for brewers. As a result, certain cities, such as New York, Milwaukee, and Chicago became brewing centers. In the South beer drinking and brewing did not really take hold perhaps because of the small immigrant population there as well as persistent illegal distilling or moonshine.[163]

Urban areas had the most breweries and also the most workers. Cities became the focal point of emerging labor and union activity. In 1886 the newly founded United Brewery Workers (UBW) engaged in a boycott of Peter Doe-

160 Victor Clark, *History of Manufactures in the United States*, 3 vols. (New York: P. Smith, 1929), 2:143; Ira Cross, *A History of the Labor Movement in California* (Berkeley, CA: University of California Press, 1935), 190.

161 Hermann Schlüter, *The Brewing Industry and the Brewery Workers Movement in America* (1910; repr., New York: B. Franklin, 1970), 92-93.

162 Clark, *History of Manufactures*, 22:143.

163 For information about moonshine and illicit distilling in the South after the Civil War, see Wilbur R. Miller, *Revenuers & Moonshiners: Enforcing Federal Liquor Law in the Mountain South, 1865-1900* (Chapel Hill: University of North Carolina Press, 1991).

gler Brewery, Brooklyn, New York. Boycotts, as well as union labels, were major weapons in ongoing union struggles with the brewers. A mass product such as beer befitted the use of both strategies. Working-class drinkers contributed greatly to the sales of malt liquors, which they purchased from local brewers. The boycott had originated in Ireland around issues of land and rent. Irish-American radicals adopted the concept of social ostracism which was the foundation of the tactic. The boycott was one element in the social adaptation of immigrants to their new world. Boycotts, parades, and mass demonstrations "provided opportunities for immigrant workers to participate in familiar patterns of protest and recreation."[164] Pervasive in labor struggles in the 1880s, boycotts, and the practice of social ostracism often went hand in hand. Both worked best in neighborhoods and small communities and helped foster consumer consciousness. The UBW strove to increase class consciousness.

The new union successfully negotiated a contract with the Brewers Association in the spring of 1886 which gave workers a weekly wage of $15 to $18 for a six day week, 10 hours a day. The young organization had certainly gained an "extraordinary victory."[165]

The year 1886 was good for brewery workers nationwide as unions developed in Baltimore, Chicago, New Jersey, St. Louis, Philadelphia, Detroit, San Francisco, and Buffalo. Many of the unions operated under the auspices of the Knights of Labor. In California Alfred Fuhrman, a sailor and the Federated Trades Council organized the Brewers' and Maltsters' Union of the Pacific Coast. Through a boycott of one San Francisco brewery, Fuhrman organized workers in five companies and achieved support throughout the Coast area.[166]

Brewery workers used tactics like the boycott and the union label to encourage workers from other industries to support their struggles with management. The UBW sought to build a strong union and to fully legitimate organized labor in the brewing industry. Towards that end, in conjunction with boycotts, the brewery workers and other unions promoted the concept of "union labor" which implied cooperation with pro-union management against anti-union owners. The average brewery laborer had a hard and grueling life before the advent of the union movement yet the UBW won changes in working conditions, hours, and wages more easily than they did advancements in recognition and jurisdiction. The early successes of the union in gaining ten hour days and increased wages in

164 Michael A. Gordon, "The Labor Boycott in New York City, 1880-1886," *Labor History* 16 (Spring 1975): 194.

165 Schlüter, *The Brewing Industry* 117; Gordon, "The Labor Boycott in New York City," 213.

166 Schlüter, *The Brewing Industry*, 117-127; Ira Cross, *A History of the Labor Movement in California*, 191-192.

various cities served as the prelude to ten years of fighting with the brewers and the Brewers Association for union legitimacy.

Many unions formed in the 1880s evolved from strong craft heritages and traditions. Brewing, in many ways, was a traditional occupation; brewers certainly sought to present their business to the public in this light. Yet, at least since the Civil War, brewing required primarily unskilled and thus replaceable labor. The second convention of the UBW recognized this fact of life. Although the union strongly supported the hiring of experienced brewery workers over inexperienced ones, the convention proposed an inclusive union for all workers and trades in the industry; an industrial union. Organizing all the workers in an industry made it more difficult for management to break strikes. Thus the UBW consisted of beer drivers, maltsters, firemen, and engineers, and became the first industrial union in the country to survive. This commitment to industrial unionism would lead to chronic jurisdictional difficulties with other unions and the American Federation of Labor (AFL). The union sought to organize all workers in the industry, yet it did not consider distillery workers as part of its jurisdiction. On this point the UBW agreed with the brewers' view of division within the liquor industry.[167]

Many different people made up the workforce of a brewery. Because beer is a food and consists of raw ingredient combined, heated, and fermented into the final drink, the brewmaster was an essential part of a brewery. In 1887 brewmasters joined together to from the Master Brewers Association of the Americas (MBAA). This organization still exists and has always focused on the technical and scientific aspects of brewing. The MBAA was not a union, but a trade association. Although most brewmasters were employees, they saw themselves as craftsmen and technicians not workers. This segment of the brewing industry generated schools and technical advancements as well as an ongoing connection to international brewing communities. Their legacy informs home and craft brewers today.

Saloonkeepers were also part of the liquor industry's workforce. As brewery ownership of saloons intensified and saloonkeepers increasingly became employees, these workers felt the need to combine. Unions often used saloons as meeting places so it was not unexpected for bartenders to form the Hotel and Restaurant Employees and Bartenders Union in 1891. The union belonged to the AFL and was craft based.[168]

---

167 James Morris, *Conflict Within the AFL, A Study of Craft Versus Industrial Unionism, 1901–1938* (Ithaca, N.Y.: Cornell University Press, 1958), 20. Another name for the UBW was National Union of United Brewery Workmen of the United States.

168 Amy Mittelman, "Labor in the U.S. Liquor Industry" in Blocker, et. al., *Encyclopedia*, vol. 1, 356-358. For more information about the present day union see Unite Here, http://unite-

Figure 9: Union House and Union Bar cards used in earlier years. Photo courtesy of UniteHere.

The United Brewery Workers saw their struggle within the brewing industry as part of a larger struggle for social justice for working people. To promote their goals, they established a journal shortly after forming the national union.

The first issue of *Brauer–Zeitung* was published on October 2, 1886. Originally a German language newspaper, the journal added an English page in 1891.[169]

The *Brauer–Zeitung* or *Brewery Worker* was committed to socialism; in 1893, it declared "the abolition of classes and class government is our object." The union had an international as well as industrial focus and established reciprocal agreements with German, Austrian, and Swiss unions; Canadian locals eventually became part of the national union. The UBW and its journal saw all workers as equal in the struggle against capitalism and thus were committed to fighting discrimination on all levels. For the journal, "the internationality of labor (was) the first principle."[170]

The UBW was not a typical late nineteenth century union. Neither its socialist ideology nor its industrial unionism was within the mainstream. The work they did also made them increasingly marginal. As the temperance movement grew some workers were drawn to it. The saloon was the symbol of the relationship between working people and alcohol, and also often served as a meeting place for unions. Despite the concrete and practical purposes the saloon served for organized labor, some labor leaders did not believe there should be such a strong connection between liquor and workers. In a survey of thirty-nine craft unions conducted by the Bureau of Economic Research in 1901, nine firmly opposed the saloon, including the Seamen's Union, Tailors and Typographers. The Brotherhood of Locomotive Engineers, founded in 1868, had from its inception sought to instill temperance values in its members. The motto of the union was "Sobriety, Truth, Justice, and Morality." The Brotherhood denied membership both to habitual drunks and saloon keepers. Other unions in the railway industry were also strongly pro-temperance. All these groups sought to insure their jobs by impressing management with the reliability and responsibility of its workers. Towards this end, the Brotherhood of Locomotive Engineers "deliberately chose to cooperate with the companies. The brotherhood maintained its own blacklist with the consent and approval of the railway managers and officials."[171]

Anti-saloon sentiments differed from compulsory prohibition sentiments although the temperance movement of the late nineteenth and early twentieth century often blurred the distinction. Thus socialists, labor leaders, and social reformers could all pursue an analysis of liquor selling consonant with anti-monopoly thought. The left wing movement for prohibition attacked the "rum-seller" instead of the drinker. Prohibition did and does mean the cessation of

169 Schlüter, *The Brewing Industry*, 130 -131.
170 *Brewery Worker* 7 (May 21, 1892):1; 9 (April 28, 1894): 1; 7 (April 23, 1892): 1; Schlüter, *The Brewing Industry*, 236.
171 Benson, "American Workers and Temperance Reform," 82.

liquor production and liquor consumption. Most labor leaders never felt comfortable with compulsory prohibition because they rejected state intrusion into their private lives.

In spite of an active temperance movement in the 1880s and 1890s, opposing it was not a consistent priority for either the United Brewery Workers or the United States Brewers Association. As we have seen, both organizations expended a significant amount of energy on labor control and union recognition. Changing economic conditions within their industry, equally important to workers, also preoccupied the brewers. A self-conscious alliance between the union and the brewers to combat prohibition forces did not really develop until about 1913.

The commitment of the UBW to industrial unionism as well as its commitment to socialism made this union unusual. These ideological principles connected it to the larger international labor and socialist movements. One figure from those movements became the historian of the brewery workers. Hermann Schlüter, author of *The Brewing Industry and the Brewery Workers Movement in America*, was from Holstein, Germany and lived in Chicago from 1873 to 1876. He helped found the Workers Party of Illinois, worked on its newspaper, and was secretary of the Chicago branch of the International Working Men's Association. He moved to Dresden in 1876 where he worked on a socialist newspaper until 1883 when the German government expelled him. He then worked as a librarian for the Socialist Party archive in Zurich. He went into exile in 1888 and landed in New York in 1889. From 1889 until his death in 1919 he was the editor of the *New Yorker Volkszeitung* (People's Newspaper) and author of several works on German-American labor movements.[172]

Schlüter was sufficiently high up within the socialist elite to have frequently corresponded with Friedrich Engels. Their discussions ranged from songs and their potential revolutionary effects to the "independent nature" of "English nations and their offspring."[173] Schlüter was perfect as the historian of the brewery workers because his ideology and status within the international left was completely in sync with the union's outlook.

Hermann Schlüter promoted the union's left wing view of temperance. The avidly socialist UBW could not easily or willingly see a harmony of interests between the brewers and themselves. The union did critically analyze liquor

---

172 Hermann Schlüter Papers, International Institute of Social History, http://www.iisg.nl/archives/en/files/s/10768538.php; (accessed November 5, 2006).

173 Engels to H. Schlüter in New York, London, January 11, 1890, Engels to Schlüter (Excerpt), London, May 15, 1885, "Letters of Marx and Engels," Marx & Engels Internet Archive http://www.marxists.org/archive/marx/works/1885/letters/index.htm; (accessed November 5, 2006).

consumption among the working class. The distribution of free beer in breweries stood as an honored tradition and workers could drink as much beer as they desired on the premises of the brewery. Schlüter, in his 1910 history of the brewery workers, pointed out that free beer properly belonged in a discussion of the "hygienic conditions of the brewery workmen" since "it cannot be denied that the excessive use of beer is injurious."[174]

Schlüter believed that alcohol consumption among the working class arose from societal conditions. Increased industrialization directly led to increased consumption. Once drinking increased, over-indulgence followed.

No labor leader would ever deny that excessive use of alcohol had bad individual and societal consequences. But the nature of the industrial workplace and the conditions of labor promoted drinking. As Schlüter noted, "Drunkenness has its roots in the excessive exploitation of workingmen by capitalism. Every improvement in the condition of the workingmen brings about a diminution in drunkenness." Schlüter believed that once prohibition advocates understood this true cause of drunkenness they would spend more time supporting trade unionism and less with the prohibition movement. He hoped that temperance reformers would realize, "together with the enlightened working class, that the battle against drunkenness can best be waged in the general class struggle of the workingmen and in the organizations which this class struggle produces."[175]

Choosing to be an industrial union was unusual for nineteenth century labor when most unions were craft based; industrial unionism did not really take hold until the 1930s. A certain degree of modernity seems to have been inherent in the brewing industry. The United States Brewers Association was a trade lobby intimately involved with the federal government several decades before this became common business practice.

Although Hermann Schlüter and others portrayed the interests of brewery workers and brewers as completely separate, more than a modern impulse linked the two sides. Self-interest demanded that brewery workers fight the prohibition movement. No matter how hard they argued for a class interpretation of the liquor question, they had to endorse an individual solution for excessive drinking. Like other workers they viewed statutory prohibition as class legislation. In a similar manner to the USBA, they also argued for the personal freedom of every American to choose whether to drink or not. Brewery workers shared the anti-prohibition ideology of brewery owners.

Brewers had first acknowledged the existence of a labor movement in 1886 at the twenty-sixth convention of the United States Brewers Association. They ex-

174 Schlüter, *The Brewing Industry*, 261-263.
175 Ibid., 306–307.

pressed the hope that any labor strife "should be settled as promptly as possible and upon such a basis of justice and equity as shall make that settlement lasting." The USBA understood that the way in which management responded to labor activity could determine the success or failure of the UBW. If brewers chose to capitalize on potential increases in sales from a boycott of a specific brewery, the UBW would gain considerable mileage in their efforts to win concessions from an individual concern. Cognizant of the situation, the USBA, showing once more its ability to perceive the larger and long term picture, passed the "St. Louis resolution" in which they agreed to restrain from interference in the markets of competitors when under boycott. This response to what the industry perceived as labor's threat to its livelihood indicated the brewers' determination to preserve industry-wide control over their business. This was much more fundamentally important than specific concessions over wages, hours, and decreases in profits. Post-Prohibition brewers rarely showed such restraint or vision. Costly strikes in specific urban areas often meant the end of one or another regional brewer.[176]

The brewers sought to reduce the problems that could occur in a competitive market during a strike. Large cities had large immigrant populations who both drank beer and participated in unions. One such city was St. Louis, Missouri which had been a center of brewing from the 1850s on. Some of the nation's largest brewers, Anheuser–Busch and William J. Lemp Brewing Company, had their origins in the city. Brewers in St. Louis, Milwaukee, and Cincinnati (all Midwestern cities with good water supplies and access to ice) were in the forefront of shipping beer and providing national coverage. The local populations of these cities were too small to continue to provide growth for the various breweries, which is why they turned to shipping. Pabst, Schlitz, Blatz, Anheuser–Busch, Lemp, and Christian Moerlein all pursued a national market through shipping in the late nineteenth century. Smaller, local breweries continued to co-exist with the shipping brewers in these cities.[177]

Once brewers had committed to a national shipping strategy, they needed to insure that they would be able to sell the beer they sent to various parts of the country. Brewers established branches at various railroad stops to facilitate dis-

---

176 Quoted in Baron, *Brewed in America*, 280, 282.

177 Martin Stack, "Local and Regional Breweries in America's Brewing Industry, 1865 to 1920, *Business History Review*, vol. 74, no. 3, (Autumn 2000): 439; Downard, *Dictionary*, 122, 47-48; Baron, *Brewed in America*, 259. The Christian Moerlein Brewing Company, based in Cincinnati, was Ohio's largest brewery at the turn of the century and the fourteenth largest in the country. Some of its agencies were located in cities that had breweries larger than its own. The business stayed in the family but dissolved at the beginning of Prohibition. During Repeal, an attempt at reorganization failed. Both Cincinnati and Cleveland were large enough to support many breweries but none developed to the extent of those in Milwaukee or St. Louis. Each city had over twenty breweries on the eve of Prohibition but most did not survive the passage of the Eighteenth Amendment.

tribution. These agencies had existed since the 1860s, but the shipping brewers developed and expanded the system greatly. By 1893 Pabst had forty branches and sold beer in thirty-five states.[178] The original excise tax law of 1862 had established that a wholesale dealer of distilled spirits and fermented beverages was someone who sold alcohol in quantities larger than three gallons while a retail dealer was someone who sold beer and whiskey in amounts smaller than three gallons. Although the specific amounts changed over time, these two categories of liquor dealers persisted until Prohibition. Dealers of only fermented beverages paid a different amount; the distribution system reflected the divisions within the liquor industry.[179]

The Midwestern brewers' pursuit of shipping was a response to the competitiveness of the brewing industry which had generated price cutting and price wars in various cities. Many industries had similar issues of competition, overproduction, and decreases in prices and profits, turning to mergers as a solution to their problems. As brewers in various cities were seeking means to control prices and competition, British investors, needing new outlets for capital investments began to buy American breweries. The goal was to convert the American companies into publicly traded firms and sell shares in London.[180]

In 1889 eighteen St. Louis breweries merged to form the St. Louis Brewing Association which an English syndicate controlled. A second merger wave occurred at the turn of the century: in 1906, an additional nine breweries formed the Independent Breweries Corporation. Both these conglomerates continued in operation until Prohibition. Lemp and Anheuser-Busch, the city's largest brewers, as well as a few small local breweries, remained independent firms in St. Louis following these mergers.[181]

Milwaukee brewers were also targets for English investors, and in 1889 a British syndicate hoped to buy the three big brewers in Milwaukee: Pabst, Blatz, and Schlitz, which the Uihlein family owned. Such a purchase would have formed a very large beer trust. The investors offered at least $16.5 million, but both the Pabst and Uihlein families refused.[182]

British syndicates controlled breweries in several American cities including Baltimore, Philadelphia, Detroit, and Rochester, New York. These mergers

---

178 Baron, *Brewed in America*, 259.

179 Charles Estee, *The Excise Tax Law* (New York: Fitch, Estee, 1863) passim; Stack, "Local and Regional Breweries," 441.

180 "The Price of Beer and Some Useless Customs," *Western Brewer*, 4, no. 12 (December, 15, 1879): 1084; Roger V. Clements, "The Farmer's Attitude toward British Investment in American Industry," *The Journal of Economic History*, 15 no. 2 (June 1955): 151-159; Duis, *The Saloon*, 20.

181 Kevin Kious and Donald Roussin, "Lemp," reprinted from *American Breweriana Journal*, http://www.breweriana.com/history/historylemps.html (accessed June 29, 2007).

182 Baron, *Brewed in America*, 269.

were part of a larger trend toward consolidation, but in general most of the large brewers of the late nineteenth century withstood merger offers and remained as sole proprietors.[183]

Blatz, one of Milwaukee's largest brewers, did sell part of the company to a British syndicate, United States Brewing Company, in 1890 for $2.5 million. Blatz Brewing had existed since 1851 and was a leader in bottling and exporting beer in the 1870s. By 1895 Blatz was the nation's seventh largest brewer and produced over 350,000 barrels. Valentin Blatz, a Bavarian, stayed on as president of the new company but died in 1894.[184] Both Blatz Brewing and the United Sates Brewing Company survived Prohibition.

After the wave of mergers, both Anheuser–Busch and Lemp remained as large St. Louis brewers. Lemp Brewery dated back to the 1850s, and its most famous brand was Falstaff Beer. The first of the Midwestern brewers to both begin national shipping and establish coast to coast distribution, at the turn of the century Lemp was the eighth largest brewer in the country. The family suffered several personal tragedies before and during Prohibition and sold the brands and trademarks to the Griesedieck family in the 1920s.[185]

The origins of Anheuser–Busch, the United States' largest brewer, are in an 1850s St. Louis brewery, Hammer & Urban. Eberhard Anheuser, a German immigrant and soap and candle manufacturer, invested in this brewery in the 1850s. In 1860 he became majority owner along with William O'Dench, who left the business in 1864. Lily Anheuser, Eberhard's daughter, married Adolphus Busch who eventually took over the brewery. Anheuser retired in 1877. In 1879 Busch assumed sole responsibility and changed the name of the incorporated company (1875) to Anheuser–Busch Brewery Association.[186]

In 1877 Anheuser–Busch produced 44,961 barrels which was not enough to be included in the country's top twenty brewers. Yuengling, a brewery which still exists today, was eighteenth and produced 62,740 barrels. During the next two decades, Anheuser–Busch used advertising and technology such as refrigerated cars to become the country's second largest brewer by 1895. In 1887 the company began producing its own refrigerated train cars. The subsidiary company responsible for the production, Manufacturer's Railway, is still part of Anheuser–Busch and provides terminal and switching services. By 1901, the company brewed over one million barrels and surpassed Pabst to become number one.[187]

183 Ibid.; "Buying Up Breweries," *New York Times*, February 15, 1889, 5.

184 Downard, *Dictionary*, 23; New York Times, May 28, 1894, 5; "Chicago Brewers Hold On," *New York Times*, August 18, 1889, 3.

185 Downard, *Dictionary*, 71-72.

186 Mittelman, "Anheuser-Busch " in Blocker, et. al. *Encyclopedia*, vol. 1, 43-35.

187 Ibid.

Anheuser–Busch named its trademark beer after a type of beer brewed in the Czech town of Ceske Budejovice, known in German as Budweis. Such a familiar name certainly meant something to Busch's immigrant customers. The company's slogan also connected to its town of origin. Residents of Ceske Budejovice called their beer the Beer of Kings. Anheuser–Busch transformed this into Budweiser, the King of Beer.[188]

The Czech "Bud" dates back to 1853 when Budweiser Burgerbrau, founded in 1795 and located in Budweis, Bavaria, began brewing lager. In 1895 a new brewer, ultimately named Budejovicky Budvar, began brewing Budweiser beer in Ceske Budejovice. Despite the growing dominance of Anheuser–Busch in the United States and Canada, the company did not gain exclusive rights to its trademark overseas.[189]

Anheuser–Busch and Czech brewers were not the only companies to seek to use the name "Budweiser." Leisy Brewing Company also produced Budweiser. Leisy Brewing began in Iowa as the Union Brewery which the Leisy family owned and ran. Iowa went dry in 1884, and the Leisy family continued brewing in Cleveland. Isaac Leisy & Co. was the 81st brewery in the United States in 1877. The brewery produced Premium Lager and Budweiser.

Isaac, the founder, died in 1892 and his son Otto took over. His mother and sister also owned the brewery. By 1898 Leisy Brewing produced 120,000 barrels; forty percent of the company's total sales went to saloons Leisy owned. By 1918 these totaled over two hundred. Cleveland was not immune to the merger mania, and an English syndicate offered Otto $3 million for the brewery. He refused because he did not believe in trusts. Cleveland & Sandusky was the combination that many Cleveland breweries joined; it received a $1,950 fine from the Ohio Attorney General for trust activities. Leisy Brewing did not survive Prohibition. It closed in 1923; employees emptied 6,000 barrels of pre-Prohibition beer into a nearby sewer.[190]

Strong economic competition had prompted the merger wave; a recession in 1907 further intensified the difficult economy facing brewers. All these conditions led many brewers into ownership of saloons as a means of controlling distribution. For the shipping brewers, ownership of saloons flowed from their

188 "Business: Can They Be Buddies? Two brewers are locked in what may be an endless struggle over one of the world's great beer brands," *Time International*, vol. 150, no. 46 (July 13, 1998): 58.

189 Ibid.; Michael Jackson, *Ultimate Beer* (New York: DK Publishing, 1998), passim.

190 Bruce Leisy, *A History of the Leisy Brewing Companies* (North Newton, KS: Mennonite Press, 1975); excerpt from Carl H. Miller, *Breweries of Cleveland*, OhioBreweriana.com, "Leisy Brewing Company, Cleveland, Ohio," http://www.ohiobreweriana.com/library/holdings/leisy.shtmlhttp://www.ohiobreweriana.com/library/holdings/leisy.shtm (accessed May 23, 2007).

marketing agenda. To guarantee sales of their beer in faraway places, they bought retail establishments, the saloon. Small breweries also bought saloons as a way to control their local market. Such ownership made them easy targets, encouraging a public perception of the industry as big business.[191]

The chief complaints against the saloon were its association with urban political machines and the sense that police protection of drinking establishments allowed crime, gambling, and prostitution to flourish inside. Although scholarly investigations of saloon conditions revealed that much of this popular image was exaggerated, and that there were many different kinds of saloons, prohibitionists were successful in establishing a sordid picture of the saloon as the definitive one.[192]

By the late nineteenth century, the brewing industry was very competitive; mergers, syndicates, and ownership of saloons were all indicative of this. Thus, most brewers focused on their internal affairs with competition and expansion occupying most of their energies. As public sentiment against the saloon intensified, the industry reluctantly paid more attention to the prohibition movement. The USBA persisted as a trade organization at this time with Thomann Gallus serving as its secretary. From 1898 to 1906, he published several books and articles that often challenged prohibition rhetoric. Still the primary identification of the brewers remained their relationship with the federal government. Unfortunately for the brewers the issues that animated public discussion about the saloon and the potential for greater federal regulation of their industry began to converge.[193]

The power of the state and its potential impact on the role of liquor in society was apparent in another arena of federal power — the army. Where soldiers should drink (and ultimately whether or not they should drink) became an issue for the federal government in the late nineteenth century. Following the Civil War, most soldiers purchased supplies and liquor from traders. In the 1880s, corrupt traders who sold large amounts of alcohol, along with problems of morale, and a rising number of desertions, led to reforms in uniforms, recreation time, and the sale of consumer goods.[194]

191 United States Brewers Association. *Proceedings of the Forty-Ninth Convention* (New York, 1909) 37; Stack, "Local and Regional Breweries," 435-463.

192 Ernest A. Grant, "The Liquor Traffic before the Eighteenth Amendment," *Annals of the American Academy of Political and Social Science*, Vol. 163, "Prohibition: A National Experiment" (September, 1932): 1-9; Royal L. Melendy, "The Saloon in Chicago," *The American Journal of Sociology*, 6, no. 3 (November 1900): 289-306.

193 Downard, *Dictionary*, 190.

194 Jack Foner, *The United States Soldier Between Two Wars Army Life and Reforms, 1865–1898* (New York: Humanities Press, 1970), 77-81.

The most significant reform was the establishment of canteens, amusement centers for enlisted men, similar to the English canteen system. For a while the canteens, which sold beer, coexisted with the traders, but inevitably the two systems came into conflict. After extensive research, the War Department recommended formally establishing canteens and phasing out traders. Since enlisted men inevitably drank, the canteen provided the best means for army control of their behavior. On the other side of the issue stood prohibitionists and their congressional allies, who still rued the day the federal government had legitimated the liquor industry by taxing it.[195]

In congressional discussions of the Army Appropriation Act of 1890, which contained a request for funds to build and equip canteens, familiar arguments about the government and alcohol repeatedly appeared. Both sides claimed they were the true advocates of temperance, similar to legislators in 1862 who had sought differential taxes for beer because of its moderate qualities. Canteen supporters pointed out its benefits and the reform nature of its existence while opponents focused on the negative aspects of drink and the inadvisability of involving the federal government in the sale of liquor. Although the temperance advocates clearly recognized the legitimizing power of the state, the vast majority of elected officials would not endorse the banning of alcohol in any general way. Despite heated debate and much legislative maneuvering, the canteen appropriation passed.[196]

For the next eight years, the army successfully operated canteens in most posts and received many favorable reports from commanders. The congressional debate, however, had raised issues that did not disappear easily. In 1898 America went to war with Spain, and the army canteen once again became the center of controversy. The Prohibition Party began its campaign against the canteen by publicizing the apparent disarray and demoralization of army camps during the war. These posts represented a temporary situation and did not reflect the on-going conditions of regular army life. Prohibitionists, seizing on the current chaos, quickly moved from concern over the morality of young volunteers to a demand for abolition of the Post Exchange system.[197]

After the war, army officials continued to support the sale of liquor at canteens, and President McKinley seemed to agree. Despite his apparent support,

---

195 House, 51st Cong. 1st sess, H. Rept. 529, Appendix C, 1890, passim.

196 *Congressional Record*, 51st Cong. 1st sess. 1890.

197 *The New Voice*, May–Sept. 1898; *New York Times*, May–Sept. 1898; Graham Cosmas, *An Army for Empire: The United States Army in the Spanish American War*, (Columbia, MO: University of Missouri Press, 1971). For reports on operation of the canteen see Extracts from SemiAnnual Reports of Post Commanders of the Canteen System, Dec. 31, 1890, roll 9, Series IX, Folder B, James McCook Papers. Microfilm edition.

the canteen issue became linked with passage of the Army Reorganization Act of 1901. The bill represented a first step in the professionalization of the military, and culminated in the creation of the General Staff in 1903. Both officials and the public had experienced changes in attitudes about alcohol.[198] A writer for *Arena* claimed that there was "a growing demand for sober men in all works of life and in all business occupations."[199] The professional army required a professional work force.

In 1901, legislators again debated the issue in familiar terms, yet the army's experience in the Spanish–American War, or perhaps more accurately the public perception of that experience, had pushed the federal government much closer to Prohibition. On February 2, 1901, President McKinley signed a bill that banned the sale of alcohol on army bases.[200]

The canteen debate, begun in 1890 and concluded by the President's action, represented a dress rehearsal for Prohibition. Both the Prohibition Party and the WCTU had focused on eliminating alcohol from a specific arena, while never retreating from their ultimate goal. This tactic prefigured the approach of the rapidly emerging Anti-Saloon League which politicized the saloon to such an extent that its abolition and the cessation of the manufacture and sale of alcohol became synonymous.

Congress had flirted with the prohibitionist approach to drink and soldiers several times, but had previously retreated at the last minute. They now endorsed prohibition in army camps. Most legislators recognized that this was a form of federal intervention that had never really existed before.

The war, the need for a disciplined work force in the army, and public opinion won out over the reluctance of federal officials to take a stand on the prohibition issue and their previous willingness to limit their involvement in the liquor industry. By banning the canteen, the federal government assumed some of the power that had been inherent in the taxation of liquor. By the time such use of this prerogative became acceptable the range of available options had narrowed. The federal government could have always regulated the liquor industry according to standards of health practices, or morality, yet it had refrained from doing so. The defeat of army officials who urged that the canteen be maintained as a temperance effort and of legislators who argued for the right of soldiers to drink seemed to affirm the belief that the federal government had a role to play in determining morality. Losing ground was the moderate position in which the

---

198 House. *Report of the Secretary of War*, H. Doc. 2, 56th Cong., 1st sess., 1899; Stephen Skowronek, *Building A New American State, The Expansion of National Administrative Capacities, 1877–1920* (New York: Cambridge University Press, 1982), 85–120.

199 *Arena*, 25 (March 1901): 300.

200 *Congressional Record*, 56th Cong. 2d sess., 1901.

government carefully regulated and controlled drinking but did not prohibit it. Prohibition would soon become the only solution to both the alcohol problem and the relationship between the liquor industry and the government.

Chapter 4. Who Will Pay the Tax? Brewers and the Battle over Prohibition, 1905–1933

Until the passage of the Volstead Act, which established enforcement procedures for Prohibition, the federal government had a limited view of its proper role in the regulation of the liquor industry. Prohibiting the sale of alcohol at army canteens was both an exception and a taste of things to come. As the nineteenth century ended and the twentieth began, brewers, the sixth largest industry in the country in 1905, could look forward to ever increasing growth and sales. Reality, in the form of the prohibition movement, led in another direction.[201]

Following the breakup of the Whiskey Ring, the administration of the Bureau of Internal Revenue stabilized. Although fraud by licensed distillers did not disappear, the Bureau shifted its attention to moonshine, particularly in the South. In March of 1875, Congress raised the liquor tax to ninety cents a gallon. During the 1880s, there were several attempts to raise the tax. Linked to efforts to reduce tariffs, none of the legislation succeeded. Although Republicans originated the liquor tax, when Democrats gained the Presidency in 1884, the patronage and power associated with liquor taxation convinced them to retain the status quo.[202]

---

201 Hugh F. Fox, "The Prosperity of the Brewing Industry," *The Annals of the American Academy of Political and Social Science*, vol. 34, no. 3, 55.

202 Amy Mittelman, "The Politics of Alcohol Production: The Liquor Industry and the Federal Government, 1862–1900" (Ph.D. diss., Columbia University, 1986), 106; Miller, *Revenuers and Moonshiners, Enforcing Federal Liquor Law in the Mountain South, 1865-1900* (Chapel Hill: University of North Carolina Press, 1991), 147–149.

The federal system of liquor taxation had come into being because of the need of the state, at first, for an emergency supply of revenue, and after the Civil War, for an ongoing secure source of finance. In 1894, the exigencies of the depression required additional revenue; Congress raised the distilled spirits tax to $1.10 a gallon. The legislation also provided relief for over-extended distillers by increasing the bonded period. The tax did not change again until the beginning of World War I.[203]

Another aspect of the legislation also had consequences for the liquor industry. Congress had first passed a personal income tax during the Civil War; in 1872 legislators repealed the tax. In the depths of the "Great Depression" of 1893, Congress again enacted income tax legislation, attempting to reverse declining revenues and address some of the issues of inequity the Gilded Age economy had raised. Although the Supreme Court subsequently ruled the law unconstitutional, the measure laid the groundwork for the Sixteenth Amendment and was the first faltering step toward a system of revenue in which the liquor industry would not necessarily make a significant contribution.[204]

In the years following the Supreme Court's ruling on the income tax, the country experienced social unrest and a recession in 1907. Although the Republican Party, firmly committed to hard money and high tariffs, remained in power, there were many people both in the party and outside who began to seek political and economic change.

The tariff had evolved from an aspect of economic policy to a shield for the nation's industries. The nation's tax structure, relying so heavily on consumption, was highly regressive. Most politicians agreed that economic conditions, as well as equity, made tariff reform necessary. Tariff reform would leave a revenue shortfall, thus leading to renewed proposals for an income tax. Although most of the discussion of the federal tax system focused on the inequities of high tariffs, many ardent advocates of the income tax also strongly supported Prohibition. Two notable supporters of both measures were William Jennings Bryan and Andrew Volstead.[205]

In 1909, after much political maneuvering and at a great political cost to President Taft and, ultimately, the Republican Party, Congress submitted the following amendment to the states. "Congress shall have the power to lay and collect taxes on incomes, from whatever source derived, without apportionment among

---

203 Mittelman, "The Politics of Alcohol Production," 131.

204 John D. Buenker, *The Income Tax and the Progressive Era* (New York,: Garland Pub., 1985), 2-3, 7-21.

205 Ibid., passim. For a discussion of the links between prohibition and other progressive reforms see James H. Timberlake, *Prohibition and the Progressive Movement* (Cambridge: Harvard University Press, 1963).

---

the several states, and without regard to any census or enumeration." Congress also passed a one percent corporate income tax. In 1913, the United States ratified the Sixteenth Amendment and established the federal income tax, marking the beginning of our present income tax system.[206]

The significance of these two actions was not readily apparent to most observers. Less than two percent of the labor force filed returns from 1913–1915. Before World War I over ninety percent of federal revenue continued to come from excise taxes and customs, but the pieces were now in place for a system of revenue that could supplant excise taxes.[207]

In 1907, the country experienced a run on banks, particularly New York trust companies. Similar panics had happened periodically throughout the late nineteenth century.[208] The panic of 1907 had negative economic consequences for industry including the brewers. At the 1909 convention of the United States Brewers Association, President Julius Liebmann mentioned that the industry had experienced only a negligible increase in comparison to significant growth the previous five years. Recognizing the outside pressures facing brewers, Liebmann commented that, "In some States, of course, Prohibition or Local Option aggravated matters considerably. But in a general way, the condition of things confirms the old experience that there is no better indication of prosperity or its opposite than the revenue report. The ups and downs in its beer column tell the story quite as plainly and reliably as the rise and fall of the mercury column in the barometer indicates fair weather or foul."[209]

Liebmann was head of Rheingold Brewing, one of Brooklyn's premier breweries. In 1850 Samuel Liebmann, a German Jew, left Württemberg with his three sons following his involvement in the political upheaval of 1848. They settled in Brooklyn and by 1914 had an output of 700,000 barrels. Julius was Samuel's grandson.[210]

---

206 Laurence F. Schmeckebier and Francis X.A. Elbe, *The Bureau of Internal Revenue, Its History, Activities, and Organization* (Baltimore, 1923), 41.

207 John F. Witte, *The Politics and Development of the Federal Income Tax* (Madison, WI: University of Wisconsin Press, 1985), 78-79.

208 Jon Moen, "The Panic of 1907," *EH.Net Encyclopedia*, http://eh.net/encyclopedia/article/moen.panic.1907 (accessed July 1, 2007).

209 United States Brewers Association. *Proceedings of the Forty-Ninth Convention* (New York, 1909), 20.

210 William Downard, *Dictionary of the History of the American Brewing and Distilling Industries* (Westport, CT: Greenwood Press., 1980), 159; Will Anderson, *The Breweries of Brooklyn: An Informal History of a Great Industry in a Great City* (New York: Anderson, 1976), 100-111; Rolf Hofmann, "The Originators of Rheingold Beer from Ludwigsburg to Brooklyn—A Dynasty of German-Jewish Brewers," BeerHistory.com, http://www.beerhistory.com/library/holdings/hofmann-rheingold.shtml (accessed November 20, 2006).

Brewers clearly cherished their place in the federal tax structure, yet reduced income made them reluctant to part with an even greater share of their profits. Amid the political wrangling over tariff revision and the income tax amendment, several legislators suggested increasing the tax on beer. Liebmann urged officials to realize the great contribution the industry had already made and not burden the brewers or the country further. "Our losses helped to swell the Federal deficit. The Treasury received 5½ million dollars less from us on account of hard times . . . . No sensible lawmaker could fail to see the suicidal policy of putting more weight on an industry already sliding along swiftly on the downward grade, and thus crippling one of the best revenue sources."[211]

Brewers were financial contributors to federal finances yet their economic activity made them vulnerable to public disapproval. The Anti-Saloon League used the bad conditions of many saloons as their key weapon in the propaganda campaign they conducted against alcohol. The industry had been ambivalent about changing its ownership of salons to improve its public image. In 1909, aware of public pressure to reform the saloon, Hugh Fox, Secretary of the USBA, said, "If beer is to be made and sold there must be some place for its sale."[212]

To Fox, the problem was not that brewers owned saloons but that they did not operate them. The independence of saloon keepers encouraged them to sell spirits; if brewers also operated the saloon this would not be the case. Fox felt that the fact that "American beer only averages three and one-half percent (alcohol)" made "the encouragement of beer-houses . . . most desirable." Despite the problems of intense competition and the existence of a few "saloons of a positively disreputable character," brewers were more than willing to "cooperate with all public and private agencies whose purpose is constructive ... but the common ground must be *regulation not elimination. . . .* There is no doubt that an enormous class wants what the saloon provides. . . ."[213]

Fox's idea that brewers needed to own saloons outright to prevent the sale of distilled spirits flew in the face of standard marketing principles. Even today, brewpubs sell wine and hard liquor to capture the greatest number of customers.

Although the brewers intensely disliked the criticism of their industry, the USBA members who attended the 1909 Convention did not include the 1909 corporate income tax or the proposed amendment among their woes. Brew-

---

211 USBA, *Proceedings of the Forty-Ninth Convention* (New York, 1909), 23.
212 Ibid., 37.
213 Hugh F. Fox, "The Saloon Problem," *The Annals of the American Academy of Political and Social Science*, vol. 32, no. 3, 536, 538.

ers remained secure in their sense of themselves as indispensable to the federal government.

Brewers, partially because of their ownership of saloons, were the most prominent aspect of the liquor industry in the decade preceding Prohibition. Distilled spirits were also part of the federally taxed liquor business. Distilling expanded tremendously after the Civil War and then faced the typical industrial problems of over-production, high fixed costs, and competition. In response to these problems, distillers tried to organize production agreements, pools, trusts, and corporations. The Whiskey Trust, a combination of neutral spirit producers, was one of the nation's earliest trusts, yet ease of entry made tight control of the market an impossibility. In the late nineteenth century the struggle to control competition, define its product, and achieve consolidation dominated the distilled spirits industry.[214]

Distillers seem to have been as unaware of any consequences of the proposed income tax as were the brewers. In 1909, the year Congress submitted the Sixteenth Amendment to the states, distillers and liquor dealers were battling over the meaning of the term "whiskey" and its possible uses within the provisions of the new Federal Drug Administration (FDA).[215]

Distillers were unable to maintain the same high profile in Washington that the brewers had through the USBA. There were divisions within the distilled spirits industry and the federal government was less favorably disposed toward their industry. Bourbon manufacturers, a distinct minority, were the most successful in winning favorable legislation from Congress. The extension of the bonded period to seven years and the subsequent Bottled-in Bond Act of 1896 were their greatest victories. In the decade preceding the enactment of Prohibition, there were two national organizations representing liquor dealers — the National Wholesale Liquor Dealers Association and the National Retail Liquor Dealers' Association. These organizations continued to grapple with the economic issues of the distilled spirits industry, but also had to acknowledge the growing threat the prohibition movement represented to their livelihood.[216]

For close to fifty years, both brewers and distillers had sustained a stable relationship with the federal government. During that period of time they resisted an evolving prohibition movement. Brewers were fairly consistent in both their

214 Mittelman, "The Politics of Alcohol," 102-150.

215 Jack Hugh and Clayton A. Coppin, "Wiley and the Whiskey Industry: Strategic Behavior in the Passage of the Pure Food Act," *Business History Review*, 62 (Summer 1988): 286-309; William Downard, *Dictionary*, 188.

216 K. Austin Kerr, *Organized for Prohibition, A New History of The Anti-Saloon League* (New Haven: Yale University Press, 1985) 32-33; Amy Mittelman, "Who Will Pay the Tax," *Social History of Alcohol Review*, no. 25, (Spring 1992): 28-38.

approach to the temperance movement and their willingness to ally with the distillers. State-wide prohibition had been in effect in Maine and Vermont since the 1850s; after the Civil War many localities, rarely distinguishing between whiskey and beer, enacted local option and high license laws which effectively made areas dry. Both Kansas and Iowa enacted prohibition in the 1880s; brewers believed that distillers in those states had taken every advantage of the situation. In Iowa, drugstores legally sold alcohol; the *Western Brewer* claimed that distillers had "the law so worded as to make every drug store a miniature distillery." Brewers gained no benefit from the law because "no 'druggist' could sell beer, owing to its bulk." Druggists and others continued to sell legal and illegal whiskey while brewers could not market their product "except in open defiance of the statutes."[217]

Although commonsense would indicate that distillers would oppose prohibition as vehemently as the brewing industry, brewers maintained that distillers had "openly aided the passage" of state prohibition. In 1886 they responded angrily to a call for a national convention of all the elements of the liquor industry in Chicago. "Malt liquor stands on its own bottom, either to rise or fall and declines to go before the public handicapped with whiskey. Whenever the brewers have consorted with the spirit makers they have got the worst of it!... Whiskey and beer are two different things as far apart as heaven and hell, light and darkness. You make the drunkards through your accursed fire water and charge it to our good beer. You cohabit with the deceit and fraud of hypocrisy to get in your condensed spirits and keep out the product of the healthful mash tub of the brewers."[218]

Despite these strong words, brewers found it necessary at different times in different states to ally themselves with distillers. In the 1880s, Personal Liberty Leagues were the main lobby against state prohibition threats and local option battles and always included brewers, retail liquor dealers, and distillers. Texas was the site of one such battle. Texas had a large German immigrant population and was a distribution site for many of the national shipping breweries. Anheuser-Busch had helped establish Lone Star Brewing in San Antonio in 1883. Lone Star brewed under its own label; Busch's role was financial. It did not survive Prohibition.[219]

The Texas temperance movement began advocating for state-wide prohibition in 1885. In 1887 they succeeded in placing a constitutional amendment

---

217 *Western Brewer*, 11 (Oct. 15, 1886): 2166.
218 Ibid., 2165-2166.
219 Stanley Baron, *Brewed In America: A History of Beer and Ale in America* (Boston: Little, Brown & Company, 1961), 266. Lone Star opened under new owners after Repeal.

before the voters. At the twenty-seventh USBA convention the brewers voted $5,000 to their colleagues in Texas who had "a big fight on their hands." In July 1887, opponents held a rally in Fort Worth which 50,000 people attended. State treasurer and former Governor Francis Lubbock read a letter from Jefferson Davis which denounced prohibition.

Texas voters went to the polls August 4, 1887 and defeated the proposed constitutional amendment by a margin of 90,000. Temperance advocates blamed the defeat on Davis's letter. Widely read, the letter cost "many thousand votes." The brewers saw the matter differently: "Crankdom met its Waterloo, and the friends of personal liberty throughout the world may well rejoice at so great a victory." [220]

The prohibition movement underwent significant change from 1860 to 1900. Middle-class professional white men dominated antebellum temperance organizations. During the Gilded Age the existence of the Woman's Christian Temperance Union and its support of the Prohibition Party showed the growing strength of the movement's female constituency. The Prohibition Party itself also represented a break with the political practices of antebellum temperance. Party activists held a deep commitment to a vision of America in which a third party dedicated to temperance ideals would remake society.

The politics of the 1890s — an era of depression and social dislocation — propelled Frances Willard, leader of the WCTU, and many of her followers toward a broader critique of American society. Willard's move away from a single issue focus prompted a crisis in the movement that resulted in a turn to the right for the Prohibition Party and the WCTU. The controversy brought a vacuum into which a new organization with a different approach stepped. The Anti-Saloon League, based in Ohio, took a completely new direction for the prohibition movement, one with lasting consequences. [221]

Unlike the Prohibition Party, the Anti-Saloon League did not object to federal involvement in the liquor industry; the organization was extremely successful in using the Bureau of Internal Revenue to enforce anti-alcohol legislation on the state level. The prohibitionists, who were acutely aware of the power of the state, seized upon the regulatory and police potential inherent in tax legislation and collection. Government officials and politicians had chosen to ignore

---

220 *Western Brewer* 12 (June 15, 1887): 1259; 12 (August 15, 1887): 1723-1724; Ernest Cherrington, ed., *Standard Encyclopedia of the Alcohol Problem*, 6 vols. (Westerville, OH: American Issue Pub. Co., 1925–1930) vol. 6, 2634; "A Big Demonstration," *New York Times*, July 27, 1887, 1.

221 For an excellent overview of American temperance movements see Jack Blocker, *American Temperance Movements: Cycles of Reform, Social Movements Past and Present* (Boston: Twayne Publications, 1989).

this potential, encouraged by the liquor industry which understandably sought laissez-faire administration of the revenue in exchange for its compliance.[222]

Despite the ultimate significance of the ratification of the Sixteenth Amendment, another event of 1913 was more compelling for brewers and distillers. The passage of the Webb–Kenyon Act which made the transportation of alcohol into dry areas illegal gave prohibitionists a major national victory. The legislation served to close loopholes in previous laws that had allowed out-of-state liquor dealers to continue to ship to dry areas. It passed over President Taft's veto which showed the growing strength of prohibition forces in Congress. The brewers as well as other opponents of the bill had not been effective. The success of the Anti-Saloon League in passing Webb–Kenyon convinced the organization to pursue national prohibition.[223]

One year after passage of Webb–Kenyon, the advancement of national prohibition continued. Nine states had prohibition and less then one-third of the country's area supported the legal sale of beverage alcohol. The Anti-Saloon League also held the balance of power in the House of Representatives and in most state legislatures.[224] The brewers realized the dire nature of the situation and joined forces with distillers, vintners, and saloonkeepers to begin a program of cooperation with government officials to regulate the saloon.[225]

In 1914 the Wilson administration faced a revenue shortfall caused by the beginning of World War I. The Emergency Revenue Act of October 22, 1914 raised the beer tax to $1.50 a barrel, raised the rates for wine, tobacco dealers and manufacturers, and instituted a stamp tax. The legislation represented a continuation of the tax policies of the Spanish–American War and did not reflect a new importance for the income tax. In 1916 the Bureau of Internal Revenue collected almost $250 million from the liquor industry; excise taxes and customs duties still accounted for 74.8 percent of the government's income.[226]

The brewers, following the same script as the legislators, maintained their position as reluctant but law-abiding taxpayers. The Revenue Act of 1914 had confirmed the continuing importance of the brewing industry; the brewers chose

222 Richard F. Hamm, *Shaping the 18th Amendment: Temperance Reform, Legal Culture, and the Polity, 1880-1920* (Chapel Hill: University of North Carolina Press, 1995), 155-174.

223 Hamm, *Shaping the 18th Amendment*, 175–202; Kerr, *Organized for Prohibition*, 138.

224 Edward Marshall, "Is National Prohibition Actually Close At Hand?," *New York Times*, April 19, 1914, SM10.

225 "Liquor Men Urge Reforms," *New York Times*, July 1, 1915; Nuala McGann Drescher," The Opposition to Prohibition, 1900–1919" (Ph.D. diss., University of Delaware, 1964), 2.

226 U.S. Office of Internal Revenue, *Annual Report of the Commissioner* (Washington, D.C., 1915), 47; Witte, *The Federal Income Tax*, 79; U.S. Office of Internal Revenue, *Annual Report of the Commissioner* (Washington, D.C., 1916), 45; Charles Gilbert, *American Financing of World War One* (Westport, CT: Greenwood Press, 1970), 76.

to stress this in their 1914 *Yearbook*. After a lengthy discussion of the industry's economic contributions, the brewers concluded with a look at the consequences of prohibition. "There would be the serious matter of finding new sources of revenue. The Federal Government would have to impose new taxes to meet deficits which would be nearly three times greater than the amount now derived from the income tax. How could this burden be met?"[227]

What the liquor industry could not have foreseen was that during World War I, the income tax gradually replaced liquor taxes as the country's primary source of revenue. As part of this process, prohibitory and financial legislation, beginning in 1917, eroded the liquor industry's ability to operate. Perceiving food as an essential element in the nation's mobilization, in the summer of 1917, Congress considered legislation to create a Food Administration that would oversee all aspects of food production and distribution. President Wilson hoped that Herbert Hoover would head the new agency. Prohibitionists sought to ban the use of grains for distilling and brewing, claiming this was a conservation measure. Although Hoover and others believed that the use of barley was a more significant drain on food resources than the use of corn, brewers were successful in exempting beer from the Lever Bill. The final legislation prohibited the use of grains in distilling and granted Wilson latitude in determining how much barley and hops the brewing industry could use. The USBA still retained its ability to influence legislation.[228]

Had the brewers really won anything? If they had combined with distillers to fight prohibition, instead of persisting in seeing themselves as distinct, could a unified industry have stopped Prohibition? The brewing industry and the USBA had, from 1862 on, held firm to the view that beer was a temperance beverage and that distilled spirit was not. The two branches remain completely distinct even today.

Some brewers, notably Anheuser–Busch, did want to join forces with distillers; the large shipping brewers had found it increasingly difficult to maintain saloons across the country. In an effort to reduce competition from local brewery ownership of saloons, national brewers such as Anheuser–Busch supported the separation of distribution and production.[229] The dismantling of the tied house system of retail distribution would certainly have helped create a more positive public perception of the brewers. Anheuser–Busch and the other brewers who

227 United States Brewers Association, *Yearbook* (New York, 1914), 262.

228 Kerr, *Organized for Prohibition*, 200-202. Kerr feels that the brewers' victory was self-defeating. He maintains that the brewers should have spent their time and energy joining with the distillers in a fight against prohibitionists.

229 Martin Stack, "Local and Regional Breweries in America's Brewing Industry, 1865 to 1920, *Business History Review*, vol. 74, no. 3. (Autumn 2000): 459.

argued for reform of the saloon and an alliance with distillers did so from a position of both self-interest, and concern for the future of the industry.

If these efforts had been consistent perhaps, together, brewers and distillers could have stopped the enactment of the Eighteenth Amendment. Even combined, they would have had few political options since state legislatures, not individual voters, enacted Prohibition. To defeat the Eighteenth Amendment, opponents — brewers, distillers, workers, libertarians — would have had to control state governments. This fact created a no-win situation for brewers. When they intervened on a state or local level — to prevent local option or woman's suffrage — such actions led prohibitionists to brand them "King Alcohol," an evil lobby interfering in the political process. Thus it is hard to see how even a united industry, engaging in self-regulation and in a widespread publicity campaign, would have been able to prevent state legislatures from voting in favor of the Eighteenth Amendment.

The USBA had always been more effective on the federal level and the income tax reduced its influence considerably. From 1914 on, the trade association faced increasingly hostile government on both the state and federal level. Both Texas and Pennsylvania conducted investigations into the brewing industry involvement in politics, and in 1918 the federal government undertook a similar investigation.

All three investigations revealed that the brewers had attempted to manipulate election results in both prohibition and women's suffrage contests. Men were the face of the saloon and public drinking; women were the face of prohibition and temperance. Brewers were determined to prevent women from getting the vote. In Pennsylvania, one hundred state breweries and forty-two members of the USBA received indictments for unlawful contributions to influence the 1912 presidential election. The brewers paid a $1 million fine rather than go to trial.[230]

Both the Texas and Pennsylvania investigations focused on anti-trust activity on the part of the brewers. In 1918 the country had 1,185 brewers. The USBA had 645 members; every economically viable brewery belonged. Although the industry was the nation's sixth largest and had a net profit of $1.5 billion in 1914, it was not highly concentrated.[231] There were a few national producers and many, many local and regional concerns. Texas and Pennsylvania were not actually concerned with the economic status of the industry but with the political

---

230 Catherine Gilbert Murdock, *Domesticating Drink: Women, Men and Alcohol in America* (Baltimore: Johns Hopkins University Press, 1998) 29; "Federal Jury Acts Against Brewers," *New York Times*, March 4, 1916, 13.
231 Drescher, "Opposition to Prohibition," 79, 103-104.

impact of brewers. Many years later in the 1950s the federal government would examine issues of monopoly and competition in the brewing industry from an economic vantage point amid concern for the vanishing small brewer. No such concern animated either Texas or Pennsylvania.

On October 3, 1917, following the United States' entry into war with Germany, Congress passed the War Revenue Act of 1917. Although the Lever Bill sharply limited their production, distillers still paid a tax of $3.20 a gallon, and brewers contributed $3.00 a barrel, doubling the 1914 rate.[232] Congress passed several revenue bills during the course of the war; all expanded the role of the income tax in generating money for the federal government.

By 1920 the income tax accounted for 58.6 percent of revenue, on average; the tariff had ceased to have any significance either as a political issue or a source of revenue. Income tax revenues now occupied the principal place in the internal revenue system that excise and customs had held for so long.[233]

As legislators were opening this door, prohibitionists persuaded them to shut down the liquor industry in the best interests of the war effort. Under the provisions of the Lever Bill, Herbert Hoover convinced President Wilson to reduce the alcoholic content of beer to 2.75 percent and limit grain allotments.[234]

The Civil War had expanded the power and authority of the federal government; the Bureau of Internal Revenue and the liquor tax were permanent consequences of that expansion. By 1918 the Sixteenth Amendment and U.S. involvement in World War I had generated further change. Commissioner of Internal Revenue Daniel Roper described the federal tax structure as a "new era of taxation." The Commissioner believed that the Revenue Act of 1917 marked "the end of one period of taxation policy and administration and the beginning of a new and essentially different period." This legislation created a "comprehensive system of internal-revenue taxes." Roper described these changes as a "transformation."[235]

Despite these dramatic developments, the liquor industry and segments of the federal government persisted in believing that the pattern of the past fifty-six years remained the same. The National Wholesale Liquor Dealers' Association's *National Bulletin* for 1916 and 1917 reiterated in editorials and cartoons their message of economic ruin resulting from Prohibition. Referring to the revenues the federal government received from the liquor industry — an amount totaling one-third of the total budget — the liquor dealers asked: "Will they tax the law-

232 Gilbert, *American Financing*, 97; Schmeckebier, *The Bureau of Internal Revenue*, 48.

233 Witte, *The Federal Income Tax*, 79; Gilbert, *American Financing*, 76.

234 Kerr, *Organized for Prohibition*, 205-207.

235 U.S. Office of Internal Revenue, *Annual Report of the Commissioner* (Washington, D.C., 1918), 2-3.

yer, doctor, the grocer, the druggist, the barber, the butcher, dry goods man and teamster? How will they raise this revenue?"[236]

Such pleas fell on deaf ears as prohibitionists narrowed the net around the liquor industry. The final blow came in the guise of the Wartime Prohibition Act, which prohibited the sale of all alcoholic beverages after June 30, 1919. The brewers responded by stating "nine reasons for liquor." The main reason was, as always, economic: "It would destroy a present Federal revenue of $250,000,000 and a future revenue of $300,000,000 almost immediately available, at a time when every dollar is needed for war purposes."[237]

Six months after Congress passed this bill, on January 16, 1919, Nebraska ratified the Eighteenth Amendment. It took affect a year later. The day after ratification, *The New York Times*, commenting on the new reality, counseled that, "It is for the country and many belated and surprised persons in it to realize that legal, to be succeeded by the constitutional, Federal prohibition will soon be in effect. Even at Washington, Congress which started the engine of virtue . . . is blind to the new light. Senate and House conferees were agreeing about the rates on distilled and divers other spirits and intoxicants just before the news from Nebraska came."[238] Old habits die hard.

Both brewers and distillers focused on their economic importance to the government in their public statements against Prohibition. Other groups also opposed the Eighteenth Amendment. The United Brewery Workers and most of organized labor fought against enactment of Prohibition. Samuel Gompers was the nation's most prominent labor leader; early in his career he provided counsel to the UBW. He was very reluctant to publicly oppose Prohibition primarily because he felt such a stance would weaken the AFL.[239]

By June 1919, wartime prohibition had caused liquor manufacture to cease. The ratification of the Eighteenth Amendment which would permanently prohibit the manufacture and sale of alcoholic beverages was complete. Congressional committees met to discuss enforcement legislation for the amendment; ultimately the Volstead Act performed this function for thirteen years.

Organized labor called for a demonstration in Washington, DC, on June 14 "against war prohibition as well as against the inclusion of beer in the national prohibition enforcement bill." A delegation from the demonstration including Samuel Gompers testified before a subcommittee of the Senate Judiciary Committee that afternoon. Senator Sterling, a Republican from South Dakota chaired

236 National Wholesale Liquor Dealers Association, *National Bulletin*, 8 (May 1916), 241.
237 "Nine Reasons for Liquor," *New York Times*, May 27 1917, 7.
238 Kerr, *Organized for Prohibition*, 206-207; *New York Times*, January 17, 1919, 12.
239 Drescher, "Opposition to Prohibition," 25.

the committee; other members included Lee Overman, a Democrat from North Carolina. Overman had recently concluded a lengthy investigation of "Brewing Interests and German and Bolshevik Propaganda."[240] A final report of over one thousand pages failed to show how the brewers and Bolsheviks were connected. The Bolshevik Revolution of 1917 alarmed President Wilson and others; the withdrawal of Russian troops served to strengthen German forces.

Overman undertook his investigation following charges by Attorney General Palmer that the brewers had engaged in illegal and un-American activities. His investigation was probably the first but obviously not the last time a congressional committee investigated communism.[241] Palmer subsequently undertook the infamous Palmer Raids, which imprisoned citizens and aliens and deported many others. Both the source of the charges against the brewers and the results of the investigation were so biased and so deeply rooted in anti-German and anti-communist hysteria that it is hard to separate fact from fiction in the report.

Gompers presented a resolution from the AFL convention about wartime prohibition and the Eighteenth Amendment. The resolution declared that these actions were "principally intended to deprive the workers of America of the means to secure legally a glass of beer after their day's labor."[242] Gompers and organized labor sought to defeat Prohibition, for beer at least, by making the case for personal liberty. Because the Anti-Saloon League had successfully linked brewing to Germany, drinking beer as a personal act was an expression of German identity and thus unacceptable. The German language community within the United States totaled five to six million people and German-Americans comprised ten percent of the American population.[243]

The German-American Alliance was the largest organization of German Americans and was dedicated to preserving German culture and language. After the outbreak of war in Europe in 1914, but before America's involvement in the war, the Alliance did send financial support to Germany. This activity became the basis of Overman's committee report. In general the Alliance's major activity was fighting Prohibition.[244]

The brewing industry was overwhelmingly German; most German-Americans drank beer as did many other Americans. Although German-Americans maintained many ties to Germany, the vast majority were second or third generation Americans. The founders of most breweries had immigrated to America

---

240 "Prohibiting Intoxicating Beverages," United States Senate, Subcommittee on the Judiciary, June 14, 1919, passim.
241 "Overman Report Accuses Brewers," *New York Times*, June 15, 919, 20.
242 "Brewing and Liquor Interests and German Propaganda," Washington, 1919.
243 Drescher, "Opposition to Prohibition," 9.
244 Ibid., passim.

in the 1840s and 1850s. World War I generated a tremendous amount of public hostility against Germans and German-Americans. For brewers and their fellow ethnic citizens, the war period was a test of their dual identities.

Some of the nation's most prominent brewers faced these issues of loyalty and cultural identification as soon as America entered the war. One of New York's most prominent brewers was George Ehret, Sr., the nation's largest brewer in 1877. In 1914, Ehret, an American citizen, returned to Germany to live. In 1918 his son, George Ehret, Jr., turned over the family property with a value of $40 million to the federal government. A. Mitchell Palmer, who was then the Alien Property Custodian, found Ehret, Sr. to be "of enemy character." Ehret had not broken any laws but appeared to be friendly with and under the protection of "powerful men." He had also given large amounts of money to the German Red Cross since 1914. Palmer stated that Ehret, who was 83, could get his property back if he re-turned to America. He would then lose "his enemy character." The Ehret family's status as influential New Yorkers and wealthy Americans apparently did not mean as much as his German affiliations.[245]

Lily Busch, widow of Adolphus Busch, suffered similar problems. The Buschs, if not the country's wealthiest brewing family then certainly its most ostentatious, owned several estates including a castle on the Rhine in Germany. Adolphus died in 1913; estimates of the value of his wealth ranged from $30 to $60 million.[246] Both Adolphus and Lily were born in Germany; Lily had become a naturalized citizen of the United States. When World War I broke out she made her German home a war hospital and served as a nurse. The German govern-ment took her property because she was an American citizen; the United States viewed her as enemy alien since she was in Germany. When she returned to the United States in 1918 the government seized her property and placed her under a form of house arrest. She died in 1928.[247]

The prosecution, if not persecution, of these prominent brewers and their families indicated the deep unease Americans felt about the presence of Ger-mans in their country. Thus, as Samuel Gompers testified before Congress about wartime prohibition, he sought to move the discussion away from the ethnic identity of beer and brewers and focus on the impact of the Eighteenth Amend-ment on workers. His resolution noted that wartime prohibition and the Eigh-teenth Amendment had "the effect of destroying part of the American labor movement and is crippling many international organizations affiliated with the

245 "Nation Gets Ehret Property," *New York Times*, May 14, 1918, 1.
246 "Adolphus Busch Dies in Prussia," *New York Times*, October 11, 1913, 15.
247 "Mrs. Lily Busch of St. Louis Dies," *New York Times*, February 26, 1928, 27.

American Federation of Labor."[248] This argument referred primarily to brewery workers and the UBW. Therefore the committee could dismiss it as self-serving. The overall point of the resolution was to advocate for an exemption for 2.75 percent beer (near beer) from the Eighteenth Amendment.

Gompers did not come before the committee to argue the merits of the recently enacted Eighteenth Amendment, but to secure an exemption for beer. He claimed that the labor movement, by securing a shorter work day, had increased "temperance among the working class." A better standard of living had reduced the need for "that exhilaration which comes from the drinking of alcoholic beverages among workers."[249] Economic change, from the Civil War on, had increased disposable income and leisure time enough to create the saloon and the drink business in the first place.

Gompers was testifying on Flag Day and he took pains to convince the committee of his patriotism. The Bolshevik Revolution was on everyone's mind; the labor leader warned the committee that "we are not wholly free from some who would imitate in the United States and encourage in the United States what has occurred and is taking place in Russia within the past year." Gompers apparently felt that keeping 2.75 percent beer for the working man would prevent a Communist takeover. Gompers passionately declared that he made his appeal "not alone as president of the American Federation of Labor, not alone as a laboring man, but as a citizen of this Republic who knows no loyalty outside of devotion to the Republic of the United States. I am apprehensive of the results should Congress fail to meet the situation. . . ."[250]

Gompers' appearance before the committee reflected the problems brewers and distillers faced in their attempts to stop Prohibition. In the heady mix of wartime fear, anti-German, and anti-Bolshevik hysteria as well as a new source of revenue from the income tax, the public apparently held the brewers in such low regard by this point that only spokespeople who were without any connection to the brewing interests had any chance of being heard. There were few available to make an intelligent, disinterested argument for the rights of individual Americans to lawfully drink. In 1919 the Association Opposed to Prohibition seemed the only possibility. They planned a national demonstration. The goal of the organization was to "preserve the rights of free men in a free country." The board of directors of the organization included the presidents of American Tobacco and B. Altman & Co. as well as Joseph Harriman, president of Harriman

---

248 "Prohibiting Intoxicating Beverages," United States Senate, Subcommittee on the Judiciary, June 14, 1919, 6.
249 Ibid., 8.
250 Ibid., 18.

National Bank. There were no brewers involved.[251] The fact that these prominent business men opposed Prohibition highlighted the anomaly of the federal government dismantling the country's sixth largest industry.

The rhetoric of the Prohibition movement for most of its existence had been positive, extolling the virtues that removing alcohol from society would bring. The final push that brought Prohibition, the Eighteenth Amendment, and the Volstead Act into being became negative and played on people's fears as American faced a world that was unfamiliar and rapidly changing.

Much of the debate over enforcement of the Eighteenth Amendment focused on whether 2.75 percent beer was intoxicating. If Samuel Gompers and other opponents of Prohibition could prove it was not, then brewers could continue to produce beer. Halting wartime prohibition would have allowed brewers a longer period of time to operate legally. The brewers and their supporters failed in both these efforts. The debate over what level of alcohol in beer led to intoxication would continue throughout Prohibition and into Repeal.

The Volstead Act defined intoxicating as one half of one percent by volume; it also enforced wartime prohibition. Because of this aspect of the legislation, on October 27, 1919 President Wilson vetoed it. Wilson stated that "Where the purposes of particular legislation arising out of war emergency have been satisfied, sound public policy makes clear the reason and necessity for repeal." The President urged lawmakers to separate the two parts of the law so that the Prohibition amendment, "which is now part of the fundamental law of the country," would be enforced.[252] Brewers and others were ecstatic, but at best Congress upholding the veto would have delayed, not stopped, the country from going dry. Within two days it was a moot point; the House overturned Wilson's veto 176 to 55, the Senate 65 to 20.[253]

The brewers and other opponents of Prohibition made one final attempt to save low-alcohol beer. Jacob Ruppert, the owner of the New York Yankees and Ruppert Brewing, petitioned for an injunction to prevent the federal government from prohibiting the sale of 2.75 percent beers. On January 5, 1920, the Supreme Court, in a 5 to 4 vote, ruled that the sections of the Volstead Act that dealt with wartime prohibition and defined intoxicating alcohol as having more than one-half of one percent alcohol were constitutional. This ruling did not involve the constitutionality of the Eighteenth Amendment or those sections

---

251 "Wets Hold Back Protest," *New York Times*, March 30, 1919, 19.
252 "House 176 to 55, Overrides Veto of Wartime Prohibition," *New York Times*, October 28, 1919, 1.
253 "Brewers Rejoice at Wilson's Veto," *New York Times*, October 28, 1919, 3; "Senate Overrides Prohibition Veto By Vote of 65 to 20," *New York Times*, October 29, 1919, 1; Richard F. Hamm, *Shaping the 18th Amendment*, 251-253.

of the Volstead Act pertaining to it.[254] Several states, including Rhode Island and New Jersey, a brewer, Christian Feigenspan, and the Kentucky Distilleries and Warehouse Company, all filed suits challenging the constitutionality of the Eighteenth Amendment and the Volstead Act.[255] On June 7, 1920 the Supreme Court unanimously upheld both the amendment and its enforcing legislation. In the National Prohibition Cases the Supreme Court ruled that the concurrent powers granted the states referred only to enforcement and did not permit states to pass laws "granting the right to produce and consume light wines and beers or liquors of not more than a certain alcoholic content." Both New York and New Jersey had passed such legislation. Governor Calvin Coolidge had vetoed a similar law in Massachusetts.[256]

The Supreme Court ruling meant that any efforts to change the dry status of the country would have to be political; activists would have to work for modification of the Volstead Act or repeal of the Eighteenth Amendment. In 1920 neither seemed very likely.

The brewers had relied on their relationship with the federal government via taxation to save them. It had not. It seems clear that the creation of a new secure source of revenue expedited the enactment of Prohibition. Although liquor manufacture was now illegal, the Eighteenth Amendment and the Volstead Act did not eliminate the relationship between the federal government and the liquor industry. Congress placed the responsibility for enforcement of Prohibition in the hands of the Bureau of Internal Revenue. Commissioner Daniel Roper, a personal supporter of Prohibition, disagreed with this decision, believing law enforcement was a "function" of the Justice Department and "essentially unrelated to taxation."[257] Yet the enforcement strategy of the Anti-Saloon League relied heavily on state and local cooperation, a policy that the Bureau had pursued for many years concerning tax compliance and evasion. The Bureau also had existing personnel; any other agency would require a new staff.[258]

Throughout the 1920s, the country seemed to enjoy economic prosperity; the federal government had a surplus of almost a billion dollars in 1924. Secretary

---

254 "Ban on 2.75 Beers In Wartime Upheld By Supreme Court," *New York Times,* January 6, 1920, 1; Baron, *Brewed in America,* 312-313.

255 "Rhode Island Fight On Dry Act Opens," *New York Times,* March 9, 1920, 11; "High Court Grants Dry Test to Jersey," *New York Times,* March 16, 1920, 7; "Urges Supreme Court to Kill Prohibition," *New York Times,* March 10, 1920, 4; "End Dry Acts Arguments," *New York Times,* March 11, 1920, 6; "Pleads States Rights To Enforce Dry Laws," *New York Times,* March 31, 1920, 18.

256 "Dry Law Upheld in Unanimous View of Supreme Court," *New York Times,* June 8, 1920, 1; Hamm, *Shaping the 18th Amendment,* 251-253.

257 U.S. Office of Internal Revenue, *Annual Report of the Commissioner* (Washington, D.C., 1919), 62.

258 Hamm, *Shaping the 18th Amendment,* 253.

---

of the Treasury Andrew Mellon, an early proponent of supply-side economics, cut taxes five times.[259] For over fifty years, prohibitionists had claimed that the removal of the liquor tax would generate untold prosperity for the American people. The economic successes of the Twenties seemed to confirm this. Opponents of Prohibition — several non-industry groups emerged following passage of the Volstead Act — tended to concentrate their rhetoric on the increasing violence and lawlessness caused by illicit production and distribution of alcohol. Fewer people drank, but those who did were completely beyond the reach of the government, for the purpose of paying taxes or any other reason.[260]

During Prohibition, the relatively few brewers that survived did so by producing items other than beer, including milk, butter, cheese, condensed milk, grain, flour, and feed. Larger breweries added de-alcoholizing apparatus to their plants and essentially became cereal beverage producers. Pabst, Blatz, and Stroh, all large Midwestern brewers, took out trademarks for malt syrup in the 1920s. Malt syrup is one of the ingredients in brewing beer. It is evaporated malted barley and has a sweet taste; sometime it contains hops. Anheuser–Busch produced malt syrup as well; the company's survival arsenal included producing yeast, corn products, ginger ale, and cereal beverages.[261] The brewers were businessmen and sought to retain their economic livelihood. They may also have hoped that Prohibition would not last; perhaps the government would once again need their financial contribution.

The Volstead Act, which prohibited even low alcoholic content beer, hindered attempts by brewers to make palatable alternatives to pre-Prohibition beer. The lack of such alternatives encouraged the infamous creation of bootleg liquor and beer during Prohibition. It also fostered new legal competition in the form of soft drinks and soda.[262]

Brewers continued to brew beer to supply doctors with amounts for prescription; to make non-alcoholic beer you had to brew beer and then remove the alcohol. The process obviously left the door open for diversion. Although none of the prominent brewers appeared to have engaged in illegal production of beer, bootleg beer was big business. Al Capone controlled at least six breweries in Chicago. His total revenue from liquor sales was $60 million; beer sales gener-

259 Witte, *The Federal Income Tax*, 88-95; Lillian Doris, *The American Way in Taxation* (Englewood Cliffs, N.J.: Prentice-Hall 1963), 27.

260 David E. Kyvig, *Repealing National Prohibition* (Chicago: University of Chicago Press, 1979); Larry Engelmann, "Organized Thirst: The Story of Repeal in Michigan," in Jack S. Blocker, Jr., ed., *Alcohol, Reform and Society: The Liquor Issue in Social Context* (Westport, 1979), 171-221.

261 *Brewer's Art* 5 (January-February 1932): 248; Charlie Papazian, *The Complete Joy of Homebrewing*, 3rd ed. (New York: Harper Collins, 2003), 15.

262 *The Brewer's Art* 1 (June 1923): 6; Stanley Baron, *Brewed in America*, 323-324.

ated much of it. Transporting the beer meant more illegal activity. Beer's bulk required trucks; protecting the trucks led to bribery of police and gang violence.[263]

Yeast and malt syrups, produced by Anheuser–Busch, Pabst, and other brewers during Prohibition, were the building blocks of fermented beverages. Enterprising home brewers bought the ingredients and brewed their own beer. Colonial women had brewed beer in their kitchens; families in the 1920s revived this tradition. In the first few months of Prohibition, officials realized the potential for diversion of the products from baking to brewing and ruled "against the sale of hops and malt to others than bakers and confectioners."[264]

In 1922 it became obvious that the line between home and business brewing as well as legal and illegal brewing had become very blurred when New Jersey police raided a "Home Brew College" in Bayonne. They discovered forty barrels and one hundred cases of beer as well as $2,500 worth of whiskey. The owner of the "saloon," Frank Orlouski, was apparently more interested in teaching others how to make their own beer and liquor than in selling alcohol himself.[265]

Home brewing as well as bootleg beer continued unabated throughout Prohibition; by 1930 officials attempted to stop this production by prosecuting producers and distributors of beer-and liquor-making supplies. Prohibition Commissioner Doran acknowledged that it would be difficult to distinguish between purchases of the supplies for personal consumption and use of the supplies for commercial gain. He also admitted that "the government is not in a position to prosecute the non-commercial home brewer."[266]

The brewers who attempted to stay in business showed some hope that Prohibition would be temporary. The individuals who maintained the brewing organizations showed even greater persistence. Jacob Ruppert, Jr. had been influential in the USBA prior to Prohibition and had sued the federal government over the constitutionality of the Eighteenth Amendment and the Volstead Act. Ruppert and the Jacob Ruppert Brewery epitomized the successful urban, non-shipping brewer.

Jacob Ruppert, Jr. was born in 1867, the son of the founder of Jacob Ruppert Brewery Company. Ruppert, Jr., a colonel in the Seventh Regiment of the New York National Guard, was a Democratic New York Congressmen for four terms. In 1914 he purchased the New York Yankees and was president of that team until his death in 1939. His ownership of the team gained him national recognition.

---

263 Frederick Lewis Allen, *Only Yesterday: An Informal History of the 1920s* (New York: Harpers 1931), 228; Peter Hernon and Terry Ganey, *Under the Influence: The Unauthorized Story of the Anheuser–Busch Dynasty* (New York: Simon & Schuster, 1991), 131.

264 "Bar Hops and Malt for Home Brewing," *New York Times*, November 12, 1920, 13.

265 "Home Brew College Found in Bayonne Raid," *New York Times*, September 15, 1922.

266 "Doran Moves to End Beer Material Sale," *New York Times*, May 7, 1930, 2.

Ruppert was the only prominent brewer to link sports and beer prior to Prohibition. After Repeal many brewers saw the advertising potential in connecting beer with sporting events and other recreational activities.

Figure 10: Jacob Ruppert and Miss Harwood, 1921. Photo courtesy of Library of Congress, Prints & Photographs Division [LC-DIG-ggbain-33197 (digital file from original negative)].

The Colonel's grandfather was a German immigrant who had worked in breweries. His father, Jacob Sr., founded The Jacob Ruppert Brewery in 1867; the company had million barrel sales prior to Prohibition. This success came solely from sales in the New York and New England areas; the brewery did no national shipping. Knickerbocker was the company's most famous brand. This beer dated from the 1950s. The firm remained in operation until 1965.[267]

Hugh Fox, secretary of the USBA, and Jacob Ruppert kept a skeleton organization going during Prohibition. Carl Nowak, former secretary of the Master Brewers Association of the Americas, began publishing the *Brewer's Art* in 1923. Nowak's goal was the "rehabilitation" of the brewing industry. This periodical has survived until today as *Modern Brewery Age* (on-line). The MBAA, an organization of brewmasters rather than brewery owners, also kept a skeleton organization going during Prohibition.[268]

Hugh Fox, a native of Great Britain and a hops dealer, was the secretary of the USBA for twenty-five years, only ceasing this work when he died at the age of 69 on November 30, 1932. Fox was secretary in the years leading up to Prohibition when the brewers rather naively believed that the wholesomeness of their product and their relationship with the federal government would protect them from Prohibition. Unfortunately he did not live to see Repeal which to some extent justified those earlier beliefs.[269]

Jacob Ruppert, Jr.'s leadership of the USBA during Prohibition and Repeal, and his determination to keep the organization strong, places him among the great figures, such as Frederick Lauer, in the history of brewing. Ruppert, however, was unable to maintain unity among brewers during Repeal, with ultimate consequences for the ongoing fate of the USBA.

During the early years of Prohibition, Christian Feigenspan headed the Brewers Association. Feigenspan was the head of a Newark, New Jersey brewery bearing his name. Prior to Prohibition the company had gained control of the Dobler Brewing Company in Albany, New York, and the Yale Brewery in New

267 "Ruppert, Jacob, Jr. (1867-1939)," *Biographical Directory of the United States Congress*, http:// bioguide.congress.gov/scripts/biodisplay.pl?index=R000513 (accessed June 14, 2007); Downard, *Dictionary*, 161-162; "Jacob Ruppert," *Dictionary of American Biography*, Supplements 1-2: To 1940, American Council of Learned Societies, 1944-1958, Reproduced in Biography Resource Center. Farmington Hills, Mich.: Thomson Gale. 2007. http://galenet.galegroup. com/servlet/BioRC (accessed June 14, 2007).

268 *The Brewer's Art* 1 (November 1923): 99; "Chronology of the American Brewing Industry," http://www.beerhistory.com/library/holdings/chronology.shtml (accessed November 11, 2004).

269 John Arnold and Frank Perman, *History of the Brewing Industry and Brewing Science in America* (Chicago, 1933), 233; *New York Times*, November 30, 1932, 19; Drescher, "Opposition to Prohibition," passim.

Haven. The company resumed brewing following Repeal. Ballantine bought the firm in 1944; Dobler beer was produced into the 1960s.[270]

In 1921 the House Judicial Committee began holding hearings on a supplement to the Volstead Act which would have prevented doctors from prescribing unlimited amounts of beer, something Attorney General Palmer had allowed. August A. Busch, President of Anheuser–Busch, telegrammed to the committee, stating "Beer for all or beer for none is my motto." Oliver T. Remmers, speaking on behalf of the company, presented a brief for the committee which sought sale of a low alcoholic content beer. If that could not occur, the company did not want medicinal beer sold because of the competition and incentive for fraud it represented. Remmers did not believe that beer was a medicine. Anheuser–Busch claimed that it had lost $5 million by obeying the law while brewers in Ohio, Pennsylvania, and Illinois were all openly violating the Volstead Act. Anheuser–Busch and other brewers were seeking to retain control over legal production of an illegal substance. The illegal brewing and distilling that went on unabated during Prohibition was very frustrating for all brewers who sought to remain in business during Prohibition.[271]

In 1922 Busch traveled to Germany aboard the *George Washington*. The United States Shipping Board owned the boat; Busch was able to buy liquor and beer while aboard. Once ashore, he telegraphed President Harding decrying the hypocrisy of the situation and that the boat and the federal government were in violation of the three-mile limit law. A.D. Lasker was chairman of the Shipping Board; he replied to Busch that the boat had been beyond the three-mile limit and therefore had not violated any laws. He also added that he believed Busch to be "thoroughly selfish, and that you are acting in the hope of creating a public revolt against Prohibition so that you may again revive the sale of your liquors." Lasker made a direct link between Busch's German ancestry and his letter to the president. "It is, of course notorious that the Adolphus Busch who founded your brewery was possibly the Kaiser's closest friend in America, and that your family for many years has maintained a castle in Germany...."[272]

This controversy raged on in the papers for a few days, demonstrating both that a prominent brewer could command public attention, and that the passions of World War I had not yet subsided. When the dust settled, legislation prohibited the sale of alcohol aboard American ships and the limit for contraband liquor was extended to twelve miles.[273]

---

270 Downard, *Dictionary*, 74.
271 "Brewer Calls For Dry Enforcement," *New York Times*, May 13, 1921, 17.
272 "Busch Protest to Harding," *New York Times*, June 14, 1922, 18.
273 Hernon and Ganey, *Under the Influence*, 144.

By 1925 those brewers who were attempting to stay afloat saw money that consumers had previously spent on beer going to the purchase of bootleg hard liquor. Sections of the brewing industry sought to restore near beer, a beer of 2.75 percent alcohol content. As one method of achieving this goal, the USBA sought talks with the Anti-Saloon League. Feigenspan was completely opposed to such negotiations and resigned as president. In the aftermath of his resignation, Jacob Ruppert became the President of the USBA. Although both the USBA and the Anti-Saloon League officially denied that there had been any contacts between the two organizations, there were signs that a representative of Anheuser–Busch had met with Wayne Wheeler, head of the Anti-Saloon League.[274]

In public statements, Hugh Fox made clear the USBA was not seeking repeal of the Volstead Act but an amendment that would permit 2.75 percent beer. The conflict within brewing, highlighted by Feigenspan's resignation, was over whether to attempt amelioration or fight for outright repeal. If modification of the Volstead Act had occurred, the larger brewers still in business would have had a better chance of converting their facilities. Prohibition remained in full force until Repeal. This controversy served primarily to thrust Jacob Ruppert into greater prominence. The other consequence was that illegal brewing and distilling continued unabated during Prohibition. After Repeal, legitimate brewers still had to face bootleg competition.[275]

Brewers began to gain hope for change in their dire situation when Al Smith, Democrat from New York, ran for President against Herbert Hoover in 1928. Enforcement of Prohibition relied upon states providing concurrent support. New York, with Governor Smith's support, repealed state enforcement of Prohibition in 1923.[276] Illegal production of alcohol thrived in the state. The Democratic Party platform did not advocate Repeal; it simply stated the party's support for the law. Smith disliked the party's plank and, in private, wrote his own version. "The Eighteenth Amendment is part of the fundamental law of the United States. We hold it to be an economic not a political question. We promise a solution of its enforcement or its amendment as experience may teach."[277]

Although many people in the country openly flouted prohibition, it was not clear that they would vote to repeal it. Will Rogers, noted humorist, saw the situation in the following manner: "If you think this country ain't Dry you just watch 'em vote; and if you think this country ain't Wet, you just watch them

---

274 *New York Times,* September 24, 1925, 27; *New York Times,* September 25, 1925, 6.

275 *New York Times,* September 25, 1925, 6.

276 "Wets are Jubilant, Drys Disappointed," *New York Times,* June 2, 1923, 2; David Fahey, "National Prohibition (United States)," in Blocker, et al., *Encyclopedia,* 440-443.

277 Oscar Handlin, *Al Smith and His America* (Boston: Little, Brown, 1958) 109, 127, 130; Richard O'Connor, *The First Hurrah, A Biography of Alfred E. Smith* (New York: Putnam,1970), 191-192.

drink. You see, when they vote, it's counted; but when they drink it ain't. If you could register the man's breath that cast the ballots, that would be great. But the voting strength of this country is dry."[278]

Smith was defeated; he received only 87 electoral votes to Hoover's 444 and did not carry his home state of New York. Anti-Catholicism, anti-urbanism, and general prosperity as well as his "wet" status all played a role in the defeat. The election results also held a harbinger of future contests. In both 1920 and 1924, the Republican Party had a plurality in the nation's twelve largest cities, but in 1928 the Democrats won New York, Chicago, Philadelphia, Pittsburgh, Detroit, Cleveland, Baltimore, St. Louis, Boston, Milwaukee, San Francisco, and Los Angeles. Prior to Prohibition urban areas consumed four-fifths of the country's total beer production.[279] These cities had all been centers of beer production before 1918, and most had never accepted Prohibition. Under the right circumstances, their population could provide support for an anti-prohibition movement.

In his capacity as president of the USBA, which the *New York Times* described as an organization of "near beer" makers, Ruppert sought to have light beer legalized which he portrayed as being in "the interest of temperance." The USBA, anticipating Hoover's inauguration, called for a commission to investigate Prohibition.[280]

One of the more obvious reasons for bootleg beer and liquor was poor enforcement of the Volstead Act. Before 1927 the Treasury Department was responsible for enforcement. In 1920 Congress appropriated $5 million for enforcement; this amount was for controlling the borders and inspecting and regulating the production of near beer and industrial alcohol as well as druggists' sale of prescription alcohol. It was a mammoth task for which the federal government supplied neither enough funds nor manpower. In 1920 there were 1,520 prohibition agents; by 1930 the number had risen to 2,836.[281]

Prohibition enabled temperance advocates, with the support of many businessmen, to dismantle a highly lucrative capitalist enterprise — a rare event in American history. The intimate connection between the federal government and the liquor industry which began in the Civil War was unusual for an era historians have often characterized as laissez-faire. The social movement against consumption of alcohol further differentiated liquor manufacturers from other businesses of the day. However, the driving need of governments for revenue ultimately contributed to the repeal of the Eighteenth Amendment.

278 Quoted in Handlin, *Al Smith*, 125.
279 O'Connor, *The First Hurrah* , 221-224.
280 *New York Times*, December 21, 1928, 12.
281 Allen, *Only Yesterday*, 215-216.

On October 29, 1929, the Stock Market crashed, bursting the bubble of the Roaring Twenties, and very quickly bringing into question the claims of the Anti-Saloon League and other prohibitionists regarding the positive economic benefits of Prohibition. The debate over the enactment of the Eighteenth Amendment had presented Prohibition as a panacea for much of industrial society's ills. Repeal became a similar "quick fix" for Depression America.

Hoover had established a commission to study Prohibition and law enforcement. In 1931, the final report of the Wickersham Commission Report opposed Repeal and modification of the Volstead Act. Although almost all of the people who served on the commission supported some change in Prohibition, and two were for Repeal, Hoover claimed the report was a validation of Prohibition. He then advocated for more efficient enforcement. As the economic situation worsened, the public found his position unacceptable.[282]

Although the prohibition movement had a long history, the enactment of the Eighteenth Amendment was a short-term phenomenon. When alcohol consumption rises rapidly or reaches a significant level of consumption, a reaction to the effects of such high consumption sets in. In 1910 the level of per capita consumption of alcoholic beverages was 1.7 gallons absolute alcohol. The level had not been that high since 1840.[283]

Thirteen years of Prohibition reduced memories of the negative consequences of widespread drinking and replaced them with visions of criminal activity around bootleg whiskey. Because people no longer associated legal alcohol drinking with anything unpleasant, in 1932, they were able to concentrate on the economic benefits Repeal would bring.

The economic situation had transformed the debate over Prohibition. Questions over its efficacy persist until today. The one thing it did clearly achieve was the destruction of the saloon and its male-centered drinking. During the thirteen years of Prohibition, patterns of public and private drinking had expanded to include women alongside men. No longer did women solely embody temperance nor were men the face of public drinking.

With the economic downturn, the Association Against the Prohibition Amendment and the Women's Organization for National Prohibition Reform, the two major anti-prohibition organizations, were able to use the prohibitionists' economic arguments against them. Proponents of repeal touted the economic benefits legalization of alcohol would bring. The liquor industry had always argued that they made an irreplaceable contribution to federal and state govern-

---

282 Thomas R. Pegram, *Battling Demon Rum: The Struggle for a Dry America, 1800-1933* (Chicago: Ivan R. Dee, 1998), 182-183.

283 Downard, *Dictionary*, 225.

ment. In 1932, most Americans agreed, electing Franklin Roosevelt as President. The Democratic platform promised legalization of near beer and repeal of the Eighteenth Amendment.[284]

From 1862 on, the liquor industry had been a primary support of the budget of the federal government. The nation's experience with expanding income taxes during World War I, coupled with a progressive impulse to shape the moral character of the country, led officials to allow the cutting off of a vital source of revenue — liquor production and distribution. The prosperous 1920s validated this decision, yet in 1933 the country again turned to the liquor industry in an hour of need. For many years the liquor industry had persistently asked, "Who will pay the tax?" The answer turned out to be themselves.

---

284 Engelmann, "Organized Thirst".

CHAPTER 5. BEER FLOWS: REPEAL OF PROHIBITION, 1933–1941

Liquor and labor interests had been the most prominent actors in the struggle over Prohibition prior to the adoption of the Eighteenth Amendment. The Stock Market Crash of 1929 allowed several strands of anti-prohibition arguments to coalesce into a ground swell against Prohibition. In 1932, the election of Franklin Roosevelt sealed Prohibition's fate.

Since Al Smith's candidacy in 1928, the Democratic Party identified with wet constituencies in the urban areas of the country. The economic crisis of the Great Depression strengthened the Repeal advocates' arguments about the negative financial consequences of Prohibition and the benefits of legal taxable liquor. The 1932 Democratic platform endorsed a constitutional amendment to end Prohibition, stating "Pending repeal, we favor immediate modification of the Volstead Act; to legalize the manufacture and sale of beer and other beverages of such alcoholic content as is permissible under the Constitution and to provide there from a proper and needed revenue."[285] Roosevelt's election was a landslide, clearly a mandate for quick economic remedies. The newly elected President, a member of America's landed aristocracy, enjoyed cocktails, and mixing drinks was one of his hobbies.[286]

When Franklin Roosevelt became the 32nd President of the United States on March 4, 1933 the country was in the worst economic depression in history,

285 Democratic Party Platform of 1932, Gerhard Peters, *American Presidency Project*, http://www.presidency.ucsb.edu/showplatforms.php?platindex=D1932 (accessed June 11, 2007).
286 Arthur M. Schlesinger, Jr., ed., *The Almanac of American History* (New York: G. Putnam's Sons, 1983), 460; Arthur M. Schlesinger, Jr., *The Age of Roosevelt: The Coming of the New Deal* (Boston: Houghton Mifflin, 1965), 570-580.

with 13 million people unemployed. Roosevelt set to work trying to repair the nation's economy. On March 12 he addressed the nation in the first of his many "fireside chats." The president declared a bank holiday. Immediately after the fireside chat, he sent a message to Congress requesting immediate modification of the Volstead Act to exempt beer with an alcoholic content no greater than 3.2 percent alcohol by weight. Roosevelt believed that "now would be a good time for beer."[287] The President was calling on the beer industry to provide the nation with a much needed boost in morale as well as assist him in his agenda of reform and repair of the economy. In turn the brewers would get a much desired chance to start anew.

As the movement to repeal Prohibition gathered steam, proponents for reestablishing legal liquor sought to remove federal control and return regulatory powers to the states. State regulation of liquor prior to Prohibition had involved licensing of retail establishments as well as sumptuary legislation. States generally did not tax liquor before 1933. The Twenty-First Amendment repealing Prohibition and legalizing the production and sale of alcohol achieved the return of regulatory control to the states. The federal government resumed its primary concern with taxation.

The states, as well as the federal government, saw the brewing industry as a source of economic relief. Following Repeal, many states established Liquor Control Boards and began taxing alcoholic beverages. The highest tax the brewers had paid prior to Prohibition had been $3 a barrel. *Modern Brewery* estimated that the newly reestablished brewers were facing tax increases of "400 to 600 percent."[288]

After fourteen years of Prohibition, on April 7, 1933 the legal production of beer resumed. The *New York Times* proclaimed that "beer flows" in 19 states. The newspaper was recording the return of legal 3.2 percent alcohol beer to many cities across the nation including Philadelphia, St. Louis, Baltimore, Milwaukee, and San Francisco. All of these municipalities held "gala night" in honor of modification of the Volstead Act.[289] Prior to Prohibition the country had approximately 1250 brewers; by June there were 31 brewers operating. In 1934 there were 756 brewers who produced 37,678,313 barrels. Production for 1914, the last "normal"

---

287 Schlesinger, *Almanac*, 461-462; Quoted in Kenneth S. Davis, *FDR, The New Deal Years 1933-1933* (New York: Random House, 1986), 63.

288 Oregon State Archives, "Prohibition in Oregon: The Vision and the Reality," http://arcweb. sos.state.or.us/50th/prohibition1/prohibintro.html (accessed January 20, 2006); *Modern Brewery*, February 1933, 20. *Modern Brewery Age* began as *The Brewer's Art* (1923-1932), and then became *Modern Brewery* (1933-1935), *Modern Brewer* (1936-1940), and then *Modern Brewery Age* (1940-2004). It is now available online only at http://www.breweryage.com/.

289 "Beer Flows in 19 States at Midnight as City Awaits Legal Brew Today," *New York Times* April 7, 1933, 1.

year prior to Prohibition, was 66,189,473 barrels.[290] The brewing industry had achieved an amazing rebirth; the public was extraordinarily grateful. The challenge for the brewers, as the nation sought to regain its economic footing, was to maintain their good public image and restore their industry.

Repeal proponents had touted increased revenue as a benefit which made liquor taxes inevitable. Amazingly, a week after beer became legal, legislators passed a tax bill. Echoing their Civil War predecessors, Congressmen sought the highest possible rate from the beer tax that would not cause fraud and corruption. They settled on a rate for legal brewers of $5 a barrel plus a $1,000 annual license fee for each brewery.[291]

In the immediate aftermath of modification of the Volstead Act and prior to ratification of the Twenty-First Amendment, the government was looking forward to the economic benefits that Repeal would bring. Postmaster General Farley predicted that "it will provide approximately $800,000,000 annually in revenue."[292] Taxes on beer had helped to reduce the government's operating deficit and Farley was optimistic that the end of Prohibition would help reduce federal taxes on everything else.

Michigan was the first state to ratify the Twenty-First Amendment and the amendment became final on November 7, 1933 when Kentucky, Ohio, Pennsylvania, and Utah voted their approval. The amendment's language made Repeal effective December 5, 1933. The Eighteenth Amendment and its antidote the Twenty-First stand as unique events in American history. The first outlawed a legal industry and deprived thousands of business people of their livelihood. The Eighteenth Amendment is the only amendment to have been repealed. The Founding Fathers used state constitutional conventions to enact the Constitution; the Twenty-First Amendment was enacted in the same manner. Joseph H. Choate, Jr., as head of the Voluntary Lawyers Committee, contributed this expeditious and successful legal approach as part of the anti-Prohibition movement.[293]

Both the government and the liquor industry were quite comfortable reestablishing their old relationship, particularly since officials were willing to limit

290 USBA, *Brewers Almanac* (Washington, D.C.: USBA, 1940), 14; "Chronology of the American Brewing Industry," Beerhistory.com, http://www.beerhistory.com/library/holdings/chronology.shtml (accessed January 16, 2002).

291 Carl Miller, "We Want Beer: Prohibition and the Will to Imbibe," Beerhistory.com http://www.beerhistory.com/library/holdings/prohibition_2.shtml (accessed January 20, 2006).

292 "Farley Holds Liquor Will Balance Budget," *New York Times*, September 1, 1933, 36.

293 *Brewers Almanac*, 1940, 60; United States Brewers Association, *Brewers Almanac* (Washington, D.C.: USBA: 1980), 110; Robert LaForge, "Misplaced Priorities: A History of Federal Alcohol Regulation and Public Health Policy" (Sc. D. diss., Johns Hopkins University, 1987), 135-136.

tax increases, citing concern over the continued presence of bootleggers. Tax revenues had fallen to $1.5 billion in 1932 — the lowest collection since 1917; following Repeal they began to rise. In the first six months that legal 3.2 beer was available, Americans drank 7,037,969,264 eight-ounce glasses. This gave the government $84,917,539 in revenue.[294] Liquor taxes continued to grow in strength; by 1936 excise taxes on alcohol contributed thirteen per cent to the federal tax system, providing fiscal support for New Deal legislation.[295]

The brewing industry, newly legal and providing a product for which there was pent-up demand, was well situated to meet the goals of New Deal legislation that sought to increase production and reduce unemployment. Unlike other industries, they also had a history of government regulation and control. The challenge for the brewers would be to flourish in a new regulatory environment.

The first major piece of New Deal legislation to affect the brewers was the Agricultural Adjustment Act of May 12, 1933. Henry Wallace, Secretary of Agriculture, was the ultimate authority for any policies that might affect the brewers. Alcoholic beverages, including beer, distilled spirits, and wine, were a unit of the Division of Processing and Marketing. The division head was W.I. Westervelt who had been the head of Sears, Roebuck. He reported to George N. Peek and Charles J. Brand who were the co-administrators of the Agricultural Adjustment Administration (AAA).[296]

The National Industrial Recovery Act (NIRA), which FDR signed on June 16, 1933, established the National Recovery Administration (NRA). This legislation had significant implications for all industries, including the brewers. Attempting to address issues of competition, monopoly, and underemployment, the architects of the NRA placed emphasis on the role of trade associations in the economy. The pre-Prohibition brewing industry had been one of the first to form a trade association — the USBA — which had continued to operate during Prohibition and now, was fully ready to participate in the NRA. The industry also had one of the nation's first industrial unions — the United Brewery Workers. During Prohibition the AFL had granted the UBW jurisdiction over flour, cereal, and soft drink workers in an effort to increase membership.[297]

Because the brewing industry used agricultural products and was a food industry it fell under the supervision of both the NRA and the Agricultural Adjust-

---

294 *New York Times*, October 28, 1933, 32.

295 Amy Mittelman, "Taxation of Liquor (United States)" in Jack Blocker, et al., *Encyclopedia*, vol. 2, 609-61.

296 George N. Peek and Samuel Crowther, *Why Quit Our Own* (New York: D. Van Nostrand Co, 1936), 92, 106-109; *Modern Brewery*, September 1933, 28.

297 Eric Foner and John A. Garraty, *The Reader's Companion to American History* (Boston: Houghton Mifflin, 1991), 777-778; Amy Mittelman, "Labor in the U.S. Liquor Industry," in Blocker, et. al., *Encyclopedia*, vol. 1, 356-358.

ment Administration (AAA). The AAA was part of the Department of Agriculture; the NRA was an independent agency.

With enactment of the NIRA the processing and marketing division of the AAA gained greater responsibilities. Executive orders by FDR gave the Department of Agriculture the final authority over codes, licenses, and marketing agreements for agricultural trades and industries in order to prevent duplication of activities.[298] The newly legal brewers faced a myriad of agencies with authority over their economic activities as well as more hurdles in their quest to maintain a positive public image while building their industry. Prior to Prohibition they had dealt fairly exclusively with the Bureau of Internal Revenue.

In the forefront of the brewing industry's response to the NRA were C.D. Williams and the USBA. Williams, former Executive Secretary of the New England Gas Association, had become the secretary of the trade association following the death of Hugh Fox in 1933. Other industry organizations included the American Brewers Association (ABA) founded in 1930 to represent near beer brewers and the MBAA which represented the technical and educational interests of the industry, had a heavily German orientation prior to Prohibition, and still exists today.[299]

Although the goal of the NIRA had been to stimulate the economy, the need to generate higher employment levels remained pressing. Motivated by the belief that higher wages were the answer, the New Dealers next put forth the President's Re-employment Agreement. Addressed "To Every Employer," the agreement mandated the elimination of child labor, limitation on weekly hours of work, and the establishment of minimum wages. Unlike the NRA codes, which also dealt with these issues, re-employment agreements were individual contracts designed to be in effect from August 1 to December 31, 1933.[300]

The brewers agreed to the wages and hours provisions of the President's Re-employment Agreement by accepting the unions' demand for shorter hours. The agreement kept the wage standard already in existence. This mandated wages above the minimum that the President's agreement set. Brewery workers would realize an hourly wage increase of ten to twenty percent.[301]

Despite the individual contractual nature of the re-employment agreements, brewers, acting in conjunction with brewery workers, responded on an indus-

298 Van L. Perkins, *Crisis in Agriculture: The Agricultural Adjustment Administration and the New Deal, 1933* (Berkeley: University of California Press, 1969), 91.

299 *Modern Brewery*, February 1933, 54; William Downard, *Dictionary of the American Brewing and Distilling Industries* (Westport, CT: Greenwood Press, 1980), 7, 78, 117. The MBA had 3,500 members organized in 24 districts in 2004. See www.mbaa.com.

300 Charles Lee Dearing, et al., *The ABC of the NRA* (Washington, DC: The Brookings Institution, 1934), 60-61; *Modern Brewery*, August 1933, 21-22.

301 "Brewers Put Code on Labor in Force," *New York Times*, July 29, 1933, 3.

try-wide basis. The USBA and other industry organizations exhorted all brewers to sign re-employment agreements as long as they could exempt those workers who were already covered by collective bargaining contracts. This activity was part of the larger effort of code writing.[302]

Although many American businesses resented the far-reaching nature of NRA activity, the brewing industry seemed predisposed to cooperate fully with the federal government as long as their business remained legal. In September 1933, an editorial in *Modern Brewery* declared that "the brewers enjoy the good will and high esteem of the American public to a degree never before recorded. This esteem can only be preserved by self-government of the entire industry by itself rather than by governmental coercion."[303] Prohibition, the ultimate form of "governmental coercion" was never far from the minds of brewers.

A joint committee of brewers from both the USBA and the ABA worked on a draft of the code. The writing of the code generated conflict within the newly legal brewing industry. Although the USBA and the ABA apparently represented "62 percent of the production volume in the industry and approximately one-third of the number of plants," some brewers questioned their motives.[304]

In October 1933, a group of "independent" brewers met in Washington, D.C. to mount opposition to the proposed NRA code. Both the USBA and the ABA worked on the code; this group of brewers represented that aspect of the industry which belonged to neither organization. The Independent Brewers Association, headed by Major Thomas G. Lanphier, claimed the USBA and ABA spoke for only one-fourth of brewers and would be a trust under the proposed code.[305] Section 3A of the NIRA authorized the President to accept a code provided "that such . . . codes are not designed to promote monopolies or to eliminate or oppress small enterprises . . . ."[306]

Modern Brewery felt that "It would be a disgrace to this industry if brewers not only delayed approval of a Code but also openly fought each other in an open meeting on the Code."[307] The NRA sought to have each industry write codes, which would address issues of production, price, wages, and ethics. After an industry had written a code, the government held hearings. The ultimate decision on adoption of an industry's code rested with the federal government. The

302 *Modern Brewery*, August 1933, 21-22.
303 *Modern Brewery*, September 1933, 21.
304 Ibid., 25.
305 "Fight on Beer Code Set," *New York Times* October 2, 1933, 4.
306 , *The ABC of the NRA*, 16.
307 *Modern Brewery*, September 1933, 28.

Secretary of Agriculture had the final say in who would administer the code for the brewing industry.[308]

The alcoholic beverage industry had six different facets that required codes: distilled spirits, brewing, wine, rectifying, wholesalers, and importing. The brewers were the only ones who fully participated in all phases of the code-writing process. They alone had a pre-existing trade association. Therefore they could write their code rather than having it written for them like the distillers.[309] Once again the USBA provided support for brewers that distinguished them from other industries.

The NIRA also established the Federal Alcohol Control Administration to pursue the agenda of the NRA, but also as an oversight agency to prevent pre-Prohibition problems, such as brewer ownership of saloons, from returning to the liquor industry. The brewers supported the abolition of the tied house system of distribution. Prior to Prohibition, Anheuser-Busch and other large shipping brewers had advocated this. Owning saloons across the country had sometimes placed them at a competitive disadvantage.[310]

Figure 11: Joseph H. Choate, Jr. Photo courtesy of Voluntary Lawyers Committee.

From the onset of Repeal, the focus of alcohol control policy was on regulating sales rather than reducing consumption. The economic impetus of generating revenue was always front and center. The administrator for brewers was Joseph H. Choate, Jr., a lawyer who had figured prominently in the Repeal effort. Choate had been chairman of the Voluntary Committee of Lawyers from 1927-1933. The new administrator

---

308 ABC of NRA, 77-92.

309 House Committee on Ways and Means, *Extension of NIRA Hearings before the House Committee on Ways and Means*, 74 Cong., 1st sess., 1935, 259-304; *Modern Brewery* 10 (July 1933): 21.

310 Martin Stack, "Local and Regional Breweries in America's Brewing Industry, 1865 to 1920, *Business History Review*, vol. 74, no. 3 (Autumn, 2000): 435-463.

saw his role as one of oversight for the industry and felt that industry cooperation was necessary for Repeal to succeed. The brewers concurred.[311]

Provisions of the NIRA repealed an additional gasoline tax, a dividend tax, a
capital stock tax, and an excess profits tax. These had generated $227 million. In
their place would be a $6 a barrel tax on beer, $1.10 on "hard" liquor, twelve cents
on a half-pint of champagne, and a graduated schedule of taxes for wine. The
codes established for the industry would govern regulation of all aspects of the
liquor trade. FDR signed the NRA code for the brewing industry on December 4,
1933 and it went into effect on December 5.[312]

The brewing industry drafted a complete code and participated in an open
hearing on the proposed code. The Brewers Code differed from those of the rest
of the industry because it did not establish a permit system and did not mandate
size of production or plant capacity. Still, for brewers, the final code represented
what *Modern Brewery* called a "compromise." All aspects of the liquor industry,
including distilled spirits, were under the control of the FACA. George McCabe,
speaking on behalf of the ABA stated that "Control by the Federal Alcoholic [*sic*]
Control Commission is especially repugnant to the brewers for the reason that
it has been the constant aim and effort of the brewing industry to achieve and
maintain a complete separation of that industry, both in fact and in appearance,
from the distilled spirits industry." The brewers continued their pre-Prohibition determination to be separate and distinct from distilled spirits, and the exemption from permits was a victory in this campaign. The Brewers Code also
minimized the federal regulatory presence at the site of production, which was
always a goal. For the rest of the industry, permits became a type of license and
helped insure compliance.[313]

Provisions of the *Code of Fair Competition for the Brewing Industry of the United
States* established a nine member Code Authority consisting of three members
from the USBA, two from the ABA, and four from neither association. John C.
Bruckmann, President of Bruckmann Co. was chairman of the Code Authority.
Members included R.A. Huber, vice-president of Anheuser–Busch and an officer
of the USBA, Donald Dailey of Genesee Brewery, C. W. Feigenspan from Feigenspan Brewery, and A.B. Bechaud, from Bechaud Brewery. Feigenspan was also an
officer of the USBA; Dailey and Bechaud represented "independent" brewers.[314]

311 LaForge, "Misplaced Priorities," 65, 136; Downard, *Dictionary*, 72; "Joseph H. Choate, Lawyer,
91, Dead" *New York Times*, January 20, 1968, 29.

312 "Roosevelt to End 4 Recovery Taxes as Dry Law Goes," *New York Times* November 11, 1933, 1;
Brewers Almanac, October 1940, 60.

313 *Modern Brewery*, December 1933, 60; LaForge, "Misplaced Priorities," 153, 155-156.

314 *Modern Brewer*, December 1933, 26, 53; *Modern Brewery*, January 1934, 27. Huber died in 1935 of
a blood infection. See *New York Times*, May 2 1935, 21.

The code established eighteen regional authorities who reported to the Code Authority, and the brewers of each region elected the members. William Piel, of the Piels Brothers Brewery of Brooklyn, was the chairman of the Regional Committee of New York State and Puerto Rico. Jacob Ruppert, president of the USBA, was a member of this regional board. Piels Brothers Brewery produced near beer during Prohibition. Wisconsin and Missouri brewers each had their own regional authorities.[315]

A significant aspect of the NRA was section 7a that dealt with working conditions and workers' right to unionize. The pre-Prohibition brewing industry had been unionized, and brewery workers were in the middle of the national wage and labor structure. In an era of craft unionism, the UBW had stood out, for its dual commitment to socialism and industrial unionism. Jacob Ruppert, in April 1934, stated "the brewing industry, cooperating with the Government and in harmony with the Code has already materially further reduced the hours of labor and given employment thereby to many more than those tens of thousands to whom it gave reemployment at the time of modification."[316]

Following Repeal, the UBW continued to have jurisdictional problems with the AFL. In 1933 the AFL sought to remove beer drivers, firemen, and engineers from the jurisdiction of the UBW. *Modern Brewery* urged brewers to "support brewery labor in their battle for their originally chartered rights." In the immediate aftermath of Prohibition and Repeal, brewers and brewery workers had resumed their historic and traditional relationship of cooperation.[317]

Labor turmoil was a fact of life during the New Deal; the brewing industry, however, seemed more or less free from labor unrest. In 1937 brewery workers were likely to make an average weekly wage of $32.26. Although these wages were evidence of harmonious relations between brewery labor and management, some union struggles did affect the brewing industry. The jurisdictional fight between the teamsters union and the UBW hampered distribution of beer. *Modern Brewer* felt the solution was that "the brewer operating his own fleet of trucks to employ operators belonging to the Brewery Workers Union: when trucks other than brewery owned trucks are required, use Teamsters Union trucks and men."[318]

The brewing industry had been out of business for fourteen years; what changes in American business did the brewers face when they returned to the legal production of beer? Prior to Prohibition, a few Midwestern brewers includ-

---

315 *Modern Brewery*, December 1933, 54; *Modern Brewery*, January, 1934, 60; Downard, *Dictionary*, 146.
316 *Modern Brewery*, April 1934, 35.
317 Ibid., April 1934, 23.
318 *Modern Brewer*, August 1937, 23.

ing Anheuser–Busch and Pabst had had national distribution and sales. These firms had already faced issues of marketing, advertising, and packaging on a wide scale. The vast majority of pre-Prohibition brewers, however, did a local business, selling beer at the point of consumption.

Among many changes, developments in bottling technology that made pre-Prohibition machinery useless were particularly significant. The soft drink industry had generated many of these changes and represented a new post-Prohibition source of competition for the brewers. The brewers soon developed their own source for new packaging options. Beginning in 1935, brewers produced canned beer.[319]

Figure 12: Krueger can. Photo courtesy of Brewery Collectibles Club of America.

The American Can Company had developed a viable beer can prior to Repeal. The company lined the can with enamel, thus earning the designation "keg-lined." In 1933, the Gottfried Krueger Brewing Company of Newark, New Jersey engaged American Can to produce cans. The can company produced a trial run of two thousand Krueger Special Beer cans which contained 3.2 percent beer, the alcoholic content allowed by the modification of the Volstead Act. The test market approved of the taste of beer in cans, and Krueger went on to produce a line of canned beer which the company put on sale in Richmond, Virginia on January 24, 1935.[320]

The Gottfried Krueger Brewing Company dated from 1852. Its original name was Braun & Laible. By 1865 the name had changed to Hill & Krueger; Gottfried Krueger took over in 1875. In 1889, the brewery became part of the U.S. Brewing Company, Ltd of New York, a British brewing syndicate. After Repeal, Krueger

---

319 Stanley Baron, *Brewed In America: A History of Beer and Ale in the United States* (Boston: Little, Brown and Company, 1962) 323.

320 Downard, *Dictionary* 64; "Beer Can History: The World's First Beer Can," Brewery Collectibles Club of America, http://www.bcca.com/history/overview4.php (accessed July 17, 2007).

reopened. A regional brewery, despite its brief moment of fame for canned beer, Krueger's closed in 1960. Narragansett purchased the brand; when Falstaff purchased Narragansett, Krueger became one of its products.[321]

By September of 1935 American Can faced competition. Both National Can and Continental Can began producing lined cans. Crown Cork and Seal produced a cap that sealed Continental's cans. American's keg-lined cans required a special opener. By 1936 Continental felt sufficient confidence in its product to announce an advertising campaign in 200 newspapers representing a market of 193 cities.[322]

Both Pabst and Schlitz got on the can bandwagon early, but other brewers remained skeptical. By 1941 only 187 of the 507 United States brewers used cans. The light weight of the cans, which reduced shipping costs, provided further advantages to the national brewers.[323] By the late twentieth century beer cans had simultaneously become highly collectible as well as a major source of environmental pollution. Cans became the focus of brewers' advertising as the trend towards off premises consumption intensified. With increased package sales, brewers changed their advertising approach. Not only did they have to promote beer as a healthy, family product, but the packaging had to sell this theme as well and be appealing in its own right.

As soon as the ink was dry on the modification of the Volstead Act, issues of competition between local, regional, and national brewers resumed. The advent of the automobile had given the few national or shipping brewers an advantage, as had the reduction in the number of brewers. Although, in 1934, there was no monopoly in brewing, the conditions for one developing existed.

Prohibition had led to the closing of many breweries; during Repeal, the industry experienced growth and decline simultaneously. Some established brewers started up again, new breweries formed, and others attempted to reopen but failed. P. Ballantine and Sons, New Jersey's largest brewer in 1914 and one of the nation's few English ale brewers, faced this fate. Although the company had planned to open following Repeal, the stockholders ultimately decided to sell their interests. Carl and Otto Badenhausen bought the company and retained the name. Ballantine continued as a successful post-Prohibition brewery until the 1960s.[324]

Another brewery which had a long history but was starting fresh in the post-Repeal era was Ehret's. Hell Gate Brewery had been the nation's largest in 1877;

---

321 Downard, *Dictionary*, 105.
322 "Beer Listed and Canned," *Time*, September 23, 1935; Baron, *Brewed In America*, 327.
323 Downard, *Dictionary*, 44; Baron, *Brewed in America*, 246.
324 *Modern Brewery*, July 1933, 73; Downard, *Dictionary*, 15.

Jacob Ruppert bought the plant in 1935. Louis Ehret, owner of Ehrets, purchased Interboro Beverage Company, Brooklyn in 1935. The brewery moved to Union City, New Jersey in 1949 and closed in 1951.[325]

Jacob Ruppert, Hugh Fox, and a skeleton organization had kept hope alive during the fourteen years of Prohibition. On February 6, 1934 the USBA convened its first convention in seventeen years. The trade association reelected Jacob Ruppert, President, R.A. Huber, Vice-president, C.D. Williams, Secretary and William C. Krueger, Treasurer.[326] Jacob Ruppert was by far the most prominent brewer of the four officers, and also ran one of the most successful non-national breweries.

The 1934 USBA convention elected Frederick Pabst, of the Premier-Pabst Corporation, a director. Pabst Brewing Company, one of the Midwestern "shipping" breweries, had merged with Premier Malt Sales Company in 1932. Harris Perlstein was the head of this company. *Modern Brewery* and the USBA had urged all brewers to cooperate with code writing and with the operation of the code. Pabst, facing a potential code violation charge, was dissatisfied with the USBA's level of support and withdrew from the trade association in 1934.[327]

Although the pre-Prohibition USBA had not always enjoyed the full participation of all brewers, it had been able to present a united face to the federal government regarding tax issues. In the more complex, bureaucratic world of the New Deal, the traditional organization was not as successful.

In June of 1935 in the Scheter decision, the United States Supreme Court declared the NRA unconstitutional.[328] Despite this ultimate failure, the brewing industry stood as one of its successes. Within its structure the industry had reemerged, employed people, raised wages, cut hours, and provided the American public with a supply of a product not available for fourteen years. The relationship the brewing industry developed with the federal government during the short tenure of the NRA set the tone for its subsequent involvement with the government for several decades. Additionally the issues that the code raised within the industry, those of competition and consolidation, also remained the standard for the next several decades.

Despite the disbanding of the NRA, the tensions code writing and enforcement had generated continued after 1935. Other brewers followed Pabst and withdrew from the USBA; Anheuser–Busch was the most prominent brewer to leave the organization. In February of 1936, August A. Busch, Jr., vice-president

325 Downard, *Dictionary*, 68-69.

326 *Modern Brewery*, February 1934, 46.

327 Thomas Cochran, *The Pabst Brewing Company* (New York: New York University Press, 1948), 356-370.

328 Foner, *The Reader's Companion to American History*, 777-778.

of the family-held company, stated that "only 132 of the more than 600 brewers in the country belonged to the association."[329] Busch, worried about the potential for the return of Prohibition, was bothered by the lack of representation. All of the brewers sought a strong organization to maintain and promote a positive public image of beer.

Busch Jr. was a grandson of Adolphus Busch, founder of the company. Adolphus Busch III was president of the company at this time. Prior to Prohibition, Anheuser–Busch had been the nation's largest brewery and was now in a race to regain that spot. Pabst was one of its primary competitors; they both operated national breweries from a base in the Midwest.[330]

Ruppert responded to Busch's defection by describing it as "contrary to the interest of unity in the industry." He also stated that he was "reluctant to divulge the real reason for the resignation of the Anheuser–Busch Company from the United States Brewers Association because I do not wish to say anything that might appear to reflect upon them or foster dissension in the industry." Whether Ruppert's response was hyperbole, or he did actually have information he wished to keep secret, his goal was a strong united industry. Ruppert represented the primarily Eastern non-shipping brewers; both Pabst and Busch were large Midwestern shipping concerns. The New York brewer was a shrewd businessman; as owner of the New York Yankees, his purchase of Babe Ruth from the Boston Red Sox in 1919 was only one example. There may have been personality conflicts between Ruppert and other brewers. The main area of disagreement was over how much the industry was doing to prevent the return of Prohibition.[331]

Anheuser–Busch did not simply leave the USBA: the company sought to establish an organization that would be more representative. Busch gathered together forty-five brewers who he claimed represented twenty percent of the industry and formed Brewing Industry, Inc. (BII). The nine directors of the new organization included August A. Busch, Jr. as president, Harris Perlstein, chairman of Pabst, Alvin Griesedieck, head of Falstaff Brewing, and Adolph Coors, head of Coors brewery.[332]

All of these founding directors were from Midwest or Western breweries. Both Pabst and Anheuser–Busch had had problems regarding NRA and the Code Authority. Late in 1934, Anheuser–Busch faced an indictment for providing "free"

---

329 "Anheuser-Busch Quits Group," *New York Times*, February 7, 1936, 39.

330 Mittelman, "Anheuser–Busch" in Blocker, et. al., *Encyclopedia*, vol. 1, 43-45.

331 "Busch Chided By Ruppert," *New York Times*, February 10, 1936, 2; Mark Gallagher and Neil Gallagher, *Baseball's Great Dynasties, The Yankees* (New York: Gallery Books, 1990), 10; Downard, *Dictionary*, 328-331.

332 *Modern Brewer*, February 1936, 9-10, Downard, *Dictionary*, 33.

---

equipment to over seventeen bars and retailers in the Lake Charles region of Louisiana in exchange for exclusive distribution rights. These practices were in violation of the brewing codes' prohibition of tied houses.[333]

Based in Golden, Colorado, Adolph Coors Brewing Company plant was located on a railroad line and near underground springs. Coors survived during Prohibition in a similar fashion to other brewers by producing near beer, malted milk, and butter. The company also produced porcelain, an activity which continues to this day. Prohibition had come to Colorado as early as 1916; before then the company's production averaged around 17,600 barrels, making them a small local brewery. After Repeal Coors quickly became a regional leader, producing 136,000 barrels in 1934. Adolph, Jr. was the son of the founder.[334]

The Falstaff Brewing Company, the fourth major brewer who formed Brewing Industry Inc., had its origins in the National Brewery, St. Louis, Missouri. Joseph Griesedieck and his brothers had founded the brewery in 1891. In 1921, the William J. Lemp Brewing Company closed, and Griesedieck Bros. Brewing Company acquired the Falstaff name and trademark. Lemp Brewing had been one of the nation's top ten brewers prior to Prohibition. After Repeal, the company renamed itself Falstaff, and Alvin became the director. In 1937 Alvin also became the president of Brewing Industry Inc. Joseph, the family's patriarch, died in 1938. At the time of his death, he was the oldest active member of the USBA. Falstaff Brewing was a publicly traded company on the New York Stock Exchange, which was an unusual activity since brewers usually retained private family ownership of their companies. The company continued to purchase other breweries in other cities including the Narragansett Brewing Company of Rhode Island in 1966 and Ballantine in 1972. Alvin Griesedieck died in 1961. At the time of his death he was an honorary director of the United States Brewers Foundation. Falstaff was the nation's eleventh largest brewer in 1977.[335]

In April of 1936, the USBA, Busch's Brewing Industry Inc., and the ABA held meetings, but reconciliation did not occur. Following the meeting, the three groups announced a plan for one unified association. In July, Jacob Ruppert stated that the directors of the USBA had voted not to join the proposed organization. In his capacity as president of the USBA, Ruppert said the following, "While mindful of the emergencies besetting the brewing industry and

---

333 "Anheuser-Busch Indicted Under NRA," *New York Times*, December 21, 1934, 3; Cochran, *Pabst*, 370; Baron, *Brewed in America*, 329.

334 Downard, *Dictionary*, 53: William H. Mulligan Jr., "Adolph Coors Brewing Company," in Blocker, et. al., *Encyclopedia*, 174.

335 *Modern Brewer*, August, 1938, 57; Downard, *Dictionary*, 72; "Griesedieck Heads Brewers," *New York Times*, February 19, 1937, 36; "Alvin Griesedieck, 66," *New York Times*, February 1, 1961, 35. For information on Falstaff stock offerings see *New York Times*, passim 1933 on.

the importance of promoting its welfare and safeguarding it against attacks, we cannot subscribe to any proposal to submerge our identity as the largest and senior association of brewers in favor of a new and untried organization without guarantee that it would be properly financed and managed and would be for the best interests of brewers and our members generally." [336] Ruppert was determined to preserve the legacy of the USBA, and by extension, the interest of Eastern brewers.

By 1937 there were a myriad of organizations seeking to represent the still evolving brewing industry. That year the USBA itself produced a new organization, the United Brewers Industrial Foundation (UBIF). According to *Modern Brewer*, the new group was "Definitely not a trade association and is in no way affiliated with any trade association." This claim was a little disingenuous since the Foundation counted Colonel Ruppert, Julius Liebmann, and Edward V. Lahey as members. All were also prominent members of the USBA. The Foundation sought to be a "clearing house of authoritative information for the public on brewing from every point of view — economics, health nutrition and history." [337] Public relations and maintaining a positive public image remained at the forefront of brewer's concerns.

The newly legal brewers were also concerned with advertising and promoting beer as a distinct and pleasurable product to a public, which might have forgotten its existence. Of particular importance to brewers were "the men and women who were boys and girls in 1919" who "represented a tremendous new market with new habits and new buying perspectives." [338] Of course the vast majority of pre-Prohibition brewers, local in nature and relying overwhelmingly on a male, working class population for its clientele in the saloon, had never approached marketing in quite this way.

Prior to Prohibition, public drinking in saloons had an overwhelmingly male face; from 1919 to 1933, both men and women drank in public at speakeasies and other illicit watering holes. Drinking became a companionate social activity. Brewers knew they would have to address their marketing to both men and women.

One way to begin to create a beverage that would appeal equally to both sexes was to employ women in the industry. Brewing was overwhelmingly male, but by 1937 *Modern Brewer* had unearthed two female beer sales personnel. The journal also had a woman, Elsie Singruen, as its technical editor. Ms. Singruen

---

336 "Brewers Merger Looms," *New York Times*, April 22, 1936, 40; "Brewing Unity Set Back," *New York Times*, July 17, 1936, 22.
337 *Modern Brewer*, May 1937, 38.
338 *Modern Brewer*, March 1933, 22.

had studied brewing in Berlin, and had written on brewing techniques and the history of the craft. The technician made further history when she addressed the Philadelphia District Master Brewers in 1938. Ms. Singruen, the first female to speak publicly before a brewers group, gave a talk on "the history of American Brewing Literature.[339]

Modern Brewery and its contributors advocated bock beer ad campaigns as one response to the need for advertising which reflected this new social environment. Bock beer originated in Bavaria as a special brew for Easter. Brewmasters roast the malt, producing a darker, brown beer richer in flavor than lager. Because bock means male goat in German, the billy goat became the symbol for the drink.[340]

On the eve of Repeal, *Modern Brewery* was looking forward to "the first Bock Beer Time in 15 years." By March of 1935, brewers had almost two years of legal production under their belt, and advertising continued as a prime issue of concern. *Modern Brewery* advocated cooperative advertising as a strategy for increasing beer sales. The USBA had developed a "Bock Beer" advertising program which the journal supported, stating that "Bock Beer Season affords a splendid opportunity for brewers to get together to stabilize prices and to start thinking in terms of profits and dividends instead of large volume sales. After all, the purposes of operating a brewery are first to brew a good beer and second to make money."

The USBA felt that a bock beer campaign would increase sales in both the short and long term. "Historically Bock has been a beer on which brewers made money because they met a natural demand." The proposed ad copy stressed the optimism and frivolity of spring which apparently was the essence of beer, particularly bock. [341]

Looking forward to the future of the renewed brewing industry, leaders continued to stress the issue of public relations and their proposed solution of "cooperative advertising." In 1938, Herbert Barclay used the example of the "allied trades" to point the way. "The glass bottle, copper and brass products, wooden barrel, steel barrel and other industries . . . have shown how such programs can be developed and operated successfully."[342]

In promoting bock beer advertising campaigns, the editors of *Modern Brewer* and the USBA were seeking cooperation on several levels. Brewers would have to agree to produce bock beer for distribution at the same time. In 1936, they apparently failed since *Modern Brewery* noted that "Brewers in New England, New

339 *Modern Brewer*, May 1937, 25; December 1937, 64; April 1938, 39.
340 *Modern Brewer*, March 1933, 21; Downard, *Dictionary*, 25.
341 *Modern Brewer*, March 1935, 19, 37.
342 *Modern Brewer*, January 1936, 32.

York, Chicago, and other places have been selling Bock Beer ignoring the agreed dates. This is a serious fumble and ruins any effort at cooperative action."[343]

Modern Brewer could not overemphasize the importance of establishing a specific "Bock Beer Day." According to the journal, the day "opens the beer season. It should be a festival time, the welcoming of spring." The impetus for the work required by sales executives and advertising men was that the day would "increase beer sales, not just for the short Bock Beer Season, but ... through out the year." Apparently the task of promoting bock beer was an easy one because "connected with Bock Beer are ancient legends, traditions and folklore — tales that many Americans have never heard — presenting an unexplored mine of material . . . ."[344]

The editors felt that setting a specific date to begin the season was imperative. "On that day, every Bock Beer campaign should break — break like the first crash of thunder announcing the awakening of Spring! Festivals and displays should be timed to start with and follow the opening blast." The possibilities for events and advertising were limitless and included potential nationwide billy goat contests which would culminate in the crowning of "King Bock." New York City held such a contest in 1936 and was the model for this proposal.[345]

Modern Brewer had suggestions for other products to help with sales in the winter months. English style dark beer was the answer. In 1933 British brewers had undertaken an advertising campaign linking heavier darker beer with winter. This resulted in an increase in sales over seven per cent. There was precedent for American brewers initiating a similar campaign. In 1914 brewers produced 9,200,000 barrels of dark beer in America. Since estimates for 1936 indicated that production of dark beer would be a little over one million barrels, *Modern Brewer* presented this as another challenge. "Salesmen, advertising men ... Is it in your power to regain 8,000,000 barrels of dark beer sales? Can you ... in the period starting with the first of November and ending the thirtieth of April 1937?" *Modern Brewer* had the whole year covered.[346]

Modern Brewer persisted in presenting bock beer as the ideal brewery promotion. In 1937 the journal detailed a campaign undertaken by New Jersey brewers to hold a "Bock Beer festival" in early March. The plans for the festival were apparently very elaborate since the New Jersey Brewers Association had a "16 foot float . . . (with) a full-sized keg from which runs a spillway and down this appears to be a constantly flowing stream of Bock Beer. The base of the float is

---

343 *Modern Brewer*, February 1936, 19.
344 *Modern Brewer*, December 1936, 18.
345 Ibid.
346 Ibid., 19.

elaborately decorated with an arrangement of Spring flowers." The plans also included a goat show in Newark.[347]

Once again, not all brewers were as supportive of the endeavor as *Modern Brewer*. Apparently some brewers jumped the gun, and placed bock beer on the market in February. This action indicated that they were ignorant of the fact that "Bock Beer was still the harbinger of Spring, the ancient votive offering to the Goddess of Plenty, the brew that more than 400 years ago in the city of Einbeck was christened "Bock Beer."[348]

In 1939 *Modern Brewer* reiterated that the promotional campaign was supposed to "sell the retailer and the public on Bock Beer as the traditional spring drink — and you don't drink a spring drink in the middle of February." Because every year was different, the journal proposed that "Bock Beer Day should be set for a definite day in the middle week of the month of March. It should be the same day every year and it should have the backing of every brewer's association in the country."[349]

Brewers in the greater New York City area apparently agreed and in February of 1939 announced plans for a joint campaign for bock beer. The proposed copy would run in all New York and New Jersey papers for ten weeks. At the same time the United Brewers Industrial Foundation planned a national campaign that would emphasize the "economic value" of beer.[350]

Figure 13: Photo courtesy Modern Brewery Age.

The type of ad campaigns and promotions *Modern Brewer* and brewing trade organizations advocated were simultaneously old fashioned and modern. Their fascination with the Germanic properties of bock beer spoke to a disregard or denial of the problematic nature of associating beer and Germans. The campaign's emphasis on the craft aspects of distinct beers ignored the standardization occurring due to mass shipping, national markets, canned beer, and the increase of off-premises sales. Not until the late twentieth century, with the revival of craft brewing and

347 *Modern Brewer*, March 1937, 31.
348 Ibid.
349 *Modern Brewer*, February 1939, 18.
350 "Bock Beer Bungs Pop Officially March 13," *New York Times*, February 9, 1939, 32.

an increased interest in home brewing, would bock beer and other specialties once again became a focal point for brewers.

The brewing industry was able to focus on issues such as bock beer days because of the legitimacy federal taxation provided. Despite the Scheter decision abolishing the NIRA, tax revenue from alcohol production remained a critical aspect of the New Deal recovery plan. To protect the revenue and insure a steady flow of production, the Federal Alcohol Administration took over the functions of the FACA following the Scheter decision. The Federal Alcohol Administration Act of 1935 established this agency as part of the Treasury Department. This legislation, with ongoing modifications, still governs the liquor industry today.

Following the Scheter decision, Joseph Choate proposed legislation that would have created the FAA as an independent agency with the same regulatory control as the FACA. A three person commission would head the proposed agency. Choate also advocated the prohibition of bulk sales of distilled spirits. Over his strong objections, the House Ways and Means Committee changed Choate's proposal in two ways. The House committee gave final authority for the new agency to the Secretary of Treasury and allowed bulk sale of distilled sprits. The House continued the FACA ban on tied houses. Brewers were anxious to remain in the public's good graces; the federal government sought to protect its revenue by preventing the return of brewer ownership of saloons.[351]

W. S. Alexander was the first administrator of the FAA and spent the first few months holding hearings which ratified the regulations and rulings of the FACA. One practice that continued in the new agency was using standards of identity for distilled sprits and wine. These regulations demarked differences between individual alcoholic beverages for tax purposes. Because the federal government taxed beer at a flat rate, the FACA had not developed or used standards of identity for it. This became yet another way in which the brewers were able to maintain their separateness from distilled spirits. Since the origination of standards of identity within the FACA during Repeal the standards have come to function as defacto labels. Since no standards of identity exist for beer, brewers have been able to maintain greater secrecy about their trade practices and ingredients.[352]

Despite the many victories the brewers won, the separate treatment of beer and distilled spirits continued as a major issue. In 1937, Alexander revisited the issue of permits for brewers that had first emerged during code writing. Because such a system would place brewers on the same footing as "distillers, rectifiers, wine producers, importers and liquor wholesalers," *Modern Brewer* opposed such

351 LaForge, "Misplaced Priorities," 205.
352 Ibid., 226-229.

legislation. The journal desired "Congress to declare beer a non-intoxicating beverage and place it under the Food Administration." The NRA had treated beer as both an agricultural commodity and an intoxicating beverage. The new agency was unlikely to change the government's perceptions or classification of the beverage. In fact the brewers, in their more realistic moments, sought to keep beer from pending food and drug legislation since "malt beverages are already covered by the F.A.A. act."[353] Ultimately the brewers accepted their role within the country's tax structure yet, like other industries, they sought to minimize regulatory control.

Alexander sought to use the FAA to promote greater regulation of the liquor industry. He continued to propose placing brewing under the permit system that already existed for distillers. Alexander contended that there was nothing to distinguish beer from liquor. "It is a scientific fact that malt beverages are alcoholic beverages and are sold and consumed with that understanding. It is further that in the opinion of the Administration that the social aspects of the beer and ale industry demand as much regulation as do distilled spirits or wines."[354]

Using this analysis as his jumping off point, Alexander also sought to prohibit the beer industry from advertising on the radio and in Sunday newspapers. The brewers, in response, could not deny that their industry needed regulation, but they maintained there was a clear distinction between beer and distilled spirits. Further they continued to seek, under the difficult circumstances that Alexander's position presented, the least amount of regulation possible. They remained committed to cooperation and self-policing. In their desire to minimize regulation the brewers were similar to any other industry, but the specter of prohibition probably prompted the brewing to behave with greater self-restraint.[355]

Radio and print advertising were key issues from the beginning of Repeal and were a battleground for determining alcohol's renewed role in American society. Distillers voluntarily agreed to refrain from radio advertising in 1936. They did this to retain some degree of control over their marketing practices. In 1948 they extended their voluntary self ban to television.[356]

Because legislators and officials usually saw beer as less alcoholic than distilled spirits, brewers did not have to make all of the hard choices that distillers did. They retained access to all media outlets, which ultimately gave them a huge competitive edge over distillers, and did more to differentiate them from the oth-

353 *Modern Brewer*, January 1937, 47-48.

354 *Modern Brewer*, February 1938, 23.

355 Ibid.

356 Center for Science in the Public Interest, Alcohol Policies Project, "Chronology of Broadcast Liquor Advertising," http://www.cspinet.org/booze/liquor_chronology.htm (accessed January 19, 2006).

er branches of the liquor industry than anything else. It also made them vulnerable to repeated attacks over their media access and marketing campaigns.

Although *Modern Brewer* and the major brewing organizations including the USBA spent a lot of time promoting bock beer, they were also interested in shaping a particular public image for beer in general. Towards this end, the journal congratulated brewers when, in early 1937, they protested action by the FAA which ruled that unless a beer contained at least five percent alcohol it could not be labeled or advertised as "ale," "stout," or "porter." *Modern Brewer* felt the ruling would "undo whatever success the brewing industry has had in educating the public in the direction that alcohol is a very minor and unimportant part of a malt beverage."[357] Of course brewers sought the widest latitude possible for promotion and definition of their product

Following this, the FAA held hearings on defining ale. Brewers found it very difficult to agree among themselves on what distinguished ale from lager; yet all could agree that they did not want the deciding characteristic to be alcoholic content. Their desire to avoid explicitly stating the alcoholic content of their product was part of their desire to portray beer as the beverage of temperance. The same revised regulations prevented brewers from calling a beer Pilsner or other any geographic names unless the brewing took place in that locality.

In the hearings brewers argued about what kind of fermentation produced ale. Frederick Lauer and other nineteenth-century brewers had sought tax relief from the federal government by stressing the special nature of bottom fermented lager. Ale, porter, and stout are all produced using top fermenting yeast. Despite this fact, post-Repeal brewers sought a definition which would not "factually or by implication limit or change brewing operations as to standards of manufacture and identity." Small brewing companies, represented by Ralph Kettering and the ABA, pushed for the vague, non-specific definition of ale. A specific definition would have required these brewers to invest in separate cellars dedicated to ale production. The ale definition was a victory for all brewers since it left them free to call their products whatever they wanted regardless of manufacturing methods.[358]

As the brewing industry reshaped, divisions between smaller breweries still using pre-Prohibition methods of local production and the shipping brewers who were transforming into national trucking concerns with large advertising budgets only worsened. Each year, the number of breweries decreased. In 1934 there were 756, but by 1940 there were 590. A smaller number of brewers began

---

357 *Modern Brewer*, January 1937, 48.
358 *Modern Brewer*, August 1938, 79, 81.

to take a larger share of the market. In 1939 twenty-one breweries held thirty percent of total sales.[359]

The remaining brewers, large and small, all faced renewed prohibition activity. When local brewers sought to organize politically to fight such efforts, they often had to acknowledge the significant presence of brewers from other states, one implication of the nationalizing of the brewing industry.

In early 1937, Virginia brewers became increasingly concerned about counties deciding via local option to go dry. The state trade association represented the ten local brewers; sixty-two other brewers from Ohio, New Jersey, New York, Pennsylvania, and the Midwest also did business in the state. The out-of-state brewers comprised the overwhelmingly majority of brewing in Virginia, representing eighty-five percent. The state association sought and achieved the creation of a new organization, representing the out-of-state brewers. The goal was to give the brewers "the opportunity to support financially and otherwise the movement to combat dry forces in the State of Virginia."[360]

The new organization, the Virginia Beer Institute, had three officers from out-of-state, including Julius Liebmann, who was the president of Liebmann Breweries, the brewers of Rheingold beer. A German Jewish immigrant, Samuel Liebmann founded the Brooklyn brewery which survived Prohibition — they sold ice cream — and persisted as an independently held brewery until 1964 when Pepsi-Cola purchased the company. In the 1950s and 1960s Rheingold was a very popular regional beer whose success came primarily from the Miss Rheingold beauty contest.[361]

Remote bottling was an issue that highlighted the differences between the resources and capacity of small local brewers and the larger, national concerns. According to John Bruckmann, president of the American Brewers Association, this was "the practice of a few brewers who bottle their beer at points hundreds of mile from their brewery." Because the shipping brewers had larger plant capacity and owned malt companies, their manufacturing costs were less. By shipping in bulk and then bottling their beer on-site, they were directly competing with the local brewer. Small brewers opposed remote bottling, because they felt it put them at a competitive disadvantage. Bruckmann claimed that remote bot-

---

359 *Modern Brewery Age*, August 1941, 11.

360 *Modern Brewer*, January 1937, 52.

361 *Modern Brewer*, (February, 1937): 36; Downard, 159; Rolf Hofmann, "The Originators of Rheingold Beer from Ludwigsburg to Brooklyn–A Dynasty of German-Jewish Brewers," BeerHistory.com, http://www.beerhistory.com/library/holdings/hofmann-rheingold.shtml (accessed November 11, 2006).

tling would lead to a "few large brewers . . . manufacturing all of the beer in the United States."[362]

The USBA, attempting to maintain both the legitimacy of the industry and their status as a national organization, supported the small brewers in their opposition to remote bottling. The large shipping brewers as well as wholesalers were in favor of the practice. Many wholesalers also bottled beer.[363]

Bottling of beer dated back to the eighteenth century. It had gradually gained in importance prior to Prohibition as technological and scientific advances including pasteurization and automatic bottling devices emerged. In 1915, fifteen percent of beer was bottled; by 1937, it was thirty-eight percent.[364]

Many of the more prominent members of the USBA were local large brewers, able to produce up to a million barrels in one urban market. Given their distribution practices, they were likely to have sympathy with the plight of the small brewers. The ABA and the USBA were, however, fighting a losing battle since the trend of the New Deal economy during the NIRA and after favored consolidation of industries.

Despite anxiety and conflict over competition and consolidation, brewers agreed that the most pressing industry-wide problem was publicity. They needed to insure that the negative images that prohibitionists had used so successfully fourteen years earlier did not gain the upper hand again. The struggle facing brewers was to "prove that beer is a refreshing, fermented beverage with a definite place in the American home and in the fight for real temperance."[365] As it faced the immediate tasks of rebuilding and expanding, the brewing industry worried deeply about the possible return of Prohibition.

How to best organize to resist the reemergence of Prohibitionist sentiment — that was the question. Brewers developed their answers within the context of the changing nature and structure of the industry. The states had greater control over the regulation of sales and marketing of liquor including advertising which fostered the development of state liquor boards and state liquor administrators. *Modern Brewer* felt these state officials were "the brewing industry's best friend."[366] The journal saw these officials as one aspect of their public relations campaign.

A unified industry would be better prepared to fight any new prohibitory efforts. The first step in the ultimate reunification of the brewing industry came in September 1938 when the ABA, the USBA, the BII, and the UBIF agreed to join in

---

362 *Modern Brewer*, October 1938, 82.
363 Ibid.
364 Downard, *Dictionary*, 27-28.
365 *Modern Brewery*, June 1933, 36.
366 *Modern Brewer*, June 1937, 23.

a public relations campaign under the auspices of the UBIF. The other organizations would have seats on an expanded Board of Directors. The redesigned foundation planned "to undertake an enlarged program including action in concert
with state and local organizations looking toward self-regulation and elimination of anti-social conditions wherever they may surround the sale of beer."[367]

Bernard Lichtenberg, of the Institute of Public Relations, developed the Nebraska Plan, a program Nebraskan brewers had used it in the summer of 1938 to
police drinking establishments and turn back a prohibitory drive by dry forces.
The Nebraska Plan would become the cornerstone of the USBA's self-regulation
activities, and the organization used it for many years.[368]

On January 14, 1939, Jacob Ruppert died at the age of 71. He had been sick
since April, and his death was front page news in New York. Besides Ruppert's
family, Babe Ruth was the last person to see the Colonel.

> When Ruth arrived at the Ruppert apartment, the Colonel was in an oxy-
> gen tent, in which he had been placed at 4:30 o'clock. He was removed from
> his tent at 7:15 P.M., and the first thing he said, according to his nurse, Miss
> Ann McGill, was:
>
> "I want to see the Babe."
>
> "Here he is, right beside you," she said.
>
> The dying man opened his eyes and reached out his hand to Ruth, but was
> too weak to speak. Ruth patted his hand.
>
> "Colonel," he said, "you are going to snap out of this, and you and I are going
> to the opening game of the season."
>
> The Colonel smiled faintly but still could not talk. Ruth turned away and
> started to leave the room, but the Colonel summoned up his strength and
> called to him weakly. Ruth returned to the bedside, and the Colonel again
> held out his hand and murmured the one word "Babe."
>
> "It was the only time in his life he ever called me Babe to my face," Ruth said
> after he heard the news of the Colonel's death. "I couldn't help crying when
> I went out."[369]

At the time of his death Ruppert had a wealth of more than $100 million.
Descended from German immigrants, he had risen to the upper echelons of New
York society. Much of his fortune was in real estate. His brewery holdings included Hell Gate brewery which he had purchased from the heirs of George Ehret in
1935. Under his leadership the Yankees won ten American League pennants and

367 *Modern Brewer*, September 1938, 33.
368 Baron, *Brewed in America*, 338.
369 "Ruppert Dies at 71," *New York Times*, January 14, 1939, 1

seven World Series. After purchasing Babe Ruth from the Red Sox for $100,000 in 1919, he made him the highest paid baseball player for many years. Prominent honorary pallbearers at the funeral included Joe McCarthy, manager of the Yankees, Mayor Fiorello LaGuardia, former Governor Alfred E. Smith, Senator Robert F. Wagner, Julius Liebmann, President of Liebmann Brewery, Babe Ruth, Edward J. Schmidt, Philadelphia brewer, C.D. Williams, Secretary of the USBA, Lou Gehrig, representing the Yankees, and Rudolph J. Schaefer, President of F. & M. Schaefer Brewing Company Brooklyn.[370]

Over 15,000 people attended the services at St. Patrick's Cathedral in New York City. Among the mourners was a delegation of beer distributors from New England. Lou Gehrig expressed his condolences as follows, "His loss is a great one. He was one of the outstanding sportsmen of the era, and a most loyal friend." Seven months later, the Yankees' talented and durable first baseman would cease playing, a victim of amyotrophic lateral sclerosis (ALS). The Iron Horse declared himself "the luckiest man on the face of this earth."[371]

Edward Landsberg, the president of the United States Brewing Company and Blatz Brewing Company, succeeded Ruppert as president of the USBA. G. L. Becker of Becker Products Company, Odgen, Utah became first vice-president and Rudy Schaefer, was named second vice-president and treasurer. George Ruppert, Jacob's brother, became a director of the USBA.[372]

Following Valentin Blatz's death in 1894, Landsberg, who had been involved in brewing and the USBA since 1885, ran the company for United States Brewing. Under his leadership Blatz Brewing became a family brewery again. After his death in 1941, his heirs owned the controlling interest in the company. His wife died a year later, and her brother, Frank Gabel, became the president of Blatz Brewing.[373]

In October 1939, the United Brewers Industrial Foundation approved the extension and expansion of its self-regulation program to close down retail outlets that did not follow the law. During the past year brewers had pursued monitoring of retail outlets in eight states. They now proposed to extend this operation to a greater geographical area; this was one way for the brewers to maintain their focus on preventing a return of Prohibition. The brewers elected Carl W. Baden-

---

370 Ibid., Downard, *Dictionary*, 68-69.

371 "15,000 Pay Tribute at Ruppert Rites," *New York Times*, January 17, 1939, 21; "Ruppert's Realty Put at $30,000,000," *New York Times*, January 14, 1939, 7; Gallagher and Gallagher, *The Yankees*, 23. The popular name for ALS is Lou Gehrig's disease. Today baseball players raise money to fight the illness, most notably Curt Schilling of the Boston Red Sox.

372 "Brewers Elect Landsberg," *New York Times*, February 2, 1939, 30; "Edward Landsberg," *New York Times*, Feb. 21, 1941, 19.

373 "Edward Landesberg," Downard, *Dictionary*, 23; "Mrs. Edward Landsberg," *New York Times*, March 7, 1942, 17.

hausen, president of P. Ballantine & Sons, as president of the Foundation. The USBA had created the UBIF as a response to the concerns over public relations that had led Anheuser–Busch, Pabst, and others to leave the association.[374]

Jacob Ruppert had been a controversial figure in the brewing industry; his death freed industry participants to seek closer cooperation. Fifteen months after his death, the American Brewers Association, champions of the small brewer, and Brewing Industry Inc., the voice of large, Western, and shipping brewers agreed to consolidate into the American Brewing Industry (ABI).[375]

On the heels of this consolidation, in January 1941, Harris Perlstein, chairman of Pabst and president of ABI and Rudy Schafer, for the USBA, announced the two organizations would merge. Now the two factions of the brewing industry, Ruppert's Eastern, local market brewers and Anheuser–Busch's national shipping firms, would coexist in the USBA.[376] Despite this new organizational unity, issues of competition and consolidation continued. Prior to Prohibition, brewers had responded to intense market pressures by owning saloons. The Twenty-First Amendment which repealed prohibition also prevented brewers from directly distributing their product and owning retail establishments. Wholesalers, who purchased beer from brewers and then sold it to retail establishments, became one tier in a three tier system of distribution. The wholesalers organized their own trade association in 1938, the National Beer Wholesalers Association — which still exists and represents over 2,000 distributors. This system of distribution meant that brewers would have to find other ways to gain market share and withstand competition.[377]

In 1940, the Federal Alcohol Administration, which had withstood a congressional attempt to reestablish an independent agency similar to the FACA with a three person board of commissioners in 1937, was disbanded and merged with the Alcohol Tax Unit of the Internal Revenue Bureau. This action put the regulation of the liquor industry more firmly under the Treasury Department then ever before. The reorganization also reaffirmed the Federal government's primary relationship with the liquor industry as one of taxation and revenue.[378]

The administrative and bureaucratic aspects of regulating the liquor industry following Repeal represented both a return to old patterns and the creation of new institutions. The NIRA and the FACA removed regulatory oversight from its traditional home in the Treasury Department, but that did not last long. By

---

374 "Brewers Approve More Regulation" *New York Times*, October 5, 1939, 39.
375 *Modern Brewery Age*, April 1940, 22.
376 *Modern Brewery Age*, January 1941, 9.
377 National Beer Wholesalers Association, "Who We Are," http://www.nbwa.org (accessed June 6, 2007).
378 Laforge, "Misplaced Priorities," 244-245.

1940 the federal government resumed its primary focus on taxation and located the regulation of the liquor industry for this economic purpose in the Internal Revenue Bureau, its home prior to Prohibition.

Seven years after Repeal, the brewing industry looked both similar to and different from its pre-Prohibition counterpart. There were many fewer breweries, and the industry was becoming increasingly concentrated. War had already begun in Europe. As the industry began its eighth year of legalization, would it face another prohibition onslaught due to world war?

Chapter 6. Beer: The Morale Builder, 1942–1952

On December 7, 1941, Japanese planes bombed the United States naval fleet stationed at Pearl Harbor. By the next day the country was at war. Twenty three years earlier the country had also engaged in a world war; one result then was national prohibition. On December 8, the brewing industry faced the dilemma of being active patriotic participants in the national war effort while fighting off any attempts to reinstate prohibition.

As early as 1939, the country had begun to be on a war footing and President Roosevelt created several agencies to deal with impending economic mobilization. A few of them, including the Office of Production Management, the Office of Price Administration and Civilian Supply, and the Supply Priorities and Allocations Board, had the potential to affect the brewing industry as well as other industries. The brewers had become accustomed to a myriad of bureaucracies during Repeal, and the war would not change that.[379]

The tax on beer increased prior to the United States entry into the war. On July 1, 1940 a $1.00 tax increase became effective; the rate became $6.00 a barrel (31 gallons). Brewers had every reason to believe that taxes would double if America went to war.[380] The recently reunified brewers had practice being useful, loyal participants in a war effort. They had been doing that since 1862, and only wished to be able to do it again, if necessary.

---

379 Richard Polenberg, *War and Society: The United States, 1941-1945* (New York: J.B. Lippincott Company, 1972), 7.
380 *New York Times*, October 27, 1939, 36; *Brewers Almanac*, 1940, 36.

Once Congress declared war, the President was free to give his full attention to economic mobilization, and he created the War Production Board. The agency and its head, Donald Nelson, were slow in establishing conversion polices to move production from consumer goods to military uses, but by June 1942, the rate of production of consumer goods had decreased by almost thirty percent. Factories that had produced refrigerators now made munitions. The brewers did not have to convert their breweries, but their raw material and supplies might be needed elsewhere.[381]

At the beginning of the war, the industry was confident that it could "continue its present level of operations and even increase them without any significant drain on the wartime needs of the nation." Brewers' material needs included steel, tinplate for crowns and cans, cork, barley, and other agricultural products. *Modern Brewery Age* felt a repeat of World War I and prohibition was unlikely because "our brave allies have found beer and ale great morale builders among the fighting forces as well as among their civilian population."[382] Brewers hoped America would follow Britain's lead in supplying beer for armed forces.

The USBA had provided institutional support for brewers since 1862. During Prohibition it maintained a skeleton structure and stood ready for interaction with the federal government during Repeal. With the onset of war the trade association would face new tests of its ability to provide leadership to the brewing industry. America's previous experiences with war had generated anxiety about soldiers in new situations consuming alcohol. The public relations arm of the brewing industry, the UBIF, would need to convince the public that beer drinking was a positive experience during wartime.

Rudy Schaefer, the owner of Schaefer Brewing, had become president of the USBA in 1941. Schaefer Brewing had begun in 1842 and was one of the country's first lager brewers. Frederick and Maximilian Schaefer emigrated from Russia and eventually operated a brewery near Grand Central Station. Rudolph, Maximilian's son, took over the brewery in 1912 and moved it to Brooklyn in 1915. During Prohibition, Rudolph Schaefer died, and his two sons, Frederick and Rudolph, Jr. took over. In 1927 Rudy, a Princeton graduate, gained sole control of the brewery. Having survived Prohibition, the company expanded with additional plants in Baltimore and Albany. In 1938 the brewery produced one million barrels and was consistently one of the nation's top ten breweries. Rudy Schaefer was a long time participant in the USBA.[383]

---

381 Polenberg, *War and Society*, 8.

382 Jos. Dubin, "The War's Effect," *Modern Brewery Age*, December 1941, 8-9.

383 Ibid; Downard, *Dictionary of the History of the American Brewing and Distilling Industries* (Westport, CT: Greenwood Press., 1980), 166; F. & M. Schaefer Brewing Company, *To commemorate our 100th year : the F. & M. Schaefer brewing co. : America's oldest lager beer* (Brooklyn, N.Y. : The

At the beginning of 1942, Schaefer, in his capacity as president of the USBA, offered his assessment of the state of the brewing industry and its planned participation in the war effort. The good news was that "public acceptance of beer as an essential food" had increased. Tax increases were a less positive development. Schaefer maintained that the industry could not withstand any additional taxes, and that an increase would have a diminishing effect on federal revenue. After all, the industry paid over $400 million in state and federal taxes in 1941, making beer brewing the fourth most heavily taxed industry in the country. Despite this strong participation in the country's economy, Schaefer wanted the industry to make a specific contribution to the war effort, and pledged sales of defense bonds to all of the over 60,000 employees in the industry. On a personal level, Schaefer became vice-chairman of the carbonated and fermented beverage committee of the Red Cross War Fund of Greater New York.[384]

Although the brewing industry had been optimistic regarding its chances of maintaining production unencumbered by supply restrictions, they soon faced the reality of a wartime economy. In February 1942, the War Production Board issued orders severely limiting the use of tin for cans. The Board considered beer cans to be non-essential, in the same class as cans for pork and beans, oil, coffee, tobacco, kidney beans, hominy, and dog food. Some 187 brewers produced beer in cans at the start of the war, and fourteen percent of consumers purchased beer in this form. Brewers also used tin to manufacture the crowns of beer bottles. The restrictions caused brewers to use blackplate and reuse crowns. They also produced beer in large containers which meant a reduced need for crowns. Bottled beer represented almost forty percent of the brewer's market at the beginning of the war.[385]

Shortly after the government restricted the use of tin, the War Production Board encouraged Americans to save their tin cans. The fall of Singapore had severely limited the country's access to tin. In New York City the government hoped to collect 120,000 tons of tin cans annually. Officials instructed the public how to prepare the various cans for collection. Only those beer cans with flat ends were suitable for salvage.[386]

The rationing of tin was part of the federal government's larger project of price controls. Other products rationed in 1942 included gasoline and shoes. The

Company, 1942); Will Anderson, *The Breweries of Brooklyn: An Informal History of a Great Industry in a Great City* (New York,: Anderson, 1976), 6, 7.

384 *Modern Brewery Age*, January 1942, 18, 82, 85; "Beer is Accorded Wider Acceptance as a Food, Says President of Brewers," *New York Times*, January 2, 1942, 39.

385 *Modern Brewery Age*, February 1942, 96-97; Downard, *Dictionary*, 44, 27-28; Stanley Baron, *Brewed In America* (Boston: Little, Brown and Company, 1962), 334-335.

386 "Tin Cans Become 'Precious' Waste," *New York Times*, March 2, 1942, 16.

rationing was effective: from 1943 until 1945 prices increased less than two per cent.[387] The brewers, well accustomed to dealing with bureaucratic agencies, now also had to contend with the Office of Price Administration.

The War Production Board's administration of the brewing industry shifted over the course of the war. Originally the industry was part of the Food Branch, but then became part of the Beverages and Tobacco Branch. J.B. Smiley, a former president of Remington Arms, headed this branch. Eventually the Beverage and Tobacco Branch had a Brewing Industry Advisory Committee headed by John E. O'Neill, a former lawyer for the FAA. Representatives from both small and large breweries were members of this committee, which dealt with beverage bottle closures and the tin restrictions. Other issues for the committee included container sizes, package styles, energy, transportation, and conservation of metals, paper, and rubber.[388]

As early as January 1942, Rudy Schaefer, addressing the sixty-sixth convention of the USBA in Chicago, called for a study of possible substitutions for brewing materials. Mindful of the rubber shortage and the need to conserve energy, he advocated decreasing the amount of deliveries and developing better distribution systems.[389] In facing these issues, the brewing industry was similar to many other American industries.

In order to be able to continue production during the war, the brewing industry needed to establish itself as an essential industry. Although by the end of the war the brewing industry had faced rationing on most of its raw materials, its production of beer for the armed forces remained exempt with fifteen percent of its supply earmarked for the military. The brewers also made an effective case for the use of brewers yeast as a nutritional supplement. The industry promoted the product as a "valuable food both for humans and animals;" brewers yeast contains the vitamin B complex.[390]

As always, the industry's most vital function was the generation of revenue for the federal government. During the war, Congress increased beer taxes twice; by 1945 the rate was $8.00 a barrel.[391] Although there was industry wide support for tax increases as part of the defense effort, the increased cost fell disproportionably on small brewers who would be unable to survive unless they passed the cost along to the consumer. Larger brewers could more easily absorb the increased costs.[392]

---

387 Polenberg, *War and Society*, 32.
388 *Modern Brewery Age*, March 1942, 81; April 1942, 18, 76.
389 *Modern Brewery Age*, February 1942, 37.
390 Peter J. F. Weber, "Brewing Is an Essential Industry," *Modern Brewery Age*, March 1942, 7.
391 Downard, *Dictionary*, 240.
392 Jos. Dubin, "The Impending Tax Increase," *Modern Brewery Age*, June 1940, 11.

The number of breweries had been shrinking, and the war was unlikely to reverse that trend. From 714 in 1934, there were now only 523. Because rationing and mobilization as well as taxes were likely to disproportionately affect small brewers, they resolved to meet to explore survival strategies. On May 28, 1942 in Detroit, Michigan, representatives of twenty-eight breweries from thirteen states met as the Small Brewers Committee. William O'Shea, one of the organizers of the Small Brewers Committee, was not a brewer. He was president of Eagle Lithographing Company, Chicago; some of his customers were brewers for whom he produced paper labels. O'Shea was secretary of the Brewers Association of America for forty-six years and was a true friend to small brewers. He died at 87 in 1990.[393]

The small brewers did not wish to form a new organization at this time, but formed a sub-committee to explore amelioration of the crown situation and tax relief, based on output. *Modern Brewery Age* felt that a tax differential would not actually help small brewers and that it was more appropriate for all brewers to argue against additional tax increases.[394] Since additional taxes to support the war appeared inevitable, the journal's advice to small brewers seemed futile. Small brewers continued to argue for tax relief for the next thirty years, in fact. They finally succeeded in 1976.

In attempting to establish a more distinct identity, the small brewers reflected the reality of the organizational structure of the reunified USBA. In 1942, 236 brewers belonged, which was about forty-five percent of all the brewers in the United States. The brewers who belonged to the USBA produced almost seventy-eight percent of the country's beer output.[395]

The problems of small brewers were emblematic of the problems small business in general faced throughout the war. The federal government was aware of the issue and established a fund to help small companies, but most government contracts went to large businesses.[396] The brewing industry was no exception.

In October 1944, the Small Brewers Committee met and Senator James E. Murray of Montana addressed the group. Murray was chairmen of the Special Committee to Study and Serve the Problems of Small Business Enterprise. The Senator called for strengthening anti-trust laws and expanding the anti-trust division of the Justice Department. He claimed that the large brewers were engag-

---

393 Lee W. Holland, "The Evolution of the Brewers Association of America," (Colorado: Brewers Association of America, 1994). William O'Shea was secretary of the Brewers Association of America from 1942 to 1987.

394 Jos. Dubin, "An Open Letter to a Small Brewer," *Modern Brewery Age*, February 1942, 9.

395 Ibid., 103.

396 Kearns, 398-99; John Morton Blum, *V Was For Victory* (New York: Harcourt Brace Jovanovich, 1976), 124-131.

ing in "reprehensible and shocking methods" and could face federal regulation if they persisted in "an endeavor to destroy small business."[397]

The curtailment of tin for producing crowns remained the brewer's most pressing issue. In 1942, they were able to only use sixty percent of the tin they had used the previous year. This led most brewers to produce larger containers, decreasing the need for as many crowns. The quart bottle became standard and brewers spent many advertising dollars promoting this size as a patriotic gesture. Slogans included "Help to win — save the tin" and "Save caps to beat the Japs."[398] Once again, the brewing industry was responding to war needs in a way similar to many other industries including chewing gum and soft drinks.[399]

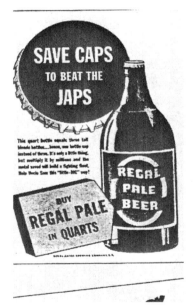

Figure 14: Photo courtesy of Modern Brewery Age.

Small brewers had sought relief from tin rationing in relation to beer bottle crowns. They did not have to decrease their use of crowns from the previous year; large brewers had to do so by a rate of thirty percent. Small brewers, overwhelmingly local in their sales, received some cessation of competition from national brewers because tire and energy restrictions reduced shipping. The crown shortage reduced supply. As demand for beer went up, brewers were able to charge higher prices for their product which benefited all brewers. There was, however, an upper limit on what brewers as well as other manufacturers could charge for the products. In April 1942, the President had established a price ceiling for the duration of the war, namely the price on March 1942.[400]

Large brewers could not continue to expand their breweries during the war because of a lack of copper and steel. Since local demand increased, this scarcity

---

397 "Fears for Future of Small Business," *New York Times*, October 16, 1944, 74.

398 Robert Crandall, "Crowns Occupy Spotlight in Current Beer Ads, *Modern Brewery Age*, 38-42.

399 Blum, *V Was For Victory*, 107-110.

400 Jos. Dubin, "A Silver Lining," *Modern Brewery Age*, September 1942, 7-8; Doris Kearns Goodwin, *No Ordinary Time: Franklin and Eleanor Roosevelt: The Home Front in World War II* (New York: Simon and Schuster, 1994), 339-340.

benefited smaller brewers. The good news for small brewers was only temporary; in general the larger brewers benefited more from governmental and army contracts. One of the nation's largest brewers, Anheuser–Busch, shipped 7,604,144 cases and 169,919 barrels overseas from January 1943 to the end of May 1944.[401]

The USBA, large brewers, and *Modern Brewery Age* all gave lip service to the idea that small breweries needed support and bemoaned the declining number of breweries. When the small breweries began to advocate for themselves and formed the Small Brewers Committee under the leadership of William O'Shea, the journal, however, was less than pleased. It disliked O'Shea and stated that "if there ever were a time when the industry needed unity, that time was right now." The USBA established a Small Brewers Relations committee which it felt was sufficient; in their opinion small brewers did not need their own organization. The brewing industry, in a time of war with the threat of a renewal of Prohibition still hanging over its head, did not wish to return to the discord and disharmony of the early Repeal years.[402]

William O'Shea and the Small Brewers Committee were determined to make an impact on government regulation of the brewing industry. In the spring of 1943, the Beverages and Tobacco Division of the War Production Board became part of the War Food Administration. The Food Distribution Administration became responsible for malt conservation, and the Brewing Industry Advisory Committee became part of that bureaucracy. The Small Brewers Committee meeting for the second year requested greater representation on that advisory committee. William O'Shea, leader of the small brewers stated their mission as follows: "Our objective is not to make giant breweries of the small breweries, not to make a lot of money, but to preserve the small breweries for the good of the industry."[403] This would remain an issue throughout the post war era.

A main focus of individual brewers during the war was maintaining their competitive position; yet public relations and popular opinion were never far from their collective minds. Drinking and the military was a perennial controversy. Concern over American boys overseas during World War I had played a role in the enactment of Prohibition. In 1943, General George C. Marshall reiterated that a 1901 law, a consequence of the Spanish American war, which had prohibited the sale of "any intoxicating" liquor at military establishments, remained in force. This legislation had abolished the army canteen and was a first

401 *Modern Brewery Age*, July, 1944, 67; A. M. McGahan, "The Emergence of the National Brewing Oligopoly: Competition in the American Market, 1933-1958," *The Business History Review*, vol. 65, no. 2 (Summer 1991): 264.

402 Jos. Dubin, "A Flukey Fuehrer," *Modern Brewery Age*, October 1942, 10; *Modern Brewery Age*, January 1944, 44.

403 *Modern Brewery Age*, June 1942, 63, 69, 25-26.

step in the march to the Eighteenth Amendment. Despite the ruling, officers and enlisted men could still drink 3.2 percent alcohol beer and wine. During Repeal, Congress had declared this amount of alcohol "non-intoxicating."[404]

Although Marshall attempted to control the consumption of hard liquor, most observers agreed that a lot of drinking was going on in the military — both at home and abroad. The acceptance of this usually led officials to encourage beer and wine over spirits; brewers heartily concurred. In any case, brewers reassured the public that the 3.2 beer was very close to the average of 3.5 percent alcohol of "ordinary" beer.[405]

The brewers actually did not agree with the casual observation of heavy drinking among U.S. soldiers. In 1943, the Office of War Information published a report which confirmed the brewers' point of view. The OWI found that there was no "excessive" drinking among soldiers, and that "no American Army has been so orderly." *Modern Brewery Age* took this finding as a sign that the brewing industry's "self-regulatory program is right on track."[406]

Soldiers from European nations had a liquor ration, and American GIs apparently wanted the same treatment. According to Bill Mauldin, well known Army cartoonist, "Drinking, like sex, is not a question of should or shouldn't in the army. It's here to stay, and it seems to us that the best way to handle it is to understand and recognize it and arrange things so those who have appetites can satisfy them with a minimum of trouble for everybody." In the absence of a liquor ration, many soldiers resorted to self-made distilleries.[407]

From the brewers' point of view, the drinking of U.S. soldiers was most significant for the impact it would have when they returned home. Having acquired a taste for alcohol while abroad, the industry hoped that soldiers would continue the habit in peacetime. In the battle for public opinion World War II represented the last stand of a prohibition movement committed to the cessation of the manufacture and sale of alcoholic beverages. The remnants of the prohibition movement and their congressional allies presented several pieces of legislation which would have curtailed the operations of the alcoholic beverages industry.[408]

---

404 "General Marshall Bans All Hard Liquor on Army Property," *New York Times*, February 4, 1943, 1.

405 Ibid.

406 Jos. Dubin, "The O.W.I. Report," *Modern Brewery Age*, January 1943, 9.

407 Bill Mauldin, *Up Front* (New York: Norton, 1995), 84.

408 Jay L. Rubin, "The Wet War, American Liquor Control, 1941-1945," in Jack S. Blocker, Jr. ed., *Alcohol, Reform and Society: The Liquor Issue in Social Context* (Westport, CT: Greenwood Press, 1979), 243.

The first attempt to limit the sale of alcohol came in the form of Senate Bill 860 which prohibition advocates introduced in 1940. The bill would have prohibited the sale of liquor to the armed and naval forces. *Modern Brewery Age* understood that prohibitionists hoped for the same results as in World War I. The journal acknowledged that enactment of the Eighteenth Amendment had been "only a question of time and our entry into the war unquestionably hastened inevitable national prohibition." Brewers now believed that "the general public, having once tried prohibition, is convinced that control and not prohibition is the answer." The brewing industry had to remain vigilant and step up its efforts to make the retail sale of beer a positive experience, "particularly in areas contiguous to military and naval establishments."[409]

Senate Bill 860 failed as did other attempts at prohibitory legislation regarding soldiers. In general, both the federal government and the military treated the industry like any other industry. This was tremendously reassuring to the brewers and signaled a greater degree of societal acceptance of alcohol than had existed before.[410]

Another issue that had been significant during World War I and the ramp up to Prohibition was the German ethnicity of the majority of American brewers. Although Germany was once again the nation's enemy in World War II, brewers' ethnicity did not become controversial. In all areas, the brewers were able to consistently present themselves as patriotic citizens fully participating in the war effort. Brewers actively participated in war bond drives, air raid drills, and blood drives. In August of 1942, employees and officers of F. & M. Schaefer Brewing Company contributed 128 pints of blood to the Red Cross, setting a record for the most blood donated in a single day.[411]

During the seven years of legal alcohol production following Repeal, *Modern Brewery Age* and brewing industry leaders had promoted the production and marketing of bock beer as the answer to many problems. Bock beer represented the craft and ethnic heritage of many American brewers. In 1943, at the sixty-seventh convention of the USBA, Herbert J. Charles, President, discussed the issue of bock beer, and declared that its production had "long been a burden, the advantages of which were outweighed by the irritants to its distribution." Many brewers had vowed not to continue to produce bock beer. Unfortunately they undertook the drive to stop production too late and many brewers had already begun brewing bock beer. Charles anticipated that "next year, unless we

409 Jos. Dubin, "The Ghost Returns," *Modern Brewery Age*, September 1942, 10.
410 Rubin, "The Wet War," 244.
411 "The Brewers Go All Out on Home Front for Victory," *Modern Brewery Age*, August 1942, 35-37.

are blessed with a return of normal conditions, . . . bock will be left out of your calculations."[412] Bock is a seasonal beer; the tightened economic and supply conditions of the war probably precluded specialized brewing.

Modern Brewery Age remained champions of bock beer. Charles' efforts succeeded, and by April there was very little bock beer production. The journal bemoaned the situation, "Stilled are the hoofs that beat a restless welcome to a new season. For Billy Bock, bellicose Billy who recognized no master remains fettered and forgotten this spring."[413]

The promotion of bock beer was an attempt to generate sales; from Repeal until the start of World War II, brewers faced slow sales and intense competition. Beginning in 1943, increased consumer spending due to greater workforce participation, the limited nature of rationing, and their required production for military purposes led to high consumption. Internal migration from rural areas to big cities also strengthened brewers' economic position.[414] The brewers certainly hoped this trend would continue into peacetime.

In September 1942, brewers sold 6,207,784 barrels of beer. This level of sales was a new record, surpassing September 1914 by 360,707 barrels. This was obviously great news for the industry as a whole, indicating that the war was not having an adverse effect. The wartime economy was promoting greater economic health than brewers had seen for a decade; other industries experienced this economic upswing as well. California and Wisconsin led the states in production. Fewer breweries were producing the greater amount of beer. By the end of 1942, there were 481 firms; there had been 667 in 1937.[415]

Brewers experienced growth in their industry both before and during the war. Areas of the country which had not previously had high rates of consumption opened new markets for the industry. Overall per capita consumption increased from 12.4 gallons in 1939 to 18.7 in 1945. California experienced a large population growth which fueled increased beer sales. The sale of beer in the South, which had been an underdeveloped market, grew more quickly than other areas.[416]

Despite the positive economic landscape, the war continued to present challenges. By the middle of 1943, the brewing industry faced further restriction on the use of its raw materials. The War Production Board limited large brewers

---

412 Ibid.

413 Robert A. Crandall, "Bock Conspicuous By Absence From Beer Ads," *Modern Brewery Age*, April 1943, 38; "As Usual There Will Be Bock Beer in '44," *Modern Brewery Age*, January 1944, 93.

414 Rubin, "The Wet War," 243; Polenberg, *One Nation Divisible*, 46-85.

415 "September Beer Sales Hit All Time High," *Modern Brewery Age*, November 1942, 29; *Modern Brewery Age*, February 1943, 12.

416 McGahan, "The Emergence of the National Brewing Oligopoly," 259.

to ninety-three percent of its 1942 use of malt and malt syrup. There was a sufficient amount of the raw material, but the government wanted to ensure an adequate amount for industrial alcohol producers. A variety of industries including rubber and smokeless powder used industrial alcohol.[417]

In April of 1943, the brewing industry celebrated ten years of legal production, taking pains to point out the many contributions the industry was making to the war effort. The industry's activities included war bonds, blood drives, scrap collection, conservation, participation in the armed forces, and the use of brewers yeast. The two most important contributions were taxes and supervision of retail establishments.[418]

That same year, Schenley Distillers purchased Blatz Brewing for $6 million. The purchase was one part of the company's plan for expansion and diversification. At the same time Schenley was negotiating to purchase Blatz from the Landsberg family, it started a protein-recovery plant for cattle feed in Kentucky and purchased the Central Winery, Roma Wine, and Colonial Grape Products Companies of California.[419]

At the time of the sale, Blatz Brewing was almost one hundred years old. Schenley Industries dated back only to Prohibition. Lewis Rosenstiel owned the company, which imported Dewar's scotch and manufactured George Dickel whisky, among many products. Distilling and brewing were usually separate activities; Schenley's purchase of Blatz represented a departure from standard practice, but Frank Gabel (and then, in 1946, Frank C. Verbest) ran Blatz Brewing like the other large breweries of the time. The company was the ninth largest brewery in 1947.[420]

Schenley purchased Blatz in an attempt to diversify. Local breweries sometimes combined to gain a competitive edge against the national shipping companies. One example of this was Sick Brewery, which benefited from purchasing closed breweries. F. Sick began a brewery in Lethbridge, Alberta, Canada at the turn of the twentieth century. During World War II, his son Emil ran over eleven breweries in the Pacific Northwest and Canada. The most famous of Sick's breweries was Rainier Beer. A Washington product, this beer dated back to 1878, but it did not survive. The Sicks bought the brewery and the brand, and began

417 "Malt Curtailment Freezes Beer Output," *Modern Brewery Age*, March 1943, 10.

418 "Relegalized Beer Marks 10th Anniversary," *Modern Brewery Age*, April 1943, 76.

419 "Blatz Brewery Deal Announced," *New York Times*, November 26, 1943; "Schenley Seek Blatz Brewing," *New York Times*, September 21, 1943, 38; "Boomlet in Stocks of Distilleries," *New York Times*, Oct. 31, 1943, 57; "Schenley Lists War Production," *New York Times*, November 26, 1943, 34.

420 Downard, *Dictionary*, 23, 160, 167.

brewing Rainier Beer in 1935. In 1977, Heileman purchased the company. Pabst currently owns the brand but does not brew it in Washington.[421]

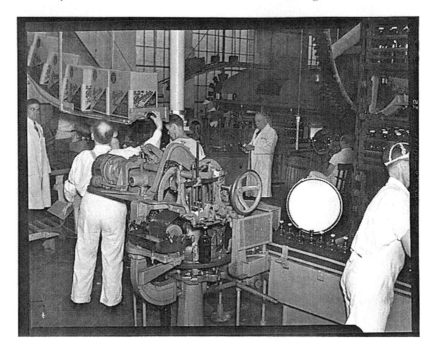

Figure 15: Workers inside Rainier Brewery, Seattle, July 17, 1939. (1983.10.13347.5.) Photo courtesy of Museum of History & Industry.

A major wartime activity was beer production for the armed forces; the government required the brewing industry to set aside fifteen percent. The whole process was under the supervision of John H. Connelly, Administrative Beer Coordinator. He felt the program was necessary because beer was "a morale factor." Connelly further indicated that all brewers, large and small, needed to contribute to this effort because the large brewers could not provide all the beer.[422]

Eventually the American brewing industry was unable to supply all of the beer the army needed for United States soldiers. In 1944 the military took over North African and Italian breweries to supplant American production. James Shakman, vice-president of production for Pabst, advised the army in this process. The United States brewing industry sent brewmasters and supplies to the

421 Rick Star, "Rainier Brewery: Rest in Peace," Beer Notes, August 1999, http://www.beer-notes.com/northwest/articles/000409.html (accessed October 10, 2006); Tom Jones Parry, "Building Brand Prestige for Eleven Regional Breweries," *Modern Brewery Age*, June 1944, 39-40; Downard, *Dictionary*, 157.

422 John H. Connelly, "Beer, The Morale Builder," *Modern Brewery Age*, June 1944, 25-26, 80.

European breweries. Robert Gadsby, an assistant brew master from Anheuser–Busch, was in charge of the operations at two breweries in Bremen, Germany. France, Belgium, Luxemburg, and Germany had a total of fifty-four breweries producing beer for U.S. soldiers. The army also planned to open the San Miguel Brewery in Manila, Philippines to provide beer to soldiers in the Pacific. American brewers obviously felt a tremendous amount of pride over this operation; it certainly further legitimated beer drinking.[423] In 1945, the industry received another shot in the arm when the federal government ordered Minneapolis brewery workers to halt a strike because beer was essential to the war effort.[424]

The brewing industry continually sought to establish and consolidate its position as a legitimate industry which provided a much-needed product to soldiers. As proof of its contribution to increasing morale, *Modern Brewery Age* recounted the following conversation between a commanding officer and a mess sergeant:

> Commanding Officer: Do I understand that the water you get here is unsafe?
>
> Mess Sergeant: Yes, sir.
>
> Commanding Officer: What precaution do you take to ensure the health of the outfit?
>
> Mess Sergeant: We filter the water first, sir.
>
> Commanding Officer: Yes.
>
> Mess Sergeant: Then we boil it.
>
> Commanding Officer: Yes?
>
> Mess Sergeant: Then we add chemicals to it.
>
> Commanding Officer: Yes.
>
> Mess Sergeant: And, then, sir, we drink beer.[425]

Providing beer to soldiers overseas helped the brewers retain the goodwill of the public, a primary goal in their campaign to prevent a return of prohibition. Controlling bad business practices was another aspect of this drive. Self-regulation under the auspices of the Nebraska Plan was the mission of the United Brewers Industrial Foundation. In 1944 it celebrated its seventh anniversary.

---

423 "GIs 'Roll Out the Barrel' as Army Boosts Overseas Brewing," *Modern Brewery Age*, July 1945, 33-34, 101.

424 McGahan, "The Emergence of the National Brewing Oligopoly," 263; *Brewers Almanac*, 1946, 2.

425 "Beer Aids Army Morale," *Modern Brewery Age*, August 1944, 73.

Advertising was a large part of the program and Rudy Schaefer chaired that committee. The committee distributed a pamphlet "The ABC of Beer Advertising" to individual brewers that provided advice on avoiding advertising that would arouse "official and public criticism." The committee also corresponded with individual brewers whose advertising it felt might "expose the industry generally to attack."[426]

Later that year, having survived two years of a war economy and relieved that the horrors of World War I had not returned, the USBA and the UBIF merged. During Repeal, Anheuser–Busch and others had felt the USBA was not devoting enough energy to self-regulation and public relations. The UBIF had been Jacob Ruppert's response. With all elements of the industry reunited within the USBA, brewers felt it was time to integrate the important functions of the UBIF into the parent organization. Herbert J. Charles, president of the USBA, remained in that position in the reformed United States Brewers Foundation. *Modern Brewery Age* hailed the merger stating that it was a "healthy sign that the industry's leaders realize that its local option work has been weak..." The journal was concerned about the spread of dry areas, reiterating that "the principal problem of the brewing industry is that of perpetuating its legal business."[427] Despite the many gains the industry had achieved in the eleven years since Repeal leaders still worried about the return of prohibition. How long would this shadow linger?

A major goal of the association was to provide training for veterans. Other officers included Adolph Coors, Carl W. Badenhausen, P. Ballantine & Sons, and Edward V. Lahey. C. D. Williams, long-time secretary of the USBA, remained secretary. Merging the two organization meant that the new United States Brewers Foundation was the second oldest trade association in the United States.[428]

The brewers' goal of providing veterans with jobs was part of a larger emphasis on post-war planning. The USBA had a sub-committee, headed by Albert Bates, president of G. Heileman Brewing Company, studying the issue and in 1944 it presented its findings. The report indicated that the post-war economy would not support war time demand for beer and production of beer. Bates declared that "seventy-five million barrels is the probable peak of the industry." Bates and the committee cautioned brewers about rapid expansion. The one area of potential growth appeared to be "the home consumption field." Bates felt that "the industry survey does not indicate an increase in the consumption of beer throughout the postwar period but, to the contrary indicates a decline."[429] The

---

426 *Modern Brewery Age*, January 1944, 90.
427 "Brewers Association, Foundation Merged for More Effective Work," *New York Times*, October 18, 1944, 29; Jos. Dubin, "Hail To USBF," *Modern Brewery Age*, October 1944, 19.
428 Ibid.
429 Albert J. Bates, "Postwar Production Planning," *Modern Brewery Age*, January 1944, 9-10, 78.

brewing industry's focus on post-war planning during the war was similar to many other business and segments of American society.

In 1944 the war had not yet ended, and the USBF was anticipating a tax increase in the coming year. Congress and President Roosevelt increased the excise tax, effective April 1944, to $8 a barrel. The distilled spirits and wine industries also received increases. Despite the tax increase, the government maintained price ceilings on those products; brewers could only increase their prices by the amount of the tax increase.[430]

Figure 16: Photo courtesy of Modern Brewery Age.

The organization hoped, however, that the government would reduce the excise tax to $5 a barrel once the war was over. The war in Europe ended on May 8, 1945 (VE Day), and the brewers realized that tax relief would have to wait at least until the war in Japan also ended. The previous month's excise taxes on beer had generated $42,969,611 for the federal government and the war effort.[431]

On April 12, 1945, President Franklin D. Roosevelt died. The country — in fact the whole world — mourned. The brewing industry was no exception; they actually had many reasons to be especially sad. The obituary in *Modern Brewery Age* lauded the president's achievements and deemed him the "greatest helmsman in the cause of freedom of our time." The picture accompanying the story was of Roosevelt when he signed the bill re-legalizing 3.2 percent beer twelve years earlier.[432]

---

430 "New Beer Tax, Higher Ceilings, Effective April 1," *Modern Brewery Age*, March 1944, 20.
431 *Modern Brewery Age*, January, 1944, 42-43; *Modern Brewery Age*, May 1945, 101.
432 "Franklin Delano Roosevelt," *Modern Brewery Age*, April 1945, 15.

The war in the Pacific ended four months later; major priorities for the brewing industry were tax relief and the end of price controls. Neither came immediately after the ending of the war. Brewers anticipated an economic recession and a reduction in demand. But, in fact, 1945 turned out to be a record year for the sale of bottled beer and home use. Of all beer, 64.3 percent was bottled. Although price controls were still in place, shortage of raw materials began to ease, and the brewing industry returned to producing beer in cans. Krueger Brewing, the first to manufacture beer in cans in 1935, proclaimed in its winter ads that it was "First Again! Krueger Beer back in Cans!"[433]

The brewing industry had continued advertising its products throughout the war; in 1945 Pabst was the only brewery to sponsor a national radio program. The program starred Danny Kaye; Pabst supplemented this exposure with an elaborate print campaign including billboards in forty states.[434] Pabst's advertising campaign was a harbinger of the post-war world.

In 1947, Schlitz and Pabst were the leading brewers in the country, with a production of slightly more than four million barrels each. Both were national companies, but the third largest, P. Ballantine & Sons, was more regional. Anheuser-Busch was fourth. Three New York breweries, Schaefer, Liebmann (Rheingold), and Jacob Ruppert occupied the fifth through seventh slots. The Greater New York area, Milwaukee, and St. Louis were the centers of brewing at this time. Acme was the largest brewer in California. Located in San Francisco, it had been sixteenth in 1940 but now ranked eighth.[435]

As brewers faced the post-war world, they had to contend with organized labor. Prior to Prohibition the United Brewery Workers had been a heavily Socialist and German union which often struggled with the AFL. As the country went through the Depression, Repeal, and World War II, the identity of the union changed considerably. The AF L revoked the UBW's charter in 1941, as a result of the long-standing jurisdictional dispute between the brewery workers and the teamsters over beer truck drivers. This dispute led to a strike in Minneapolis-St. Paul against all of the brewers in the city including Pabst, Schlitz, Miller, and Gettelman. The teamsters won representation of all outside workers while the Brewery Workers Union retained inside workers. In 1946 the UBW joined the Congress of Industrial Organizations (CIO), becoming the International

433 Jos. Dubin, "A Way To Build Volume," *Modern Brewery Age*, September 1945, 25; Jos. Dubin "The Local Brewer's Market," October 1945, 15; *Brewers Almanac*, 1946, 1; "Ads Herald Return of Beer In Cans," *Modern Brewery Age*, vol. 34, December 1945, 45.

434 *Modern Brewery Age*, January 1945, 54.

435 "Schlitz, Pabst Lead Field," *New York Times*, June 10, 1948, 42.

Union of United Brewery, Flour, Cereal, Soft Drink and Distillery Workers of America.[436]

In 1949 New York City had fourteen breweries. In April the seven locals went on strike. Their demands included a shorter work week and two man teams for delivery trucks rather than one. This was the first New York City brewery strike in sixty years; 7,000 people were out of work. Because New York brewers could not supply their usual production of 31 million gallons during May and June, national firms from the Midwest were able to penetrate the market. Blatz became a big seller in the city as a result of the strike which lasted eighty-one days. That year Wisconsin led the country in beer production, a position New York brewers had previously held.[437] After the strike was over, New York brewers sought to regain the market and the customers they had lost. Ruppert Beer advertised that it had posted a bond guaranteeing "the maturity of Ruppert Beer."[438]

The same year as the strike, the United States Brewers Foundation claimed that it was "an organization representing ninety percent of the brewery production of the United States." There were 440 breweries at this time. Packaged beer was seventy percent of consumption and the per capita consumption of beer was 17.9 gallons. Edward V. Lahey was now president and R. T. Riney from Sterling Brewers, Indiana, was secretary. The officers of the organization included representatives of all the major brewers from Anheuser–Busch to Schlitz.[439]

Advertising, which had played a small role prior to Prohibition and an increasing role during Repeal, continued to grow in importance during the immediate post war period. In 1940, seven years after Repeal and one year before the onset of World War II, brewers spent ninety-six cents per barrel on advertising. By 1950 the amount had risen to $1.09. The larger the brewer, the more the company spent. Breweries that produced over 500,000 barrels spent $1.36 per barrel. Television advertising was becoming increasingly important. In 1949 the largest brewer spent only a penny a barrel on this venue. A year later the amount was twelve cents. Brewers were the eighth largest user of television advertising. Distillers did not advertise on television. This may have been a factor in the Ameri-

---

436 Mittelman, "Labor," in Blocker et. al., *Encyclopedia*, 357-359; *Modern Brewery Age*, June 1945, 99.

437 Will Anderson, *Breweries of Brooklyn: An Informal History of a Great Industry in a Great City* (New York: Anderson, 1976) 26-27

438 *New York Times* March 21, 1951, 46; July 1, 1949, 40.

439 *Brewers Almanac*, 1949, 2, 32, 111-112; 1950, 7, 19, 3. Edward Lahey was president of Smith Brothers, Inc., a New Bedford, Massachusetts brewer. He had been the treasurer of the USBA since 1942 and in 1947 he became the president. The brewery closed in 1950. In 1963 he became an honorary director and he died in 1964. See "Edward Lahey, 71, Bay State Brewer," *New York Times*, August 9, 1964, 76.

can people spending as much for fermented beverages as for all other alcoholic beverages combined.[440]

Beer advertising as well as beer sales still relied on a seasonal cycle despite refrigeration and widespread national and year round access to beer. Winter, particularly February, was the low point for sales. To offset the perceived decease in consumption brewers generally spent more in advertising. By March, the brewers could look forward to spring and bock beer. Pictures of goats abounded, and brewers once again sought to highlight this specialty beer. Brewers had a deep fondness for "Billy Bock" — but April and then the summer months represented their prime selling season.[441]

Television was changing the nature of beer advertising; the intended recipient was also changing. Brewers began to direct their advertising at the consumer instead of the wholesaler or retailer. This shift reflected the ever increasing home-sales market.[442]

As the home consumption market increased, brewers experimented with a variety of packages for their product. Brewers usually sold their beer in twenty-four 12-ounce can or bottle cases; other sizes included three and twelve can or bottle packages. Coca-Cola and other soda manufacturers had consistently packaged their product in six packs of returnable bottles. This was the only size package that soda makers offered. *Modern Brewery Age* admired the fact that "Coca-Cola and the other soft drink firms have made the unit '6' *the* accepted package for soft drinks." The journal felt brewers had not developed this kind of marketing to "the fullest extent." Although brewers had used some six-can packs, because of continuing war-related shortages, the journal encouraged brewers to develop a six pack of returnable bottles and follow Coca-Cola, "the acknowledged leader in the entire beverage industry."[443] Eventually the six pack of one-way beer cans became the industry's favorite package and emblematic of a typical beer drinker's buying habits.

The brewing industry still paid taxes; for the federal government, this was a prime reason for the industry's existence. In 1950, the excise tax on beer stood at $8.00 a barrel. In the spring of that year the House considered tax adjustment legislation, but ultimately chose to leave both the distilled spirits and beer tax at their current levels.[444]

---

440 *Modern Brewery Age*, January 1951, 37; May 1951, 100; July 1951, 42.

441 *Modern Brewery Age*, February 1951, 49; March, 1951, 47-48; April, 1951, 55.

442 "Brewers Promotion Aimed At Consumers," *New York Times*, October 29, 1952, 50.

443 *Modern Brewery Age*, April 1945, 21.

444 John D. Morris, "House Unit Spurns Cut in Liquor Tax," *New York Times*, May 5, 1950, 15.

From Frederick Lauer on, the brewers had friends and allies in Congress who attempted to get the best advantage for the industry in their relationship with the federal government. In 1951, there were still price and production controls in place. The brewers once again faced rationing on tin, used primarily for beer cans. The sale of beer in cans had been increasing steadily since the production of the first can in 1935. When the National Production Authority announced plans to limit the use of tin for beer and other "nonessential" products, Rep. John D. Dingell Sr. of Detroit, Michigan was concerned about the impact such a policy would have on tax revenues. He planned to introduce legislation that would repeal the board authority in this matter.[445]

Dingell was from a city that had been a center of brewing in the late nineteenth century; Detroit had thirty-three breweries in 1890. Stroh's was the most famous and long lived; the owners were descendants of Germans who had been brewing since 1775. By selling ice cream as well as beer it existed as an independent brewery until 1999.[446]

The United States government had essentially remained on a war footing since 1945, and the Korean War continued this approach. In the spring and summer of 1951, Congress considered legislation to finance rearmament. Military spending had more than tripled since 1950, and the armed forces had more than doubled in size. As part of the overall package, legislators planned to increase excise taxes on liquor, beer, wine, tobacco, automobiles, gasoline, and sporting goods. The House wrote legislation that included tax increases for both distilled spirits and beer which would help to generate $7.2 billion in revenue. The Senate held hearings on the legislation; various representatives of the different branches of the liquor industry appeared.[447]

The increases in taxes that President Truman presented to Congress would have a multi-level effect on the brewing industry. An increase in the excise tax would of course directly impact brewers. At the same time, an increase in the income tax would "have a deflationary effect." The taxes were part of the President's plan to get the country back on a war footing due to the hostilities in Korea.[448]

Clinton Hester presented the United States Brewers Foundation's concerns over the proposed $1 increase. All the wartime increases which had brought the

445 "Curb on Tin For Beer Cans Opposed as Bad Strategy," *New York Times*, March 19, 1951, 18; *Brewers Almanac*, 1951, 3.

446 William H. Mulligan, "Stroh Brewing Company," in Blocker et al., *Encyclopedia*, 598-600; Downard, *Dictionary*, 56-57, 185-186.

447 "Tax Bill 7.1 Billion; No Rise on TV Sets," *New York Times*, May 26, 1951, 8; "Bootlegging Seen in Liquor Tax Rise," *New York Times*, July 31, 1951, 15; Lawrence S. Wittner, *Cold War America: From Hiroshima to Watergate* (New York: Praeger, 1974) 79.

448 *Modern Brewery Age*, January 1951, 13, 20.

tax to $8 a barrel had resulted in a steady decline in sales. Hester also protested the continuing restrictions on tin, claiming that if they continued the "Federal Government will lose millions more in beer excise taxes."[449]

Ralph T. Hymsfeld was president of the Distilled Spirits Institute, a trade association and vice-president of Schenley Industries, which owned Blatz Beer. Hymsfeld felt that the tax increase for the liquor industry would actually decrease tax revenues because of decreased sales. The states and the federal government stood to lose $67 million a year.[450]

Karl Feller, speaking for unionized brewery workers, felt that any tax increase supported prohibitionist forces. He also expressed concern about the effects of a tax increase on the small brewer, and the growing concentration in the brewing industry. Feller claimed that many small brewers would not survive.[451]

The congressional discussion of the proposed tax increase focused more on the distilled spirits industry, which continued to have problems with bootlegging and illicit distilling. This emphasis demonstrates the continuing division of the liquor industry, something the brewers always promoted.

Congress was discussing the proposed tax increase within the context of a scandal in the Bureau of Internal Revenue; the early years of the Bureau had witnessed one of the country's largest scandals, the Whiskey Ring. Since 1940 the Alcohol Tax Unit of the B.I.R. had responsibility for regulation of the liquor industry. The larger bureau, which had existed since 1862, had not had any reorganization since 1917. Two wars and Prohibition had occurred as well as a dramatic increase in tax collections and employees. By the end of World War II, a person might wait twelve months or longer for a tax refund. In 1944 the federal government collected $42,125,986,550 in income taxes. This was an increase over 1943. Although income taxes played the largest role in the country's tax situation, brewers and the liquor industry had also been significant contributors throughout the war.[452]

Staffing of the Bureau and its sixty-four collection districts had been done on a purely patronage basis with predictable results. An investigation of the agency in 1951 by Senator John James Williams, (R. DE) revealed that at least four different collectors in St. Louis, Boston, Brooklyn, and San Francisco had been engaged in fraud, embezzlement, bribery, and tax evasion. The most promi-

---

449 Senate Committee on Finance, *Revenue Act of 1951*, Hearings, 82nd Congress, 1951, 1839-1961.
450 "Bootlegging," 15.
451 Ibid.
452 Andrew J. Dunar, *The Truman Scandals and the Politics of Morality* (Columbia, MO: University of Missouri Press, 1984), 96; William Pemberton, *Bureaucratic Politics: Executive Reorganization during the Truman Administration* (Columbia, MO: University of Missouri Press, 1979), 162; "Federal Tax Yield $42,125,986,550 in 1944," *New York Times*, February 13, 1945, 36.

nent member of the Administration to face corruption charges was Matthew J. Connelly, the President's appointments secretary. Connelly received a two year sentence for tax evasion and influence peddling. He served six months in prison after the end of the Truman presidency: Truman eventually persuaded President Kennedy to pardon Connelly.[453]

Although not as large a scandal as the Whiskey Frauds of the late nineteenth century, President Truman did respond by reorganizing the Bureau, reducing the number of collection districts to twenty-five, and turning appointment power over to the Civil Service. John Wesley Snyder, a close friend of and powerful fundraiser for President Truman, was Secretary of the Treasury and was in charge of reforming the Bureau of Internal Revenue.[454]

The final legislation raised $5,691,000,000 in taxes and included a $9 a barrel beer excise tax. Brewers had to decide whether or not to pass the increase directly along to the consumer. The Office of Price Stabilization would have the final say on any price increases. At least one company, Genesee Brewing of Rochester, New York declined to pass on the increase to consumers. Genesee Brewing began in 1857 under the name Reis and Spies. In the late 1890s it became part of a British syndicate, Bartholamay and Company. After Prohibition the family which had worked as brewmasters at the brewery for several generations purchased Bartholomay and renamed it Genesee Brewing. The company was a large regional brewery until the 1990s. Its most popular product was Genesee Cream Ale. High Falls Brewing now owns and brews the Genesee brand.[455]

Although Genesee and other brewers were determined to hold the line on prices, retail establishments could not do the same. A week after the tax went into effect, tavern owners in Manhattan raised all their prices. Beyond the effect of the tax increase, the bar owners were facing union demands from bartenders, including a reduction in hours, more holidays, and better health benefits. Many places already sold beer at fifteen cents a glass, but the owners assumed that those who didn't would now raise their prices.[456]

453 Dunar, *The Truman Scandals*, 98-99, 150-155. All had received appointments as collectors during the tenure of either Robert E. Hannegan or Joseph Nunan as Commissioner of Internal Revenue. Hannegan had been instrumental in helping Harry Truman win re-election to the Senate in 1940 and later served as chair of the Democratic National Committee when Truman received the vice-presidential nomination at the 1944 convention. See "Truman is Seventh Elevated by Death," *New York Times*, April 13, 1945, 3.

454 Dennis Merrill, ed., *Documentary History of the Truman Presidency*, University Publishers of America, 2000, vol. 28, xxxix, 271-272; Rick D. Medlin, "Snyder, John Wesley," *American National Biography Online* www.anb.org/articles (accessed January 9, 2003).

455 Excise Tax Rises to Force Prices Up," *New York Times*, October 26, 1951, 15; "Brewer to Hold Price Level," *New York Times*, October 31, 1951, 58; www.highfalls.com (accessed June 19, 2007).

456 "Beer, Liquor Prices Raised in Bars Here," *New York Times*, November 7, 1951, 1.

Eventually brewers also had to raise their price; in early 1952 the four major breweries from Milwaukee all raised the cost of a case of beer. Consumers wound up paying a penny more a bottle. The Office of Price Stabilization allowed Schlitz, Miller, Blatz and Pabst to increase the price to compensate for increases in production costs.[457]

Six months after the tax increase, the Research Company of America released statistics concerning the brewing industry. Brewing production had not yet reached the 87,076,141 barrels high of 1947, but consumption was above that of 1951. Taxes had hurt consumption as well as the "booming infant population." Yet the baby boom represented a silver lining in the cloudy picture. "When this group of new kids reaches maturity, the per capita pattern should rise materially, provided no other detriments appear to retard an anticipated increase in consumption."[458]

In general brewers felt that the additional taxes put a damper on consumption rates. In 1952, the Schaefer Brewing Company celebrated its 110th anniversary. R. J. Schaefer had been president of the company for twenty-five years. On this auspicious occasion he expressed his concern over the effect of high taxes on the "working man."[459] The brewers also paid a large amount of state taxes on their product.

Schaefer Brewing continued as a leader in the brewing industry; production peaked at 5,000,000 in 1975. Rudy Schaefer ceased active leadership of the company that year. He characterized the industry as "a virtual fraternity with strong social ties that spread over more than a single generation." When the historic Brooklyn brewery closed in 1976 an era ended.[460]

The brewers continued to have congressional allies who sought tax relief for the liquor industry. In November of 1952 the country elected Dwight D. Eisenhower as President; the promise of peace was in the air. Representative Dingell took this occasion as opportunity to urge across the broad reductions in excise taxes.[461] Although Congress did not reduce the beer tax, the new administration did abolish price controls and the Office of Price Stabilization. The final step toward peacetime occurred when the Korean War ended on July 27, 1953. The

457 "Milwaukee Beer Going Up," *New York Times*, January 28, 1952, 29.
458 Greg MacGregor, "Beer Output in '51 83,718,067 Barrels," *New York Times*, July 5, 1952, 18.
459 "Beer Consumption May Hit New High," *New York Times*, Sept. 20, 1952, 26.
460 Downard, *Dictionary*, 166; Schaefer, "Our One Hundredth Year," *New York Times*, November 11, 1923, 23; Anderson, *The Breweries of Brooklyn*, 6, 7.
461 "Democrat Insists G.O.P. Slash Taxes," *New York Times*, November 29, 1952, 24.

brewing industry conducted business, "for the first time in years, with relatively no wartime controls or restrictions, affording a comparatively free market."[462]

The brewers accepted the 1951 increase of the excise tax as part of their continuing patriotic participation in the government. They would not have to worry about that role again for forty years. The familiar issues of competition and consolidation, however, still remained, and the brewing industry would confront yet unimagined issues as the post-war world unfolded.

---

462 United States. *United States Government Organization Manual, 1953-1954* (Washington, D.C.: Division of the Federal Register, National Archives Establishment, 1953), 88-89, 96-103, 624-625; *Brewers Almanac*, 1954, 3.

CHAPTER 7. MILLER TIME, 1953–1986

From the mid-nineteenth century on, families ran most American breweries — fathers passing the properties and business down to sons. Among the founders of the United States Brewing Association were men like Frederick Lauer whose father had been a brewer in Bavaria, and John Katzenmeyer, bookkeeper for A. Schmid & Co. Katzenmeyer was the first secretary of the USBA, and his son Richard followed in his footsteps.

The Miller Brewing Company followed this familial pattern as well. Frederick J. Miller was born in Germany in 1824 and came to the United States in 1850. He founded Miller Brewing in 1855. The Milwaukee based company was a large regional brewery prior to Prohibition. Frederick Miller married twice and had a total of eleven children. Five survived; these three sons and two daughters provided the heirs for the brewery. The sons, Ernst, Emil, and Fred, never married.[463]

When Frederick J. Miller died in 1888, Ernst, the oldest son, became president. The three boys, along with a brother-in-law named Carl Miller (no relation), kept the brewery going during Prohibition. Fred A. Miller, one of the brothers, was president of the company at the beginning of World War II. When he died

---

463 William Downard, *Dictionary of the American Brewing and Distilling Industries* (Westport, CT: Greenwood Press, 1980), 119-120; Miller Brewing Co., Communications Department, Corporate Affairs Division, "Miller History," Fall 1991, Beerhistory.com, http://www.beerhistory.com/library/holdings/millerhistory.shtml (accessed January 4, 2006); Associated Press, "150 years of Miller Beer," 2005, WKBT.com, http://www.wkbt.com/Global/story.asp?S=3633152; (accessed December 20,2005).

in 1943, he left an estate valued at $6.9 million including 3,444 shares of Miller Brewing Company stock. The stock was worth $1,033,333.[464]

Often the children and grandchildren of successful businessmen are unable to continue the business. Ultimately the Miller family suffered this fate. Carl was married to Frederick Miller's daughter Clara. Frederick Miller's other daughter, Elise, was married and had two children, Harry and Lorraine John. Clara and Carl had a son, Frederick C. Miller Sr. Frederick Miller's grandchildren, Harry, Lorraine, Fred, and other relatives all had shares in the Miller Brewing Company. When Fred A. Miller died, the majority of his shares went to Harry John, his favorite nephew.[465]

Through inheritance, Elise John, one of founder Frederick Miller's daughters, had a fifty-one percent share of the company, which gave her the authority to name its officers. In 1946 she chose her son Harry John, born in 1919, to become head of the company. Harry had not worked in the brewery but had concentrated on farming and a growing interest in Catholicism. His cousin Fred had been an officer of the company since 1936.[466]

Elise saw Harry's presidency as an experiment; after one year she decided it had failed and removed him. Soon after, she gave Lorraine stocks that had been in a trust for Harry. Harry's large charitable contributions alarmed Elise; she strongly believed that control of the company should remain within the family. Harry sued his mother and sister, winning back his stocks and gaining direct control over their disposition.[467]

After the family ousted Harry as company president, Fred took over the reins. Fred C. Miller was born in 1906 and graduated from Notre Dame in 1929, having been a star football player. He became vice-president of Miller Brewing in 1936 and then president in 1947. Fred was a competent executive who modernized and expanded the company. In 1953, under Fred's leadership the company moved into the top five brewing tier, displacing Liebmann Brothers and Rheingold beer. The company's output increased from 800,000 barrels (31 gallons) to three million in five years. Fred exemplified most World War II brewing executives with his commitment to sports. He played a pivotal role in bringing the Boston Braves baseball team to Milwaukee. He was also involved with promoting professional

---

464 Tim John, *The Miller Beer Barons* (Oregon, WI: Badger Books, 2005), 260; *Modern Brewery Age*, January 1944, 74; March 1945, 90.

465 John, *The Miller Beer Barons*, 263.

466 Ibid., 267.

467 Paul Wilkes, "Harry John Was Not Your Average American Catholic," *National Catholic Reporter* vol. 17 (September 1993): 13-21; *Modern Brewery Age*, January 1944, 74; John, *The Miller Beer Barons*, 272-314.

basketball in the city. Fred Miller died tragically, along with a son also named Fred, in an airplane crash in 1954.[468]

Figure 17: Fred C. Miller. Photo courtesy of Miller Brewing Company Archives.

As the family searched for a replacement, it became clear that they would not find one from within the family. Fred Miller had six daughters and a surviving son; the oldest was twenty-two. Harry John, Frederick Miller's grandson, had already failed as a chief executive and moved on to other endeavors. Married to Erica Nowotny in 1956, Harry was deeply involved in philanthropic activities and established a Catholic non-profit foundation, the de Rancé Foundation. Harry funded de Rancé in 1946 with his forty-seven percent share of the Miller fortune. Harry named the foundation for Armand Jean de Rancé, a seventeenth century Trappist monk.[469]

The other surviving grandchild was Harry's sister, Lorraine, who had married Henry C. Mulberger, the company's advertising director, in 1936. They divorced in 1947. Lorraine was also deeply religious and attended the Waukesha Bible Church. The church belonged to the Independent Fundamental Churches of America.[470]

Although Lorraine was on the company's board of directors, the family turned to Norman Klug, Miller's general counsel, as its choice to head Miller Brewing.[471] By this choice, Miller became the first of the brewing dynasties led by a non-family member. The family still had the controlling interest in the company, and Miller Brewing pursued a similar course to the other major breweries in the late 1950s and 1960s.

In 1950, the nation's top ten brewers held thirty-eight percent of the country's beer sales. The number one brewer, Joseph Schlitz Brewing Company, brewed 5,096,840 barrels of beer. Anheuser–Busch was number two. Schlitz, another of the nation's old breweries, dated back to 1849. August Krug, a German

468 "Brewer and Son Die in Air Crash," *New York Times*, December 18, 1954, 16; Dave Herrewig, "Fred C. Miller," unpublished manuscript in author's possession.

469 "Brewer and Son Die in Air Crash," *New York Times*, December 18, 1954, 16; Frank Trippett, "Harry John's Holy War," *Time*, May 26, 1986, time.com, (accessed January 2, 2006).

470 "Marketplace," *New York Times*, September 23, 1966, 50; John, *The Miller Beer Barons*, 229, 380.

471 Downard, *Dictionary*, 120; John, *The Miller Beer Barons*, 339.

immigrant, opened a saloon and brewery in Milwaukee. A year later he began to focus solely on brewing. Krug and his wife had parental responsibility for their nephew, August Uihlein. The Uihleins became one of the nations' brewing dynasties and had control of the company for over a hundred years.

Krug died in 1856, and Joseph Schlitz took over both his business and family, marrying his widow, Anna Maria Krug. He renamed the brewery Joseph Schlitz Brewing Company. In 1873 the brewery became a stock company. Schlitz was president, August Uihlein secretary, and August's brother, Henry superintendent. Joseph Schlitz died at sea in 1875; the Uihleins gained control of the company. The Uihlein brothers grew the company so successfully that by 1902, it was the world's largest brewer, producing over one million barrels a year.[472]

During the 1950s Schlitz and Anheuser-Busch traded the top spot in beer production several times. Schlitz was number one in 1950–1952 and 1955–1956. In 1952, the brewery set a world record for the most production in a single year, producing 6.35 million barrels of beer.[473]

At the same time that Miller Brewing was undergoing change, moving from family leadership to a more corporate style, other breweries were also changing. From 1950 to 1980 there was much movement among the top ten producers of beer as the industry continued its trend towards greater concentration.

Liebmann Bros owned and brewed Rheingold Beer, which was sixth in 1950. After Repeal, the company expanded through acquisitions, but Pepsi Cola United Bottlers purchased it in 1964. At that time, only the Brooklyn and New Jersey plants remained in operation. Chock full o'Nuts, the coffee company, bought Rheingold in 1974 and closed the Brooklyn brewery in 1976. In 1977 C. Schmidt and Company, tenth in 1980, bought the brand.[474] In the 1990s, and again in 2003, the owners of Rheingold Brewing Company attempted to revive both the company and its famous Miss Rheingold contest. In 2005, Drinks America bought the brand; the company also distributes Willie Nelson's Old Whiskey River Bourbon and Trump Super Premium Vodka.[475]

Although in 1953 Schlitz lost its number one ranking due to a Milwaukee strike, the brewery continued to expand, purchasing four breweries that all went out of business between 1949 and 1964. The biggest acquisition was, in

472 Bob Skilnik, "Schlitz, Joseph Brewing Company" in Blocker, et al., *Encyclopedia*, vol. 2, 544-545.

473 Victor J. Tremblay and Carol Horton Tremblay, *The United States Brewing Industry* (Cambridge, MA: MIT Press, 2005), 68; Michael R. Reilly," Joseph Schlitz Brewing Co.: A Chronological History," 1995 http://www.chiptin.com/schlitz/history6.htm (accessed January 4, 2006).

474 Downard, *Dictionary*, 159; Will Anderson, *The Breweries of Brooklyn: An Informal History of a Great Industry in a Great City* (New York: Anderson, 1976), 100-111.

475 Patricia Winters Lauro, "Advertising," *New York Times*, February 2, 2003, C8; "Rheingold Beer," http://www.drinksamericas.com/brands/rhein.htm (accessed January 24, 2007).

1961, Burgemeister, located in San Francisco and the third largest brewer in California. In 1964 Schlitz also purchased a thirty-four per cent share of Labatt of Canada which controlled General Brewing Company, San Francisco. Burgemeister and General were responsible for twenty-seven per cent of the California beer market.

Following Schlitz's purchases in the early sixties, the federal government filed an anti-trust suit against the brewery. At the same time the government was also suing Pabst for its acquisition of Blatz in 1958, Falstaff for purchasing Narragansett, and Rheingold for buying Jacob Ruppert.[476] In the 1950s the government had pursued anti-trust action against Anheuser–Busch for its purchase of the Miami Regal Brewery.[477] In 1965, Norman Klug, president of both the USBA and Miller Brewing testified at the Schlitz trial that the company's acquisition of Burgemeister had adversely affected Miller's sales. In 1966 United States District Judge Stanley A. Weigel ruled that Schlitz had to divest itself of Burgemeister and could not acquire any new United States plants for ten years.[478]

In 1958 Pabst bought Blatz Brewing, which was the country's eighteenth largest at the time. The company had been ninth in 1950; Schenley Distillers owned it. Because both Pabst and Blatz were Milwaukee brewers, the federal government sued under anti-trust laws, seeing their combination as monopolistic. Pabst denied the government's claim, stating in its defense that the company was "a failing firm at the time of the acquisition and that therefore, there was no adverse effect on competition."[479]

Although the combination of Blatz and Pabst would have created a concentration of brewers in Milwaukee and the surrounding states, it would have also created a larger company to compete with Anheuser–Busch and enabled Pabst to stay more competitive on a national level. Over ten years later, Pabst sold Blatz to Heileman following completion of litigation. Pabst Brewing currently owns the brand; Miller brews the beer under contract. It is for sale in Wisconsin, Michigan, Illinois, Indiana, Ohio, Pennsylvania, and Minnesota. Blatz was one of the big three of Milwaukee brewers in the nineteenth century and was the first to go national.[480]

476 Leonard Sloane, "Problems Are Brewing in Beer Industry," *New York Times*, December 14, 1966, F1; Tremblay, *Brewing Industry*, 86.

477 Anheuser–Busch Companies. *Annual Report* (St. Louis, Mo: Anheuser–Busch Companies, Inc, 1958).

478 "Sales Cut Cited," *New York Times* August 18, 1965, 45; "Schlitz Ordered to Drop Holdings," *New York Times*, March 25, 1966, 59.

479 "Pabst Suit Revived by Court," *New York Times*, June 14, 1966, 65.

480 "Advertising: Blatz Goes to Campbell-Mithun," *New York Times*, August 18, 1969, 52; www.pabst.com Pabst Brewing Company (accessed January 1, 2007); Downard, *Dictionary*, 23.

Figure 18: Blatz Beer. Photo courtesy of Pabst Brewing Company.

Breweries responded to the intense market competition and the shift from on-premises to off-premises competition by developing draft beer in bottles and cans. Advertising was another main strategy of the large brewers. Per barrel expenditures for advertising ranged from one to two dollars.[481] This figure did not include sponsorship of sports teams, an activity more and more brewers were pursuing.

Brewers were spending those advertising dollars on an ever increasing product line. The early sixties saw the development of malt liquor, beer with a large amount of hops and malt with a resulting higher alcoholic content. Some of the brands included Colt 45 from the National Brewing Company, Schlitz Malt Liquor and Big Cat from Pabst.[482]

By 1966 the industry was more concentrated. The federal government continued to pursue anti-trust litigation. Per capita consumption in 1965 had actually decreased from that of 1947. From 1959–1965 beer sales rose fifteen per cent while distilled spirits sales were almost twice as high. Soft drinks advanced forty-two per cent and wine twenty-six. Both increased affluence and the more widespread use of air conditioning appeared to work against beer drinking. The one bright spot for the industry in 1966 was the coming explosion in twenty-one- to forty-year-olds as the baby boom matured. This demographic group was responsible for more than half of the beer sold.[483]

When Heileman purchased Blatz from Pabst in 1969, the acquisition was part of a larger expansion program. The brewery's origins were in City Brewery, La Crosse, Wisconsin. Gottlieb Heileman and John Gund were the original owners. Heileman's son-in-law, Emil T. Mueller, developed the brewery's most

---

481 Sloane, "Problems Brewing."

482 Peter Bart, "Advertising: Brewers Uncork Malt Liquor," *New York Times*, February 18, 1964, 56.

483 Sloane, "Problems Brewing."

famous brand, Old Style Lager in 1902. From 1956 to 1970, under the leadership of Roy E. Kumm, Heileman purchased thirteen regional breweries including Rainier, Wiedemann Brewing of Kentucky and Grain Belt, located in Minnesota. In 1969 the company purchased Carling National Breweries. The acquisitions enabled Heileman to increase its capacity from 7 million barrels to over 10.5 million. It continued its acquisition program by buying Associated Brewing in 1971. Heileman rose to sixth place from thirty-ninth in 1960.[484]

The tenth brewery in the United States in 1950 was Pfeiffer Brewing Company with a barrelage of 1,618,077. Pfeiffer was a Detroit brewery that had been in existence since 1890. In 1962 Pfeiffer merged with the E. & B Company to become Associated Brewing Company. Associated Brewing eventually included other breweries not from Detroit including Jacob Schmidt Brewing Company, St. Paul Minnesota, Hampden–Harvard Brewing Company of Massachusetts, and Piels Brothers, New York.

Figure 19: Piels beer tray. Photo courtesy of Pabst Brewing Company.

---

484 Downard, *Dictionary*, 89-90.

Piels was famous for its early television commercials featuring Bert and Harry. The comic team of Bob Elliott & Ray Goulding provided the voices. In 1970, Associated Brewing was the tenth largest brewer and had a barrelage of 3,750,000. Heileman purchased all the brands except Piels in 1971. Schaefer purchased Piels in 1973; Pabst currently owns the brand which Miller brews.[485]

In 1957 Anheuser–Busch overtook Schlitz and has remained number one ever since. Anheuser–Busch produced 4, 928,000 barrels of beer in 1950. In 2005 the company produced 21.9 million barrels, an increase of 4.4 percent from 2004. Anheuser–Busch is a publicly traded company, but the ancestors of Adolphus Busch still run it.[486]

Beer has had an affinity with baseball dating back to Jacob Ruppert's purchase of the Yankees in 1915. Anheuser–Busch, like other large brewers during the 1950s, got involved in sports by purchasing the St. Louis Cardinals and its minor league clubs in 1953. For its one hundredth anniversary a year earlier, the company had broken ground on a new brewery in Los Angeles, California with a shipping capacity of 920,000 barrels. In 1958 Anheuser–Busch, along with the rest of the brewing industry, celebrated the twenty-fifth anniversary of Repeal. "The end of the 'noble experiment' was a second beginning for Anheuser–Busch from which it has progressed to its present state of stability."[487]

The United States Brewers Foundation also celebrated the twenty-fifth anniversary of Repeal; the organization felt the observation of the date "drew public attention to the brewing industry's beneficial impact on the nation's welfare." California, "which has the distinction of growing all ingredients necessary to brewing, celebrated with a Beer Festival."[488] Perhaps that was why Anheuser–Busch was building that large brewery in Los Angeles. California would become a leader in the revival of craft brewing and the growth of home brewing from the 1970s on.

Miller was consistently in the top twenty-five breweries during this period as Klug expanded the company which now had national distribution. Miller Brewing opened plants outside of Milwaukee and expanded both its productive capacity and markets by taking over failed breweries, of which there were many.

---

485 "Shakeout in the Brewing Industry," Beerhistory.com, http://www.beerhistory.com/library/holdings/shakeout.shtml (accessed January 16, 2002); Downard, *Dictionary*, 144, 12, 170, 88, 146; "Piels Brother, Advertising Mascots People," TV ACRES, http://www.tvacres.com/admascots_pielsbrothers.htm. (accessed January 30, 2007); Pabst Brewing Company, www.pabst.com (accessed January 30, 2007).

486 "About Anheuser–Busch," Anheuser–Busch Companies Environmental Health and Safety Report, http://www.abehsreport.com/docs/about.html (accessed January 24, 2007).

487 Anheuser–Busch, *Annual Report*, 1952, 1957.

488 USBA, *Brewers Almanac*, 1959, 3.

As one of the country's major breweries, Miller participated in the organizational life of the industry. Successive generations of the prominent brewing families usually sat on the board of the USBA, following the same familial pattern that governed management choices in the industry. Brewers had founded the organization but from its inception it had a professional structure. A secretary was in charge of the day-to-day operations of the USBA while prominent brewers served as president, vice-president and board members.

The mission of the USBA had always been to promote the brewing industry. As American industry grew, so did trade associations. By 1933 the brewers' organization, like other industries, had a professional secretary. C. D. Williams had previously been Executive Secretary of the New England Gas Association, an industry wholly unconnected to brewing or beer.[489]

In 1961 Henry B. King, following service in the Navy during World War II and a career in the food industry, became the head of the USBA, a position he held for twenty-two years. The organization employed over one hundred seventy people and had twenty-six divisional offices in thirty states, working on coordination of retailers, wholesalers, and brewers. In 1961 beer generated $796,217,000 in taxes; in 1863 it raised $1,629,000. In 1863 the beer barrelage was 1,765,827 barrels; in 1960 it was 94,547,867. As both production and consumption were going up the number of breweries was going down. In 1960 there were 229 breweries, the lowest number to date.[490]

In 1962 the United States Brewers Association, located in New York City, its traditional home, celebrated its centennial. The industry had grown tremendously over its one hundred year existence. The celebration at the USBA's one hundredth annual convention included speeches by Warren G. Magnuson (D. WA), chairman of the Interstate and Foreign Commerce Committee and Dwight E. Avis, director of the Alcohol and Tobacco Tax Division of the Treasury.[491] The USBA persisted in cultivating the friendship of government officials, a tradition Frederick Lauer started.

The organization declared beer "a national beverage" and claimed that Americans consumed only milk and coffee in greater quantities than beer and ale.

489 *Modern Brewery*, February 1933, 54; *New York Times*, March 9, 1961, 30.

490 "The production of beer in the United States, 1870-1970," *Historical Statistics of the United States, Colonial Times to 1970* (Washington, DC: Government Printing Office, 1975), 689-91; Martin Stack, "A Concise History of America's Brewing Industry," *EH.Net Encyclopedia*, ed. Robert Whaples, http://eh.net/encyclopedia/?article=stack.brewing.industry.history.us (accessed July 5, 2003); *New York Times*, February 5, 1962; Peter K.V. Reid, "Henry King, 1921-2005, Naval Officer, Professor and Industry Leader," *Modern Brewery Age*, November 1 2005, 27. http://www.breweryage.com/pdfs/2005-henry percent20king percent207-05.pdf. (accessed February 12, 2007) 7; *Brewers Almanac* 1961, 4.

491 "Beer Makers Mark Groups Centennial," *New York Times*, February 5, 1962, 48.

Brewers emphasized the economic role the industry had played and continued to play. Taxes, both federal and state, were apparently thirty per cent of the cost of a glass of beer.[492] By 1962, however, fewer and fewer people drank beer that way.

The brewers had only good things to look forward to. Prohibition was twenty-nine years behind them, and per capita consumption had been rising steadily since 1933. In just a few years a historic number of young people would be legally able to drink. The last tax increase had been ten years ago and no new increases were in sight.

The brewery workers union was strong and, in 1961, celebrated its seventy-fifth anniversary. Members declared themselves a union "with a heart." The union was an AFL–CIO affiliate, now called the International Union of Flour, Cereal, Soft Drink and Distillery Workers. The largest number of members came from the brewing industry. Karl Feller had been president of the union since 1949. The union's journal, *Brewery Worker*, was the successor to the *Brauer–Zeitung*. Although the paper no longer ran German language stories, the journal did have a four page section in French for Canadian members.[493]

The USBA had a national focus, continuing to be the face and voice of the brewing industry on issues of public relations and self-regulation. Regional offices worked on USBA issues as they pertained to specific issues and also monitored local option and electoral contests. One important aspect of the USBA's ongoing work was the compilation of statistical information about the brewing industry including production, sales, and tax figures. Each year the USBA, under the leadership of Phil Katz, senior vice president for research and a member of the organization's staff since 1957, produced the *Brewers Almanac*.[494]

The industry had grown and changed; over the years many brewers had modified the original recipe for beer that their ancestors had brought from Germany. From the 1870s on, brewers had added corn and rice to beer to produce a lighter, less bitter tasting beer that was uniquely American. Anheuser–Busch used rice exclusively.[495] By the 1960s this beer had evolved into a standard, light-colored, low hops, effervescent beverage with an abundant foamy head. Many breweries used their creamy full head of foam as a marketing point.

Electric dishwashers apparently left residues that impeded the development of a full head of foam. Brewers began using cobalt, an essential element that humans need to produce vitamin B12, to counteract this effect. In 1966, thirty-seven

492 *Brewers Almanac*, 1962, 3.
493 International Union of Brewery, Flour, Cereal, Soft Drink and Distillery Workers of America, "Union with a Heart" (Cincinnati: The Union, 1961).
494 Donald Shea, interview by author, Washington D.C., September 13, 2005.
495 Anheuser–Busch *Annual Report*, 1951-1958.

Canadians and seventeen Americans died from a mysterious heart disease. Another fifty-four people survived the illness. All the victims had been heavy beer drinkers. The men from Quebec drank twelve quarts a day on average, and the Americans averaged a six pack a day. Symptoms included a rapid heart beat, difficulty breathing, and blue skin. The cause appeared to be the addition of cobalt to the beer.[496]

In his capacity as head of the United States brewers Association, Henry King took the lead in convincing American brewers to stop adding cobalt to beer. The trade association was the public face of brewing during this crisis. King used information from the Seibel Institute of Technology, a brewing school and research center, to formulate his public statements. The deaths from cobalt in beer could have caused a tremendous crisis for the brewing industry. Most observers attributed the fact that it did not to Henry King's leadership. King himself gave a lot of credit to the Siebel Institute, saying "they were great brewing patriots."[497]

The potential crisis of cobalt in beer did not prevent the USBA from continuing with its traditional annual conventions. In 1966 Norman Klug, CEO of Miller Brewing, was also president of the USBA. Klug, president since Fred Miller's death in 1954, expanded the company, and Miller now operated nationally. The company's market share was 3.91 percent. Anheuser–Busch had 12.81 percent, Schlitz 8.93 percent, and Pabst, the number three brewer, 8.54 percent. Miller was the twelfth largest brewery in 1966. Since 1956, Lorraine Muhlenberg, one of the Miller heirs, had been chairman of the board of directors. Thus Miller was in a position to continue to expand, but family control, personified by Harry and Lorraine, may have contributed to less vigorous management and left Miller vulnerable to sale offers.[498]

Every year following Repeal the number of breweries had decreased. Very few new breweries had opened since the end of World War II. Surviving breweries often purchased the failed ones in a form of horizontal expansion. Brewing was a closed, contracting world. Yet brewing is a profitable business, and it was only a matter of time before outside interests would look to acquire breweries as a means to increase profits and diversify.

---

496 Donald G. Barceloux, "Cobalt," *Journal of Toxicology: Clinical Toxicology* 37:2 (March 1999): 201; Jane Brody, "A Heart Ailment Is Linked to Beer," *New York Times*, July 26, 1966, 37; "When Beer Brought the Blues," *Time*, January 20, 1967, time.com (accessed June 22, 2007).

497 Quoted in Reid, "Henry King, 1921-2005"; Brody, "A Heart Ailment." Doctors prescribed cobalt to treat anemia. The cobalt worked to prevent the thyroid gland from taking up iodine. Both the United States and Canada stopped using cobalt to treat anemia following the death from cobalt-laced beer. See "Canada Removes 9 Cobalt Drugs," *New York Times*, December 25, 1966, 34; "U.S. Acts to Suspend Shipments of Iron-Cobalt Drugs for Anemia," *New York Times*, December 29, 1966, 34.

498 Tremblay, *Brewing Industry*, 70; "W.R. Grace & Co. and Miller Brewing Co.," *New York Times*, September 20, 1966, 66; Robert Metz, "Marketplace," *New York Times*, September 23, 1966, 50.

In 1966 W.R. Grace, an old American shipping company, led by the founder's grandson, Peter, purchased Lorraine Mulberger's fifty-three percent of Miller Brewing stock. Lorraine's explanation for the sale was that she felt "the brewery was not the will of God for me." Although in the past Lorraine had occasionally drunk a Miller High Life, she was now opposed to alcohol consumption. The alcoholism of both her father and her ex-husband may have been a factor in her position. The sale had a value of over $36 million. Harry John and the de Rancé Foundation retained a minority share of forty-seven percent.[499]

Grace retained Miller's management structure. Klug proceeded with plans to brew Miller High Life in California, a first for the company, when he died suddenly of a heart attack at 61. Charles W. Miller, (no relation) a former marketing professor and a long-time member of Miller's board of directors, replaced him. W.R. Grace was not a brewing company; its base of operation was not in Milwaukee or even the Midwest. The company owning a majority share of Miller Brewing, however, did not augur significant change for either the brewery or the brewing industry at large.[500]

The forty-seven percent share that Harry John continued to hold represented a significant impediment to Peter Grace's plans for Miller brewing. As a result, in 1969, W.R. Grace began negotiations with PepsiCo regarding the sale of the company. Grace, who had purchased the company for $36 million in cash and stocks thirty-two months earlier, was now planning to sell Miller Brewing for $120 million.[501]

PepsiCo made more sense as the producer of beverages, but analysts usually characterize the soft drink industry and brewing as very distinct segments of the overall beverage industry. The purchase of a brewery by a soft drink company would be significant. Given the soda company's place in the American economy, it would also mean that a large number of new resources would be available to Miller brewing. PepsiCo, perennial second to Coca-Cola, was a larger company than any of the top brewers and spent considerably more on advertising — as was typical of the soft drink industry.

Grace's negotiations with Pepsi proceeded, but conflicts developed, and with some suddenness, Peter Grace announced the sale of Miller Brewing to

---

499 "W.R. Grace & Co. and Miller Brewing Co."; Metz, "Marketplace"; John, *The Miller Beer Barons*, 380.
500 "Miller to Produce Beer in California," *New York Times*, September 21, 1966, 64; "Norman R. Klug, President of Miller Brewing Co., Dies," *New York Times*, October 26, 1966, 47 ; "Miller Brewing Names Head," *New York Times*, November 2, 1966, 69.
501 "Pepsico to Buy Miller Brewing" *New York Times*, May 9, 1969, 63.

Phillip Morris, the country's second largest tobacco manufacturer.[502] Grace and by extension, Miller Brewing, had landed a bigger fish than PepsiCo.

As the second largest company in a highly competitive industry, Phillip Morris brought a completely different orientation to the brewing industry. Although tobacco and beer were completely different industries, smoking and drinking often go together. Phillip Morris believed it could market beer in they same way that it had marketed cigarettes.[503]

In 1969, as soon as the sale was final, Phillip Morris began making changes. Charles Miller, Miller's president, returned to his university position, and the cigarette company installed its own team. At the same time, it began work on securing complete control of the company. In 1970, the de Rancé foundation sold its forty-seven percent of Miller Brewing to Phillip Morris. As a result of the sale, Miller Brewing became the first United States brewing company to be a strictly corporate entity with no family presence or input. The de Rancé Foundation became the focus for the Miller family, or at least Harry John, formerly the heir apparent. The $97 million Phillip Morris paid Harry John for his Miller stock made de Rancé the nation's largest Catholic philanthropy.[504]

The impact of Phillip Morris on the brewing industry was immediate. The United States government, from the 1950s on, focused a great deal of attention on the growing consolidation of the brewing industry. The Justice Department pursued several anti-trust actions against the largest brewers, Anheuser–Busch, Pabst, and Schlitz, which prevented them from growing via combination. The government also prevented regional brewers from combining, which had the ultimate effect of strengthening the top three.[505] Yet the purchase of Miller by Phillip Morris did not concern the federal government because Phillip Morris's acquisition of Miller Brewing was across industries rather than within the brewing industry. By becoming part of the very large Phillip Morris, Miller Brewing gained access to a greater amount of capital and resources than any that would have accrued to a single brewer from the various mergers the federal government prevented during this time period. In 2000, when Philip Morris was the nation's largest tobacco manufacturer, it also owned Kraft Foods, the country's largest

502 "Grace Cancels Miller Purchase," *New York Times*, June 12, 1969, 65; "Philip Morris is Seeking Miller," *New York Times*, June 13, 1969, 67.

503 John Gurda, *Miller Time: A History of Miller Brewing Company 1855-2005* (Milwaukee, WI: 2005), 147.

504 "Top Officers Selected by Miller Brewing Co.," *New York Times*, January 22, 1970, 59; "Acquisition is Set by Phillip Morris" *New York Times*, July 30, 1970, 68; Wilkes, "Harry John."

505 Tremblay, *Brewing Industry*, 233-247.

food producer, and Miller, the second largest brewer. Products of Philip Morris were in nine out of every ten American homes.[506]

In 1971, John M. Murphy became chairman and chief executive officer of Miller Brewing. Murphy had no brewing background and was not German, but was a successful businessman who was determined to make Miller Brewing as successful as its parent Phillip Morris. His ultimate goal was to overtake Anheuser–Busch and became the number one brewer in the country.[507]

In the late 1960s most American breweries had relatively few different products or brands. The largest brewers, Anheuser, Pabst, and Schlitz all shipped and competed nationally, but even they had only a few different products. Most breweries brewed lager exclusively although lager could vary in alcoholic content and lightness. Miller's premier brand was High Life, which had the slogan, "the champagne of bottle beer" for many years. Ernst Miller had developed the beer in 1903. When John Murphy assumed control of the brewing company he spearheaded a new advertising campaign for the venerable High Life — Miller Time.[508]

Since Repeal, brewing had been interested in developing beers that would appeal to different segments of the population. Early on they had discussed adding vitamins to beer. *Modern Brewery* had persisted in promoting bock, with its traditions and history as a prime marketing strategy. One market that particularly interested brewers was women, and by extension, health conscious people from both sexes. Rheingold developed Gablingers, a low calorie beer but it was a marketing disaster.[509] Rheingold's failure did not dissuade other brewers from attempting to develop similar beers.

In 1972, Miller bought the rights to Meister Brau, Inc. of Chicago which had a light beer. By buying the company, Miller got both the beer and the Chicago company's marketing strategy. In 1965, a group of private investors purchased the Peter Hand Brewery which had been in existence since 1891; the new owners renamed the company Meister Brau which was the brewery's top brand. The new owners of the old Chicago brewery pursued an aggressive advertising and marketing campaign that focused on the connections between sports and beer drinking. They saw its prime consumer as a male aged twenty-one to thirty-four. Meister Brau sponsored Chicago Bulls basketball games on the radio and had

506 Dave Flessner, "Nation's Biggest Tobacco Firm Reaches Out to Critics, Changes Promotions," *Chattanooga Times/Free Press*, September 20, 2000.

507 "Executive Changes," *New York Times*, September 3, 1971, 42.

508 "150 Years of Miller Beer"; "John A. Murphy, 72, Creator of Brands at Miller Brewing," *New York Times*, June 19, 2002, C15.

509 Philip Van Munching, *Beer Blast: The Inside Story of the Brewing Industry's Bizarre Battles for Your Money* (New York: Times Business, 1997), 30-32.

a one fifth share in broadcasts of the Chicago White Sox in both Chicago and Milwaukee.[510]

Meister Brau's sponsorship of sporting events placed the company in the mainstream of larger breweries and was well within the tradition of both the brewing industry and recreational habits of beer drinkers. Out of his love of baseball and the New York Yankees, Jacob Ruppert had linked beer with sports and sporting events. In the late nineteenth century working class men and women had drunk beer at July 4th celebrations, ethnic festivals, and in beer gardens with entertainment. As noted earlier, Anheuser–Busch bought the St. Louis Cardinals in the 1950s. Meister Brau's advertising campaign was a local one; sports and beer still retained a local quality with brand loyalty an essential ingredient for both teams and breweries. Phillip Morris and Miller Brewing kept the connection between sports and beer but changed the terms of the relationship.

Following the purchase of Meister Brau, Miller began working on its own low calorie beer. In 1975 Miller unveiled Miller Lite and made history. John Murphy, the McCann Erickson advertising company, and Miller Brewing, using the resources of Phillip Morris, unleashed an advertising campaign on an unprecedented level for the brewing industry. With their clever, sports-driven television commercials, Miller created a new product and greatly accelerated the consolidation of the brewing industry. Miller expended vast sums to market and promote Miller Lite which eventually prodded Anheuser–Busch to develop its own light beer, Bud Light, and match Miller's advertising spending. Ultimately most of the country's other brewers could not keep up. Miller steadily and rapidly gained market share, not at the expense of Anheuser–Busch but by incapacitating Pabst, Schlitz, and others.[511]

Miller wanted people who liked sports to drink Miller Lite; the company's advertising used sports heroes to drive home the point that men drank the new beer. Matt Snell, a New York Jet who had played in Super Bowl III in 1969 when the Jets beat the favorite, the Baltimore Colts, was in the first Miller Lite commercial. This first ad was not funny and used the tag line "new lite beer from Miller is all you ever wanted in a beer and less." The focus was on carbohydrates; eventually "less filling" became the key message.[512]

The second commercial was with Mickey Spillane, the crime writer, and Lee Meredith, a Playboy Bunny of 1973. Meredith was "the doll" in the commercials that tried to be funny about athletes and their unsuccessful flirting with a beau-

510 Downard, *Dictionary*, 87-88; Bob Skilnik, *Beer: A History of Brewing in Chicago* (Fort Lee, N.J.: Barricade Books, 2006), 222.

511 "150 years of Miller beer"; Frank Deford, *Lite Reading: The Lite Beer From Miller Commercial Scrapbook* (New York: Penguin Books, 1984), 30.

512 Deford, *Lite Reading*, 31.

tiful woman. The appearance of the athletes in the commercial legitimated the masculinity of drinking Miller Lite and indicated that the market for sports was nationalizing as was the market for beer.

Figure 20: Lite Point of Sale, 1976. Photo courtesy of Miller Brewing Company Archives.

The final tagline for the commercials became "Lite Beer from Miller. Every-thing you wanted in a beer . . . and less." Many of the spots featured athletes and other figures debating between "tastes great" and "less filling." It took Anheus-

er–Busch over a year to respond. The company essentially copied Miller's advertising strategy and lured away several of the athletes including Mickey Mantle.[513]
Ironically, Mantle would die in 1995 following a liver transplant that was necessary due to advanced alcoholism and cirrhosis of the liver.[514]

In 1976, the Joseph Schlitz Brewing Company which brewed Old Milwaukee,
a popularly priced beer, Schlitz Light, Schlitz, and Schlitz Malt Liquor, was the
country's second largest brewer with a 16.1 percent market share. A major strike
at Anheuser–Busch bolstered Schlitz's sales in 1976. Although many of the brewing industries problems were a direct result of increased competition fueled by
Miller, Schlitz's problems were more internal.

Schlitz had been developing a new fermentation process for ten years; in
1974 accelerated batch fermentation became operational. The process, which
was yeast centered, reduced fermentation time from twelve days to four, reduced
costs, and produced a more uniform beer. It had no effect on taste. Popular opinion disagreed, believing that Schlitz was making "green" or unripe beer. In the
1870s when brewers began using corn and rice to brew beer, the public accused
them of "adulteration." Once again the public image of beer was in conflict with
the actual process of brewing.

The new fermentation process was an attempt to gain a competitive advantage through cutting costs. Towards this same end, Schlitz had been using corn
syrup instead of barley malt. This beer did taste different — it was both lighter
and cheaper.[515]

Schlitz's cost cutting came at a time when the industry leader, Anheuser–
Busch made a point of stating that they were committed to maintaining quality
by continuing to use more expensive ingredients. Coors, which was beginning
to operate on the national level, also promoted the naturalness of its beer. Coors
beer was not pasteurized; the company shipped the cold filtered beer in specially
insulated trains and trucks.[516]

Schlitz's attempts to build market share through cost cutting undermined
their long standing image as a premium beer. These attempts reached a nadir in
1976 when the use of a new foam stabilizer caused Schlitz beer to appear flaky or
cloudy. The company tried to fix the problem, but the solution only made mat-

513 Ibid., 34, 43, 49.
514 Joseph Durso, "Mickey Mantle, Great Yankee Slugger, Dies at 63," New York Times, August
   14, 1995, A1.
515 David A. Acker, Managing Brand Equity: Capitalizing on the Value of a Brand Name (New York: Free
   Press, 1991), 79-81.
516 Ibid., 82; William H. Mulligan, Jr. "Coors, Adolph, Brewing Company" in Blocker, et al.,
   Encyclopedia, 174-175.

ters worse. The beer now had a short shelf life and was flat. Schlitz eventually removed 10 million bottles and cans from store shelves.[517]

From the 1960s on, Schlitz had produced memorable ads that emphasized the "gusto" of their beers and had the tagline, "when you are out of Schlitz you are out of beer." In 1977, on the heels of the foam stabilizer problem, Schlitz turned to a new advertising campaign that most people perceived of as overly aggressive — the tagline was "You want to take away my Schlitz? My Gusto?" Industry observers described this ad campaign as "Drink Schlitz or I'll Kill You." Although Schlitz returned to its original formula in 1978, the company was not able to convince the public that the beer was of a high quality.[518] By this time Schlitz needed a greater amount of advertising dollars to match Anheuser–Busch and Miller's expenditures. This was a problem for most of the brewing industry. Ad executives noted that "except for Budweiser and Miller there's panic all over the place."[519]

By 1980 the brewing landscape was completely different from that of 1950. The '80s would bring even greater transformation. Ballantine, Inc., one of the nation's few ale brewers as well as one of the few brewing families that were not of German ethnicity, had been the number three brewer in 1950. After Repeal, Carl and Otto Badenhausen, brothers, purchased the company. They hired a Scottish brewmaster so the company could continue to sell its distinctive ales. Ballantine sponsored radio broadcasts of New York Yankees games in the 1940s and 1950s. In 1969 Investors Funding Corp of NY, investment bankers with no brewing experience purchased the declining company from Carl Badenhausen and his partners. The new owners failed to change the direction of the brewery; in 1972 Falstaff Brewing purchased the brands. Pabst Brewing brews some Ballantine beer today.[520]

Falstaff Brewing was seventh in 1950. In 1972, Falstaff purchased Ballantine which also gave the company the brands of the Christian Feigenspan brewery of Newark, New Jersey. The main brand was Munich. Feigenspan headed the USBA during Repeal. In 1975, Paul Kalmanovitz, head of General Brewing (S & P Corp) gained the controlling interest in Falstaff Beer. Falstaff Beer continued as a corporate entity with its own breweries until 1990 when the last brewery in Ft. Wayne closed. It is now an apartment complex. By that time S & P also

517 Acker, *Managing Brand Equity*, 83.
518 Ibid., 79, 83.
519 Philip H. Dougherty, "Advertising: Schlitz and Ferment in Beer Industry," *New York Times*, January 6, 1978, D7.
520 Downard, *Dictionary*, 15; "Ballantine XXX Ale," http://www.falstaffbrewing.com/ballantine_ale.htm (accessed January 24, 2007). Carl Badenhausen died in 1981.

owned Pabst. Small amounts of Falstaff beer were available for sale until 2000. The shield trademark was over one hundred years old.[521]

Figure 21: Falstaff Brewing Corporation, Logo from 1933–1940. Photo courtesy of Pabst Brewing Company.

Pabst Brewing Company was the country's fourth largest brewer in 1950 with a barrelage of 3,418,677. Pabst had long been a leader in the industry, and some observers saw the company as the prototypical, well-run, efficient corporation. From 1950 to the 1970s Pabst expanded through mergers and acquisitions. In 1958 the company purchased Blatz from Schenley. Pabst had to divest itself of the company in 1969 and sold Blatz to G. Heileman. In 1975 Pabst purchased some of the brands of Theodore Hamm Brewing. The company continued its acquisitions; in 1979 the Blitz–Weinhard Brewery and then in 1982, Olympia Brewing Company. Olympia was the country's eighth largest brewery in 1980. These purchases did not solve Pabst's financial problems; in 1984 Paul Kalmanovitz purchased Pabst for $63 million. Kalmanovitz died in 1988.[522]

Today Pabst does not own any brewery and does not brew any beer. The company is a marketing concern, a virtual brewer which manages various brands of some of the most loved breweries of the twentieth century. Pabst Blue Ribbon, the nation's most popular beer in 1895, has recently acquired a cachet among young drinkers. It is possible to buy one for two dollars in bars where draught craft beers sell for six. Buyer beware!

Although the number of breweries had been declining since Repeal, and there were distinct segments of the brewing industry representing national, regional, and local producers, the beer industry had to a large extent retained its ethnic family oriented approach. The USBA, as a trade association, reflected this

---

521 "The History of Falstaff Brewing," www.falstaffbrewing.com (accessed January 24, 2007).
522 Thomas Cochran, *The Pabst Brewing Company* (New York: New York University Press, 1948); Downard, *Dictionary*, 140; William H. Mulligan, Jr., "Pabst Brewing Company" in Blocker, et al., *Encyclopedia*, vol. 2, p 471-472.

orientation. Miller, led by people who had no connection to the brewing world or its over one hundred year history, ramped up spending and competition and the USBA could not withstand these changes.

Henry King had shown his leadership skills in dealing with the 1966 cobalt crisis. In 1978, a similar issue arouse when American brewers learned that German research showed trace amounts of nitrosamines in some European beer. Americans were becoming increasingly alarmed about the link between nitrates in meat and cancer. Coors was the only brewery in the country which did not have nitrosamines in its beer because the company used steam heat to dry the malt. Other brewers used direct heat.[523]

King once again responded promptly to the health scare and informed both the BATF and the FDA of the German research. The cobalt scare had prompted the USBA to form the Medical Advisory Group (MAG). The Johns Hopkins University School of Medicine administered the program. In 1982 the group merged with a similar Canadian organization and became the Alcoholic Beverage Medical Research Foundation (ABMRF). It still exists as an independently funded research and granting agency.[524] Donald Shea, the last president of the USBA, saw Henry King's role in forming the ABMRF as a positive example of his leadership. "He defended the industry, represented the industry, at both the federal, state, and indeed local levels . . . ."[525]

The nitrate scare coincided with increased public interest in product labeling as well as the push for warning labels on alcohol. Beer ingredients were not on any label; this practice dated back to Repeal. Brewers did not respond to this crisis by putting ingredients on their labels. They did, however, change their drying process for barley malt. By reducing the temperature of the open flame they lengthened the drying time and reduced the formation of nitrosamines. By 1980, a USBA survey showed that ninety-five per cent of brewers were compliant.[526]

In 1978, Phillip Morris, the parent company of Miller Brewing, opened an office in Washington. Miller Brewing simultaneously withdrew its membership from the USBA. Although the USBA had been located in Washington, D.C. since 1970, Miller wanted to be able to pursue its own agenda separate from the unity and cooperation a trade association such as the USBA would promote. G. Heileman Brewing Company, the nation's fifth largest brewer, undertook a similar

---

523 Reid, "Henry King, 1921-2005."

524 "About the ABMRF," Alcoholic Beverage Medical Research Foundation, http://www.abmrf. org/ (accessed February 12, 2007).

525 Donald Shea, interview by author, Washington, D.C., September 13, 2005.

526 "Brewers Say They're Reducing Nitrosamines," *FDA Consumer*, December-January 1980, 26.

move. Miller's animosity toward the USBA may have stemmed from disputes with Anheuser–Busch over the issue of warning labels.[527]

In 1978, when Miller left, the USBA had field representatives in all fifty states, as well as five regional vice-presidents and legal counsel in every state. Prior to Prohibition, there had been many active state organizations that mirrored the USBA on a more local level. By 1978 very few still existed — Wisconsin may have been the only one. Thus the USBA, along with the much smaller Brewers Association of America, represented the brewing industry. In 1970, the USBA moved its headquarters from its historic home in New York to Washington, where individual breweries did not have representation.[528]

In 1978 Henry King remained the head of the USBA for his eighteenth year. New societal concerns over drinking and its social costs had begun to emerge. The heightened societal concern coincided with an increase in per capita consumption linked to baby boomers becoming legal drinkers beginning in 1966. As this huge birth cohort worked its way into the drinking public, drunk driving, fetal alcohol syndrome, warning labels, and calls for controls on television advertising all emerged as issues. Brewers held a virtual monopoly on television alcohol advertising since distillers had voluntarily refrained from such practices since Repeal.

The USBA represented the brewing industry on all of these issues prior to 1978 and continued to pursue such representation after Miller and Heileman left the organization. The trade association's ability to continue such work was severely limited due to a reduced budget and staff. Assessments based on barrel production of the members provided the budget of the USBA; losing two of the top five producers hurt.[529]

In 1976 Congress passed legislation giving small brewers a tax differential. The tax rate, set in 1951, was $9 a barrel for the large brewers; small breweries, about 39 of the nation's 53, who also produced less than 2,000,000 barrels, paid $7 on their first 60,000 barrels. The USBA, under Henry King's leadership, heavily promoted this legislation, and the large brewers including Miller offered no objection. Donald Shea called the small brewers "the conscience" of the industry. This legislation indicated large brewers' acknowledgement of that fact. The tax differential legislation was the last time the industry acted in a united way that

527 "8 Trade Groups Are Leaving City," *New York Times*, February 20, 1970 1; Sara Fitzgerald, "Washington Update: People; the Washington Office," *The National Journal*, vol. 10, no. 50, December 16, 1987, 2037; "USBA Dissolve," *Beverage Industry*, April 1986, 14; Van Munching, *Beer Blast*, 56.
528 Shea interview, 2005.
529 Ibid.

reflected its long history. The Small Brewers Association, founded in 1941, also claimed the legislation as a victory.[530]

One of the most significant transactions which indicated that brewing was moving firmly away from its nineteenth century heritage occurred on June 10 1982, when the Stroh Brewing Company of Detroit purchased Schlitz. Stroh's, a long established regional brewery based in Detroit vaulted itself into the first tier of the industry by acquiring Schlitz, one of the country's largest brewers. Donald Shea, a vice-president of the USBA at the time of this acquisition, assessed the deal and its implication for the industry as "constant concentration within the industry, and as that happened, more and more larger breweries were building up their own shops."[531]

In 1983, Henry King retired after twenty-one years of service to the brewing industry, leaving behind a business which had changed tremendously from 1961. Anheuser–Busch was still first, but many brewers from 1950 were gone, and Miller was firmly in second. King returned to the brewing industry in the early 1990s, serving as head of the Brewers' Association of America, the craft and small brewers' organization. When King died in 2005, the industry lauded him as an iconic leader of brewing.[532]

What was the state of the brewing industry in 1983? The USBA, the industry's trade association, was smaller as was the industry itself. In an address to the National Beer Wholesalers Association, Phil Katz, the USBA's longtime statistician, presented a grim picture. "First of all there would have been more of us around in the early 1970s. Today there are 44 brewing companies and 91 plants. Ten years ago there were 78 companies and 147 plants." There were also fewer wholesalers.

The ever increasing concentration of the industry led Katz to claim "survival" as the top priority for brewers and wholesalers.[533] Such a competitive atmosphere was in conflict with trade association cooperation. Donald Shea, commented on the ill effect on competition, saying, "it would appear to me that the competitive vituperousness [sic] that was between those two (Anheuser–Busch, Miller) spilled over. Which is a danger with any trade association. You've got to make sure that those perfectly legal and appropriate marketing affinities do not spill over into association, because there's no place for them there."[534]

---

530 Ibid.; W. Holland, "The Evolution of the Brewers Association of America," (Colorado: Brewers Association of America, 1994).

531 "Shakeout in the Brewing Industry"; Shea interview, 2005.

532 "Henry B. King Dies at 84," *Washington Post*, April 29, 2005, sec. B7.

533 *Beverage Industry*, January 28 1983, 10-15.

534 Shea interview, 2005.

Shea, the USBA vice president for alcohol programs, succeeded King. According to Shea, his appointment was itself an indication of the reduced status of the organization. His first priority as the head of the USBA was to bring Miller and Heileman back to the fold. He was not successful. Miller and John Murphy met his attempts at reconciliation with derision. At a meeting to discuss Miller rejoining the USBA, Miller executives referred to the venerable trade association as the Anheuser–Busch association. Shea deemed such behavior "juvenile."[535]

As president of the USBA, Shea focused on the issue of drunk driving and social issues. Shea also spent time during his presidency reading the minutes and other documents from previous administrations of the USBA. The USBA library located in Washington, D.C. had the records going back to 1862. Many of the documents were in "Hoch Deutsch." It was a unique historical trove.[536]

The brewing industry, however, was becoming increasingly less interested in history. As the strength of the USBA lessened, other organizations stepped forward. The National Beer Wholesalers Association (NBWA), founded in 1937, represented beer wholesalers. During Repeal, federal legislation established a three tier system of distribution. The wholesalers were a key element in this system; as breweries dwindled, there were many more wholesalers than brewers or brewery workers.

Brewers and wholesalers did not have identical issues, however, and elements in the brewing industry continued to seek representation for all large brewers within one organization. Following meetings among various parties, in February 1986, Miller and the other large brewers announced they would join in a new organization called the Beer Institute. Miller seemed to feel it was necessary to start over, so the USBA had to be dissolved. Shea received the dissolution of the USBA as a *fait accompli*. Miller so wanted a new face and shape for the brewing industry it was trying to lead that it dismantled the over one hundred-year-old library, and moved to new offices.[537]

A measure of how far the USBA had traveled from the center of the brewing industry, and how changed the industry was came in the reaction to the ending of the USBA and the beginning of the Beer Institute. Only a few journals noted the events, and most analysts felt it was for the best. In March 1987, *Modern Brewery Age*, a trade journal that dated back to Prohibition, bemoaned the demise of

---

535 "USBA Takes New Direction with Shea at the Helm," *Beverage Industry*, October 1983, 20-25; Shea interview, 2005.

536 Shea interview, 2005.

537 *Washington Post*, Feb 3, 1986, 19; Shea interview, 2005. Some of the volumes from the USBA library wound up in the Anheuser–Busch archives.

the USBA, but felt that the diminished membership had "crippled its resources as well as its clout."[538]

The journal was hopeful that the new organization would "represent the entire domestic brewing industry. . . . The realization that the top five could indeed join forces to fight off industry opposition and promote the benefits of malt beverages was long needed."[539]

Although observers blamed the demise of the USBA, the nation's oldest trade association, on internal factors such as a "slow moving bureaucracy," it is clear that marketing rivalries between Miller and Anheuser–Busch led to the organization's dissolution. When brewers got together outside of the USBA to work on issues such as the "alcoholic ad ban, neo-Prohibitionism and alcohol abuse," they were duplicating much of the long standing work of the venerable association.[540] The fact that Miller and the others established a new organization reflected the necessity of trade associations in the modern world of big business. Ironically, Frederick Lauer and others had recognized the importance of industry-wide organization when they first founded the USBA.

James Sanders was the first president of the Beer Institute which originally claimed to represent large brewers and no importers; the membership did not include any craft or micro-brewers. Sanders had previously headed the Small Business Administration. Donald Shea remained as a consultant to the new organization but this was in name only. The only staff from the USBA to move to the Beer Institute was Phil Katz.[541] Apparently the only historical legacy from the USBA Phillip Morris and Miller Brewing wished to retain was the statistical analysis of the *Brewers Almanac*, leaving to others the resurrection of the family and craft ethos that Frederick Miller had pioneered in the 1850s.

---

538 *Modern Brewery Age*, March 16, 1987, 7.

539 Ibid.

540 Marty Westerman, "USBA Dissolved," *Beverage Industry*, April 1986, 14.

541 Ibid.; Cecelia Blalock, "Big Battles Ahead for Beer Institute," *Beverage Industry*, July 1987, 1-2; Shea interview; "Top S.B.A. Official Leaving by April 1, *New York Times*, Jan 28 1986, D2. The Small Business Association (SBA) faced dissolution in 1985. The Heritage Foundation advocated for the disbanding of the agency. There had been a long standing dispute over the SBA; some officials argued for the merging of the SBA into the Commerce Department. The SBA had existed since 1953. Small Business Administration, www.sba.com (accessed January 31, 2006).

CHAPTER 8. JOE AND JANE SIX PACK, 1970–2006

From the 1970s on, American society began re-exploring the social costs of drinking and a wave of neo-temperance activity ensued. Following Prohibition the temperance movement's focus shifted from cessation of the manufacture and sale of alcoholic beverages to marketing issues, access, and controlling personal behavior via taxation. One major aspect of this new regulatory landscape was the change in the minimum drinking age.[542]

Ironically, in America, a drinking age of eighteen was a relatively new phenomenon and represented a mid-point in rapidly changing societal values. As the baby boom grew to maturity, its huge size impacted society. The social activism of the 1960s and the Vietnam War prompted the federal government, in 1971, to lower the voting age to eighteen. One compelling argument for the decrease in the voting age was the connection between the draft, the war, and the vote. A popular slogan was "Old enough to die for my country, old enough to vote."[543] Ultimately twenty-nine states followed suit in regard to the drinking age, apparently believing that fighting in a war entitled you to both vote and drink.[544]

As soon as states lowered the drinking age, car accidents and deaths increased dramatically. By 1980, the negative connection between eighteen year

---

542 Pamela Pennock, "Public Health Morality and Commercial Free Expression: Efforts to Control Cigarette and Alcohol Marketing 1950s – 1980s" (Ph.D. diss., Ohio State University, 2002), 21.

543 Ruth Clifford Engs, *Clean Living Movements: American Cycles of Health Reform* (Westport, CT: Praeger, 2000), 211; C. Louis Bassano, "The Legal Drinking Age: Should It Be 21 Again?" *New York Times*, July 12, 1981, NJ, 24.

544 Iver Peterson, "Drinking Age Tied to Fall in Crashes," *New York Times*, November 4, 1981, A18.

olds drinking and car safety raised concerns nationwide. Both Massachusetts and New Hampshire raised the drinking age and other states were planning to do the same. Although some legislators argued for increased alcohol awareness education, the images of young victims of drunk driving were ultimately more persuasive.[545]

When individual states raised the drinking age, studies showed that car accidents decreased. A state-by-state response still enabled eighteen- to twenty-year-olds to find places to legally drink (and then drive). This minimized the positive effects of the higher drinking age. Many people now believed a more appropriate slogan regarding eighteen-year-old behavior was "Old enough to vote, old enough to die for a six pack."[546]

A large national movement focused on drunk driving emerged; two key organizations at the forefront of the movement were Mothers Against Drunk Driving (MADD) and Remove Intoxicated Drivers (RID). Candy Lightner founded MADD following the death of her thirteen-year-old daughter, Cari, in 1980. The driver had three prior arrests for drunk driving. Cari had been on her way to a church carnival. Lightner was a divorced California real estate agent prior to forming MADD; she modeled herself on Jacqueline Kennedy and used her grief and anger to pursue an activist legislative agenda. The grieving mother became the "human face" of the victims of drunk driving. In retrospect, she felt she "only began grieving" after she left MADD in 1985. She also acknowledged that her "insistence that people who are drinking should not drive — made me a latter-day Carrie Nation in peoples' mind."[547]

Figure 22: Candy Lightner. Photo courtesy of Candace Lightner.

The modern consumer movement had begun with Ralph Nader and his exposé of the car industry, *Unsafe at Any Speed.* Although Nader focused his attention on the automobile, the movement against drunk driving placed all the responsibility for safety on the driver. MADD gave greater visibility to the victim rights movements which focuses on victims of crimes.

---

545 "Increase in Highway Deaths Tied To Lower Drinking Age," *New York Times*, October 28, 1973, 47; "Rise in Drinking Age Becoming Issue Over Nation," *New York Times*, May 18, 1980, 22.

546 Peterson, "Drinking Age Tied to Fall in Crashes," A18; Bassano, "The Legal Drinking Age".

547 Nancy Stedman and Kelly Carter, 2006, "Profiles in Courage," *People* vol. 51, no. 10 (March 15, 1999): 104. Candy Lightner and Nancy Hathaway, *How to Cope with Grief and Get On with Your Life* (New York, 1990), 7, 12, 14.

By the early 1980s America was no longer fighting a war in Vietnam and thus the fatalities that were mounting from traffic accidents seemed more relevant. Over a sixteen-year period the United States suffered 47,752 casualties in Vietnam while in the single year of 1981 drinking was a factor in over half of the 49,125 traffic deaths.[548]

In 1982, the National Transportation Safety Board concluded that the link between drinking and young people dying in car accidents was "irrefutable." The Board was an independent federal agency, which, from 1967 on, had responsibility for investigating aviation, railroad, and marine accidents. The Safety Board also advised state and federal authorities on issues of transportation safety. In this capacity Jim Burnett, chairman and a former Arkansas judge, now called for all states to raise the drinking age to twenty-one. The Board rejected a tiered approach to drinking where eighteen- and nineteen-year-olds would be able to drink beer and wine only because the members believed that even beer could lead a driver to be incapacitated. This was the first time the Board had expressed an opinion on drinking and driving.[549]

At the end of the same year a Presidential commission chaired by John Volpe, former Secretary of Transportation, gave President Reagan its report calling for a twenty-one-year-old drinking age, increased penalties for first driving under the influence (DUI) offenses, and federal funds for state and local education programs. Reagan, in conjunction with the report, designated the third week in December "National Drunk and Drugged Awareness Week." The President claimed that "people were ... mad. They want the slaughter on the highways to stop."[550]

In 1983, the Presidential Commission on Drunk Driving of which both Candy Lightner and Henry King, president of the USBA, were members, gave another report, proposing that Congress deny Federal highway funds to any state that did not raise the minimum drinking age to twenty-one. President Reagan, although endorsing a uniform drinking age of twenty-one, did not support withholding federal funds.

The Commission had gotten the idea of using Federal highway funds as the stick to gain a uniform drinking age from a campaign in 1974 to set a 55 mph national speed limit. Thus the tactics of the drunk driving movement acknowledged the larger issue of highway safety, but the rhetoric remained firmly focused on the individual teenage driver. "The lack of uniformity among state laws is especially critical regarding the minimum legal drinking age because an incen-

548 William Dicke, "States Heeding Plans To Strengthen Laws on Drunken Driving," New York Times, April 16, 1982, A1. Street crime had also declined.

549 Ernest Holsendolphs, "Safety Board Asks All States to Fix 21 as Drinking Age," *New York Times*, July 24, 1982, 6.

550 "Reagan for Tougher Laws," *New York Times*, December 14, 1982, B6.

tive to drink and drive is established due to young persons commuting to border states where the drinking age is lower."[551]

Brewers, who had actively participated in the societal trend toward individualization of both problem drinking and problem drinkers, quickly saw that it was in their best interests to support the drunk driving movement. Brewers endeavored to keep the movement focused on measures to control, limit, and even punish individual drinkers, and away from any attempts to curtail societal access to alcohol.

The leaders of the USBA were proud of their work on this issue and their involvement in Students Against Drunk Driving (SADD). Donald Shea, the final president of the USBA, claimed that "We were the first major corporate group to sponsor students against drunk driving. I think it's fair to say that they would not have gotten off the ground without our contribution." The trade association's contribution was often financial, which could have placed neo-temperance advocates in a compromising position. Shea met with an "avowed prohibitionist" and inquired of him, " 'Bill, what are your people going to say if they know you came here to raise money? Aren't they going to think it's tainted money?' 'And Bill in his squeaky voice . . . says, 'Yeah, goddamit, they'll say 'tain't enough!'"[552]

Brewers responded to public concerns about drinking and driving by developing public service advertisements which emphasized responsible behavior and moderation. The most famous was Anheuser-Busch's campaign, "Know When to Say When." The Department of Transportation, with the help of the Ad Council, also developed pubic service announcements. "Friends Don't Let Friends Drive Drunk" was an example.[553]

Brewers were determined to protect the legitimacy of beer and promote individual moderation and responsibility in drinking. On the subsidiary issue of the minimum drinking age, brewers chose to remain neutral. Realizing it was a no-win situation, the USBA and Donald Shea refused to go on record on the issue, describing it as a "loser's proposition."[554]

Potentially the baby boom represented a very large pool of drinkers and was one factor in a steadily increasing per capita consumption of alcohol. In 1934, the

---

551 Shea interview, 2005; Marjorie Hunter, "Commission Urges 21 as Drinking Age," *New York Times*, December 14, 1983, A24.

552 Shea interview, 2005.

553 John C Burnham, *Bad Habits: Drinking, Smoking, Taking Drugs, Gambling, Sexual Misbehavior, and Swearing in American History* (New York: New York University Press, 1993), 81; William DeJong, Charles K. Atkin, Lawrence Wallack, "A Critical Analysis of 'Moderation' Advertising Sponsored by the Beer Industry: Are 'Responsible Drinking' Commercials Done Responsibly?" *The Milbank Quarterly*, vol. 70, no. 4. (1992): 661-678; Ad Council, "Drunk Driving Prevention (1983-Present)," http://www.adcouncil.org/default.aspx?id=137 (accessed June 25, 2007).

554 Shea interview, 2005.

first year following Repeal, per capita consumption of ethanol or absolute alcohol was .97 gallons. By 1980 the rate stood at 2.76 gallons. The comparable figures for beer were .61 gallons in 1934 and 1.38 gallons in 1980. All of these figures represented the highest levels of alcohol consumption since 1910.[555] A national minimum drinking age of twenty-one had the potential to cost the overall liquor industry $11 million.[556]

When alcohol consumption rises above a certain level, societal damage and problems from the drinking are more readily observable. As has happened at other historical moments of high per capita drinking, a movement against the drinking developed. Fashioning themselves as public health advocates, these activists attempted to stay far away from anything that smacked of prohibition. They did not espouse the banning of the sale of alcohol. The new public health focus of anti-alcohol advocates was part of a larger concern over the societal costs of behavior. They had much in common with anti-tobacco activists, as well as crusaders who spoke in favor of seat belt use or against obesity.

Prohibition and Repeal had ended the movement for a societal, national response to the problems of drinking. It also ended the saloon. These changes created a vacuum which the disease model of alcoholism filled. This academic and medical approach to alcohol problems fits in with the brewing industry's desire to normalize social drinking. Alcohol problems became individual problems resulting from individual choices.[557]

The brewing industry from the nineteenth century on has always argued for the societal benefits of moderate consumption of the moderate beverage — beer. The brewers' self-interested concepts about patterns of consumption and the consequences for society roughly correspond to the sociocultural model for understanding the causes of modern alcoholism. Proponents of this school argue, among other things, for a greater integration of alcohol with society. A competing model is the distribution of consumption school which argues that an increase in the overall amount of alcohol consumed, exactly what the brewers promote, is detrimental to society. This analysis is the theoretical underpinning of the neo-temperance movement.[558]

555 Nekisha E. Lakins, Gerald D. Williams, Hsiao-ye Yi, Barbara A. Smothers, *Surveillance Report, no. 66: Apparent Per Capita Alcohol Consumption: National, State and Regional Trends, 1977-2002* (Bethesda, MD: National Institute on Alcohol Abuse and Alcoholism (NIAAA), 2004).

556 Frank J. Prial, "Criticism of the alcohol industry has grown lately," *New York Times*, February 22, 1984, C13.

557 Jack S. Blocker, *American Temperance Movements: Cycles of Reform* (Boston: Twayne Publishers, 1989), 130-163.

558 For a discussion of these issues and the implications for public policy, see Dan Beauchamp, *Beyond Alcoholism: Alcohol and Public Health Policy* (Philadelphia: Temple University Press, 1980).

Temperance and prohibition advocates had always had special concerns about youthful drinking, and the new public health focused movement did not differ. By the mid-1980s, societal concerns about teenage drinking and driving had reached new heights, giving the neo-temperance advocates, particularly MADD, a fair amount of political sway. This coalesced into the passage in 1984 of the Federal Uniform Age Act. The legislation mandated withholding federal highway funds if states did not change the drinking age to twenty-one within three years. In the space of four years, Candy Lightner had pushed the issue, which had tremendous personal meaning, to the front of the country's political agenda. She stated that the bill's passage left her "shocked but delighted."[559]

The groundswell of public support for the legislation had been enhanced by the showing, in 1983, of a made-for-television movie, *Mothers Against Drunk Driving*. The movie starred Mariette Hartley and stressed the guilt of the drunk driver. Such a portrayal was at odds with an interpretation of alcoholism as a disease. Senator Frank Lautenberg and Representative James J. Howard, Democrats from New Jersey, sponsored the bill. The drinking age in New Jersey was already twenty-one. Representative Howard was chairman of the House Public Works and Transportation Committee and was the author of the legislation that created the national fifty-five mph speed limit. Although MADD's greatest national victory was the Uniform Minimum Age Act, the driver who struck Cari Lightner was forty-seven with a history of similar offenses.[560]

Consumer issues such as drunk driving were more often Democratic issues especially when the solution involved the use of federal power. Republicans felt that the states should retain the rights and authority over drinking standards. Some lawmakers and governors continued to maintain that involving the Federal government via withholding highway funds was inappropriate. A few southern representatives from both parties argued for the rights of young people, but that issue had lost all currency. In a similar fashion to brewers, legislators found it difficult to be against controlling drunk driving.[561]

President Reagan had originally threatened to veto the legislation since it did not really reflect the Republican states rights' philosophy. In the end he supported the bill because it had a large amount of public support behind it.[562] By 1988, all fifty states had complied. The states still retained the right to define

---

559 Jane Perlez, "Teen-age Drinking Vote: Crusader is 'Delighted'," *New York Times*, June 9, 1984, 5.

560 *MADD: Mothers Against Drunk Driving*, VHS, directed by William A. Graham, Universal Studios, 1983; Steven V. Roberts, "House Approves Plan for Raising Age on Drinking," *New York Times*, June 8, 1984, A1; Perlez, "Teen-age Drinking Vote".

561 Roberts, "House Approves Plan"; Perlez, "Teen-age Drinking Vote".

562 "Reagan Said to Drop Opposition to a Bill to Set Drinking Age," *New York Times*, June 13, 1984, B14.

what constituted drunk driving by determining individual blood alcohol content levels as well as individual penalties for DUIs.[563] By enacting a drinking age of twenty-one, the United States became the country with the highest minimum drinking age in the world. Ten countries have no minimum while most, including Argentina, the United Kingdom, the Czech Republic, and South Africa set it at eighteen.[564]

Lightner remained the head of MADD until 1985; interestingly enough, she later worked with the American Beverage Institute to keep the legal blood alcohol level at .10 g/dl. Lightner believed that emphasizing blood alcohol levels was misplaced. She wanted the police to focus on repeat offenders and prevent them from driving. Mindful that the man who killed her daughter had committed similar crimes, she stated, "I am still amazed that the man who killed my daughter is barred from ever owning a handgun, but he can own a car."[565]

The fact that Candy Lightner, a woman, created the most visible neo-temperance organization links this new public-health focused movement to the historic temperance and prohibition movement. In the nineteenth century, women, the protectors of the home, had been at the forefront of the prohibition movement. Similarly many of the issues of the neo-temperance movement seemed to particularly resonate with women. Drunk driving, with its emphasis on youthful offenders and youthful victims, fetal alcohol syndrome as well as underage drinking all spoke to women's ongoing societal role as moral guardian. This "retro" view of women's place in society occurred at a time when more women than ever were in the workforce, outside of the home, and advertising from the 1950s on stressed the "domestication" of drink.

Despite the claims of the neo-temperance advocates that they were not promoting prohibition, such a massive display of federal coercion must have raised the specter of prohibition for the liquor industry — particularly with women in the forefront. For brewers who sought to establish drinking beer as a habit early on, the increase in the legal drinking age to twenty-one dramatically changed the

563 Richard McGowan, *Government Regulation of the Alcohol Industry: The Search for Revenue and the Common Good* (Westport, CT, 1997), 52.

564 David J. Hanson, "Legal Drinking Age," Alcohol Problems and Solutions, http://www2.potsdam.edu/hansondj/LegalDrinkingAge.html (accessed November 1, 2005). The ten countries with no minimum drinking age are Armenia, Azerbaijan, China, Fiji, Nigeria, Poland, Portugal, Soviet Georgia, Thailand, and Vietnam.

565 Stedman and Carter, "Profiles in Courage: Candy Lightner," *Encyclopedia of World Biography Supplement*, vol. 19, Biography Resource Center. Farmington Hills, MI.: Thomson Gale. 2007. http://galenet.galegroup.com/servlet/BioRC. The American Beverage Institute is a restaurant trade association. See http://www.abionline.org/. Blood alcohol content (BAC) or level measures the grams (g) of alcohol in a deciliter (dl). A person with a BAC of .10 has alcohol in one-tenth of one percent of his or her blood.

demographics of their market and revealed the political weakness of the liquor industry on the federal level.[566]

The rise in the minimum drinking age was not the only thorn in the brewers' side; the popular non-returnable six pack that many beer drinkers, old and young, bought also became a problem. Beginning in 1972, when Oregon passed the first container deposit law, the brewers, as well as soft drink manufacturers, had to worry about the implications of their packaging and marketing strategies. Since 1935, when Krueger Brewing sold the first can of beer, beer packaging and sales had sifted form public establishments such as bars to home purchase and consumption. Most of this was in the form of cans. In 1985, the beer can was fifty years old. The Gottfried Krueger Brewing Company was no longer an independent company; Falstaff owned the brand. Although many old brands have continued via the virtual Pabst brewery, Krueger Beer is not one of them. Today eleven states have container recycling legislation; the deposit ranges from five to ten cents.[567]

Although brewers faced increasing activism around the environmental and social costs of drinking, from 1980 on, the brewing industry primarily worried about a possible tax increase. The last tax increase had been in 1951. The brewers had gotten used to a stable rate which had not kept up with the rate of inflation; at the same time they appeared to have a sense of foreboding and doom about a possible increase.

In 1982, the beer industry was already dealing with bottle deposits as an issue, when the journal, *Beverage Industry*, proclaimed increased taxation "another threat." Because of decreases in personal taxes as well as reduction in social service funding, the trade journal felt that "new income sources are going to have to be found." Brewers feared they would wind up paying double the current rate.[568]

The brewing industry had continued to maintain its historic distance from the distilled spirits industry; in terms of both television advertising and taxes beer appeared to have the competitive advantage. Facing diminishing sales and market share, the Distilled Spirits Council of the United States (DISCUS), a trade association, decided to strike back. They launched a highly effective ad campaign, which showed that twelve ounces of beer had the same alcohol content as five ounces of wine and as one and one half ounces of hard liquor. These

566 McGowan, *Government Regulation*, 56.

567 The Container Recycling Institute "Bottle Bill Resource Guide," www.bottlebill.org (accessed January 23, 2007); "Beer Cans Celebrate *Golden Anniversary*," *Beverage Industry*, January 1985, 55.

568 "An Emerging Threat: Beverage Tax Increases," *Beverage Industry*, February 5, 1982, 1.

ads which established that a drink is a drink is a drink may have played a part in convincing the public that it was time for beer to pay its fair share in taxes.[569]

Figure 23: Beverage alcohol equivalence.

In 1986, the Reagan administration, seeking additional revenue to offset losses from the tax cuts of the previous year, discussed raising the excise on liquor, beer, wine, and tobacco. A *New York Times* editorial termed such levies "sin taxes" and Treasury Secretary Donald Regan described them as "painless."[570] This language conveys the special place liquor taxation has had in the economic and bureaucratic history of the federal government as well as the assumptions officials have brought to taxation and the administration of internal revenue. Such attitudes have governed the nation's liquor taxation policy since 1862. Judgments about the ease and ability of the federal government to raise revenue via liquor taxation often have proved false.

Although a tax increase would require the brewers to play a familiar historical role, the context for a tax increase in the 1980s and early 1990s differed from previous moments when government had presented the brewing industry with demands for a greater contribution to the federal coffers. The passage of the Federal Uniform Age Act had certainly demonstrated that the brewing industry

569 Shea interview, 2005; DISCUS, "History of Social Responsibility," http://www.discus.org/responsibility/history.asp#90s (accessed May 15, 2007). One and one-half ounces of distilled spirits represents a shot or a dose of liquor.

570 *New York Times*, October 20, 1981, 30, 21; October 20, 1981, sec. 4, 6.

which contemplated a tax increase also faced a much greater degree of scrutiny and regulation.

The neo-temperance movement, which had played a role in the change in the drinking age, also sought to limit the societal damage from drinking and attempted to recover the economic costs of excessive drinking from its manufacturers. This approach was similar to the tactics that anti-smoking activists had used effectively. Thus neo-temperance advocates were part of the increasing drum roll for an increase in liquor taxation throughout the 1980s.

Along with the fear of an increase in the federal excise taxes, during the 1980s brewers also faced legislation around bottle and can deposits, warning labels, and advertising restrictions. Such legislation would also have a financial impact. By the summer of 1990, the federal government had an over one billion dollar deficit and President George H. W. Bush was contemplating tax increases to raise the needed revenue. Bush had made a pledge, "read my lips, no new taxes" when accepting the Republican nomination in 1988.[571]

Similarly to the Reagan administration, the Bush administration felt that "sin taxes" would be the best way to raise at least some of the $54 million the government needed.[572] The Beer Institute made clear from the start that they felt such increases would impact the working person most severely. Peter Coors was the president of the Institute; he stated that "The members of the brewing industry are concerned about the budget deficit, but no solution should place an unfair burden on working Americans."[573]

The Office of Management and Budget Director Richard Darman announced plans to raise the beer tax from sixteen cents a six-pack to eighty-one cents. The current barrel tax rate was $9; the proposed increase would set that rate at $44, an increase of over 400 percent. Senator Bob Kasten, a Republican from Wisconsin felt such a drastic increase would cost his state 6,000 jobs. The beer industry in Wisconsin employed 35,000 workers. Kasten also felt that the proposed beer tax increase unfairly penalized middle class consumers. He suggested that Congress raise the needed $7 million by "enacting my capital gains tax reform plan which would put more people to work by sparking economic growth."[574] Kasten's proposal was an attempt to appeal to both middle-class and elite consumers at the same time.

---

571 George Bush, "Address Accepting the Presidential Nomination at the Republican National Convention in New Orleans," August 18, 1988, American Presidency Project http://www.presidency.ucsb.edu/ws/index.php?pid=25955 (accessed June 25, 2007).

572 Stephen Barlas, "Alcohol Excise Taxes Almost Certain to Rise," *Beverage World*, September 1990.

573 "Beer Institute Helps Fight Tax Hike," *Modern Brewery Age*, July 23 1990, 4.

574 "WI's Kasten Blasts Beer Tax Hike Plan," *Modern Brewery Age*, August 1990.

Both large and small brewers joined together to fight the 1991 tax increase. The sole purpose of the Small Brewers Coalition, an offshoot of the Brewers Association of America, was to maintain the tax differential for small brewers. Proposed legislation would have narrowed the definition of a small brewer from a producer of two million or less barrels to 60,000 barrels. The Institute for Brewing Studies, which was the technical arm of the American Homebrewers Association, donated $1000 to support the Coalition. The Institute also joined with the Beer Institute against the overall tax increase. A spokesperson for the Institute for Brewing Studies explained their political action as follows: "While everyone at this point needs to carry their fair share of taxes during this time of fiscal crisis, we need to have an honest appraisal of the burden small breweries are already carrying."[575]

House Majority Leader Richard Gephardt, Democrat of Missouri and Anheuser-Busch, major manufacturer of St. Louis, Missouri, turned out to be key players in preventing the 400 percent tax increase on beer. Gephardt was a longstanding opponent of excise taxes; he believed they were "regressive". Anheuser-Busch launched a multi-media, multi-million dollar campaign against a tax increase. The company's efforts included using its 960 wholesalers to gather 2.4 million names on petitions as well as television, radio, and print advertising around the slogan "Can the Beer Tax."[576]

The brewers were much more visible in the campaign to prevent a tax increase than the distilled spirits industry, but in the end the beer tax doubled to $18 a barrel or thirty-two cents a six-pack. The small brewers' differential remained the same. The law went into effect on January 1, 1991; the tax on distilled spirits increased to $10.50 a gallon and wine went to $1.07 a gallon. Although the brewers had prevented even higher taxes, the increase was the first for the industry in forty years.[577]

Both the industrial and institutional landscape had changed tremendously from 1951 and the last tax increase. The United States Brewers Association no longer existed to advocate for protection from taxes; in its place stood the Beer Institute. The leaders of the brewing industry were also different: in the forty years since the last tax increase, Coors Brewing had emerged as a top brewery.

---

575 Lee W. Holland, "The Evolution of the Brewers Association of America" (Colorado: Brewers Association of America, 1994); "Institute for Brewing Studies backs tax fight," *Modern Brewery Age*, February 4, 1991.

576 "Gephardt, A-B key players in holding down beer tax," *St. Louis Business Journal*, October 22, 1990.

577 Stephen Barlas, "Post mortem," *Beverage World*, November 1990; Amy Mittelman, "Taxation of Liquor (United States)," in Blocker, et al., *Encyclopedia*), vol. 2, 609-611.

Until the late 1970s Coors was a regional brewer; the beer was available in sixteen Western states. The Coors family sought nationwide distribution of their beer, but faced several problems. Their appeal and brand recognition flowed from the Rocky Mountain springs that supplied the water for the beer. Building another brewery somewhere else would negate those advertising claims. Coors planned to compete in both beer types and advertising. By 1979, the company had a light beer and hoped to produce a super premium beer in the near future.[578]

Coors' plans to diversify its products reflected the changing nature of the beer market since Repeal. Nineteenth century brewers brewed fresh lager for patrons at saloons. A few brewers persisted in brewing English ale. Although the German brewers had argued for the uniqueness of their product when confronting federal taxes in the 1860s, for much of their pre-Prohibition history they presented and promoted beer as beer. Most brewers had only a few different products and they didn't really advertise one over the other.

During Repeal, brewers returned to a world of consumer products and brands. Slowly they began to develop different beers. *Modern Brewery Age* was a leader in promoting product differentiation, advertising, and marketing campaigns around specific items. Of course the brewers pushed for great latitude in production definition when producing the industry's NRA code. They continued to resist ingredient and alcoholic content labeling.

True product differentiation began in the 1960s with malt liquor; it accelerated after Miller and Phillip Morris introduced light beer in 1975. Other categories of beer included super premium, dry, reduced alcohol, non-alcoholic, and beer coolers.[579] Anheuser-Busch has over sixty beers including Michelob, its super premium entry which the company has produced since 1896, as well as O'Douls, a non-alcoholic beer, and Bud Light.[580] Most other breweries do not have that many products; craft brewers usually have a few different beers. Boston Beer, makers of Sam Adams, produces about twenty-five different products.[581]

Coors was obviously hoping to move onto the national level and begin producing a variety of beers. The company developed a plan to move into two or three new states a year. By 1986 people in forty-five different states could buy Coors beer. The company maintained its number five position in the industry through massive advertising expenditures. Coors spent more than $10 a barrel

---

578 Jerry Knight, "Coors Plans Expansion," *Washington Post*, 79.

579 Beatrice Trum Hunter, "More Informative Beer Labels," *Consumer Research Magazine*, vol. 79, no. 10 (October 1996): 10-15.

580 http://anheuser-busch.com/ (accessed April 2, 2007).

581 http://samueladams.com/verification/ (accessed April 2, 2007).

on advertising and its total marketing expenses were $165 million in 1985. The company's net income was $53.4 million from sales of $1.28 billion.[582]

By 1986 the fourth generation of Coors family members was running the company. Jeff Coors stated that the brewing industry "was much more of a marketing game today." Beyond problems of market expansion, throughout the 1970s and 1980s, the company faced a series of controversies. In 1977, Local 366 of the Colorado UBW began a strike against Coors. Coors, under the leadership of Bill Coors, consistently supported conservative causes; the company attempted to change the seniority system which would have resulted in a less powerful role for the local and its influence on discipline. Claiming union busting the local was on strike for two weeks when half of the workers returned to work. The company hired replacement workers for the remaining strikers. Coors wanted an open shop despite the fact that the brewery had had union representation for forty-two years. In 1978 employees decertified the union.

The union and other interested parties including Hispanics, homosexual rights activists, and feminists undertook a national boycott. Many groups believed Coors engaged in discriminatory labor practices. By initiating a boycott the UBW was returning to its nineteenth century roots. This boycott caused California sales to diminish by fifteen percent; California represented more than forty-five percent of Coors market. The boycott was a large impediment to the company's attempts to produce beer and market beer for the national market.[583]

Ten years later, in 1987, the union and Coors came to an understanding. Coors agreed to non-interference with union organizing and to support a union contract for a proposed building project. In response the union ended the boycott. Coors changed its hiring practices and advertising focus. Coors had also completed an agreement with the Coalition of Hispanic Organizations in 1984. Jeff Coors was determined to avoid controversy.[584]

By 1991, all fifty states sold Coors beer, and the company had risen to the number three spot in the industry. It has the largest capacity brewery in the world at its headquarters in Golden, Colorado. That same year Anheuser-Busch's market share was forty-four percent.[585]

---

582 Steven Greenhouse, "Coors Boys Stick to Business," *New York Times*, November 30, 1986, 162. The family had suffered a tragedy in 1960 with the kidnapping and murder of Adolph Coors III, the eldest grandson of Adolph Coors, the company's founder.

583 Ibid.; Amy Mittelman, "Labor in the U.S. Liquor Industry" in Blocker et al., *Encyclopedia*, vol. 1, 356-358.

584 Ibid.; Ruth Hamel and Tom Schreiner, "Coors Courts Hispanics," *American Demographic*, November 1988, 54.

585 William H. Mulligan, Jr. "Coors," in Blocker, et. al., *Encyclopedia*, vol. 1, 174; Rick Desloge, "Anheuser-Busch on path to 50 percent share of market," *St. Louis Business Journal*, February 11, 1991, 1B-2B.

In the nineteenth century a brewer was a brewer; there was little distinction between large and small brewers. Observers called Midwest brewers, including Anheuser–Busch, Schlitz, and Pabst, "shipping brewers." During Repeal, small brewers emerged as a separate tier of the industry. By the 1970s, the industry had consolidated sufficiently so that there were at least two distinct tiers — the large national brewers and the smaller regional companies.

In 1977, in this competitive atmosphere, Jack McAuliffe, a former Navy electrician, started New Albion Brewery in Sonoma, California. The brewery, which produced ales, porter, and stouts, was open until 1980. Most industry observers consider New Albion to be the country's first micro-brewer.[586]

A second pioneer of American craft brewing is Fritz Maytag who has had much more success than McAuliffe. In 1965, Maytag, a member of the well-known washing machine family, purchased the almost defunct San Francisco Anchor Brewing Company. The company produces steam beer, a product of higher fermentation temperatures which results in strong carbonation and a buildup of steam. This process developed in the Pacific coast because of shortages of natural ice. The company also owns a micro-distillery.[587]

In 1978 President Jimmy Carter signed legislation that legalized home brewing; this also helped spur the development of craft brewing. The law allowed anyone who was eighteen or older to brew up to 100 gallons of wine or brew a year. Such activity had been illegal since Repeal.[588] The states followed suit but some, including New Jersey, did not legalize home brewing until the 1990s.[589] Although the Federal Alcohol Administration Act of 1935 had outlawed home brewing, many people had continued brew beer at home, using baker's yeast and a kettle. By the early twenty-first century there were two million home brewers, three hundred home brewing clubs, and multiple brewing competitions and festivals.[590]

The founding father of home brewing and a great friend to craft brewing is Charlie Papazian. Papazian is the author of *The Complete Joy of Home Brewing*, the founder of the American Homebrewer's Association, the Association of Brewers, and the current president of the Brewer's Association. The Association of Brewers, founded in 1978, represented both home brewers and micro-brewers while the Brewers Association of America was the organization of regional brewers which had existed since 1941. Despite the proliferation of craft beers, Papazian

586 Jack Erickson, *Star Spangled Beer* (Reston, VA: RedBrick Press, 1987), 5-6.
587 Ibid., 9-10; Downard, *Dictionary*, 181.
588 "Home Breweries: They're Legal Now," *New York Times*, February 7, 1979, C10.
589 "Changing the Law on Brewing Beer at Home," *New York Times*, January 19, 1992, A1.
590 Ken Wells, *Travels with Barley: A Journey through Beer Culture in America* (New York: Free Press, 2004), 148.

maintains there is still a need for home brewing, stating "developing your skills as a home brewer is the best insurance you can have to assure that you will always have the beer you like."[591]

Not all brewers who have attempted to revive local or regional companies have been as successful as Fritz Maytag. Minnesota Brewing, which could claim a lineage dating back to 1855, sold beer in forty-eight states, and was the twelfth largest brewery in 1999, closed its doors in 2002. The company was $14 million in debt and could not keep up with production orders. From 1972 to 1990 Heileman had owned the brewery which had a huge industrial plant. For the smaller scale craft brewer, this meant unused capacity.[592]

Other historic breweries suffered the same fate as Minnesota Brewing. Rainier Beer, the iconic beer of Seattle, Washington, had been a large regional brewery for almost seventy years. Stroh's was the final owner of both the brewery and the beer. Stroh's acquired Rainier in its purchase of Heileman in 1996. When it sold the company to Pabst, Rainier's million barrel capacity made it "too small to be big and too big to be small."[593]

Craft brewing has four segments; micro-breweries, brewpubs, contract brewers, and regional breweries. Micro-brewing is small-scale production of beer in major industrial societies where large brewers can brew up to 100 million barrels (at 31 gallons per barrel) a year. Micro-brewing in Great Britain, Canada and the United States began as a response to the ever-increasing concentration of their national brew markets.[594]

Micro-brewing is one segment of the craft beer industry which is itself a subsection of the beer industry. A micro-brewery produces less than 15,000 barrels (31 gallons) a year. For over a decade beginning in the 1980s micro-breweries were hot commodities with an ever-growing market share. Craft beer appealed perfectly to baby boom generation Americans with its standards of quality and high pricing similar to imports. The strength of the boom gave micro-breweries a two percent market share by 1996. In 2001 United States craft breweries produced 6.2 million barrels.[595]

Micro-brewers brew beer in a consciously distinctive style that is quite different from the large American brewers. They have attempted to bring back older

591 Charles Papazian, *The Complete Joy of Homebrewing*, 3rd ed. (New York: Harper Collins, 2003) 10.
592 Greg Glaser, "Pre-1900 Regional Brewers," *Modern Brewery Age*, March 26, 2001; "Minnesota Brewing Closes," June 25, 2002, RealBeer.com http://www.realbeer.com/news/articles/news-001736.php (accessed June 26, 2007).
593 Rick Star, "Rainier Brewery: Rest in Peace," *Beer Notes*, August 1999, http://www.beernotes.com/northwest/articles/000409.html (accessed October 6, 2006).
594 Amy Mittelman, "Microbreweries (United States, United Kingdom, and Canada)" in Blocker, et. al., *Encyclopedia*, vol. 2, 416-417.
595 Ibid.

styles of beer, moving away from a focus on lager and pilsner. Many craft brewers produce Indian Pale Ale (IPA) and other ales; they have brought back barley wine as a modern drink. Indian Pale Ale has a large amount of hops and can range in color from pale to deep copper. IPA was a product of the British colonization of India. Brewed in Britain and sent to India, the colonists favored this style of beer because the high alcohol content and the hops acted as preservatives. Barley wine is also ale; it has malt sweetness and is high in alcohol.[596]

Most micro-breweries are quite small and operate on the local level. In a survey of Portland, Oregon breweries, number one on the list, Deschutes Brewery, had barrelage of 54,965. The twenty-fifth produced 701 barrels. Deschutes Brewery represents 2.2 percent of the Oregon beer market. Due to its level of production Deschutes is actually a regional brewer. Regional breweries have capacities ranging from 15,000 to 2 million barrels. Deschutes also has a pub.

Another aspect of the industry is restaurants connected to breweries, known as brewpubs. A brewpub sells over fifty percent of its beer on site in a restaurant which is physically connected to a brewery. As of 2000 there were 1,023 brewpubs in the United States and 3,000 micro-brew labels. The joining of dining and brewing represented a change in post-Prohibition alcohol control legislation, which usually prohibited such facilities.[597]

Dogfish Head Brewing, located in Rehoboth Beach, Delaware, is one of the nation's fastest growing breweries, and began life as a brewpub. Delaware had legislation dating back to Repeal that prevented retail operations on the premises of a brewery. Sam Calagione, the founder of Dogfish, worked personally to get the laws changed; he then promoted his establishment as "the first brewpub in the first state."[598] Delaware was the first state to ratify the Constitution.

Contract breweries are companies that use the facilities of a pre-existing brewery to produce their beer. The brewer, not the brewery, distributes and sells the beer. Utica, New York is a center of contract brewing. Brooklyn Brewery, New Amsterdam Beer, Boston Beer, and others are all brewed in Utica. In the nineteenth century the city had twelve functioning breweries. Matt Brewing, founded in 1888, still brews its own brands. The company developed Saranac beer in 1985. The Matt family has always owned the brewery; today both the third and fourth generation run the brewery. Much of a craft brewer's appeal

596 Klein, *Beer Lover's Rating Guide*, 6; Wells, *Travels with Barley*, 53.

597 Mittelman, "Microbreweries."

598 Sam Calagione, *Brewing Up a Business: Adventures in Entrepreneurship from the Founder of Dogfish Head Craft Brewery* (Hoboken, N.J.: John Wiley 2005), 97-98.

comes from the perceived uniqueness of the product. Not brewing the beer in its own brewery can diminish that image.[599]

Boston Beer Company, producer of Sam Adams beer, is the United State's most well-known contract brewer. Jim Koch founded the company in 1984. Although Boston Beer's corporate headquarters are in Boston, Sam Adams is primarily brewed at the Pittsburgh Beer brewery, Pittsburgh, Pennsylvania. The company went public in 1995. As of 1997 Boston Beer was the nation's seventh largest brewer with an output of 1, 352,000 barrels.[600]

Sam Adams, the eighteenth century patriot, was not a brewer, and barely made a financial go of his family's malting business. For Adams, politics defined his life. Why then did Jim Koch, a descendent of German brewers, choose the patriot to be his symbol? Micro-brewers staked their fortune on their authenticity in opposition to the generic nature of large American brewers. By the mid-twentieth century most of the world drank lager, not just the American consumers of Bud, Pabst, and Falstaff. Micro-brewers wished to further distinguish themselves by brewing ale, an older style of beer, rather than lager. Sam Adams, Publican Sam, met both of these ideological demands.

In 2006 Boston Brewing dug deeper into historical troves and began brewing beers in honor of four patriots, Sam Adams, George Washington, Thomas Jefferson, and James Madison. Although the company sought to establish itself as the next link in the English chain of brewing, its promotional literature also states that Jim Koch uses his "great, great grandfather's recipes."[601] Those would be for lager beer.

Smuttynose Brewing Company, founded in 1994 and located in Portsmouth, New Hampshire, exemplifies how craft brewers use historical themes to legitimate their product. The company claims that it is named for Smuttynose Island, part of the Isles of Shoals which are "steeped in history and legend," including pirates, ghosts, and fishermen. The mission of the brewery is to "brew fine, fresh distinctive beers, characteristic of our New England origins." A, "genuine craft brewery," Smuttynose brews an IPA which is a "tribute to those big, hoppy nineteenth century ales that made the long sea voyage from England's temperate

---

599 Klein, *Beer Lover's Rating Guide*, 15, 350-359; Gary Regan, "There's a Contract Out on America's Craft-brewed Beers," *Nation's Restaurant News*, November 25, 1996; Glaser, "Pre-1900 Regional Brewers"; "Family History," Matt Brewing Company, http://www.saranac.com (accessed August 22, 2007).

600 "Boston Beer Company History," Business and Company Resource Center, Farmington Hills, MI: Thomson Gale, http://infotrac.galegroup.com/galenet (accessed December 12, 2002); Frank J. Prial, "A Microbrew Gets a Macromug: A Homemade Beer Goes National," *New York Times*, May 29, 1996, C1; "Top U.S. Brewers in 1997," beerhistory.com, http://www.beerhistory.com/library/holdings/top10.shtml (accessed January 1, 2002).

601 http://samueladams.com/verification/ (accessed June 15, 2006).

shores, 'round the Cape of Good Hope to the sultry climes of the faraway East Indies."[602]

Relations between the big national breweries and craft brewers have not always been cordial. Anheuser–Busch has tried at various times to impugn the integrity and marketing legitimacy of Boston Beer.[603] More often, however, the big brewers have pursued a strategy of "if you can't beat them, join them." Miller owns Jacob Leinenkugel, one of the country's largest craft breweries. Leinenkugel dates back to 1867 and is a separate operating unit from Miller. On its own it is the nation's fourteenth largest brewery. Leinenkugel has had better sales recently than Miller.[604] Coors manufactures Killians and Anheuser–Busch has part ownership in several craft breweries.[605] Through these actions the big three have acknowledged the appeal and market share of craft beer. By keeping the craft aspects of their business separate, they also express a determination to maintain their core products without any changes.

The emergence of craft brewing highlights a battle within the brewing industry over authenticity and identity. Since World War II the national brewers have connected beer to all things American — baseball, barbeques, race cars, and pretty, sexy women.[606] Yet the nationalizing of the beer industry removed one of the most potent aspects of beer's identity — localism. The new generation of brewers emphasizes its connection to place and community even more than taste. They stake a claim to authenticity via their roots in a specific locale.

Craft brewers, whether or not they start as home brewers, are entrepreneurs. In this way they are similar to the many hundreds of people who start a business every day. What is interesting about the thousands of people who started breweries and brewpubs since the late 1970s is that they created these businesses in an industry dominated by some of America's biggest companies.

Craft brewers have been able to exploit a hole, a gap, in the huge edifice of American brewing. Some three to fifteen percent of the American beer drinking population didn't and still doesn't like drinking Bud, Schlitz, Miller, or Pabst. In the nineteenth century ten percent of Pabst's customers wanted pure malt beer; craft beer drinkers of the twenty-first century are their descendants.[607]

---

602 Information obtained from Smuttynose IPA package.

603 Van Munching, *Beer Blast*, 256-262.

604 Bill Yenne, *The American Brewery* (St Paul, MN: MBI Publishing, 2003), 135-136.

605 Glaser, "Pre-1900 Regional Breweries."

606 For examples of these themes and their use in alcohol advertising and marketing see Lynn Walding, "Alcohol Marketing 2005" (powerpoint presentation), Iowa Alcohol Beverages Division, http://www.iowaabd.com/index.jsp (accessed July 20, 2007).

607 Thomas Childs Cochran, *The Pabst Brewing Company: The History of an American Business* (New York: New York Univ. Press, 1948), 122.

Drinkers seeking stronger tasting, more flavorful beer, first turned to imports in the post-World War II period; Heineken benefited greatly from this. From the 1930s on Van Munching and Company was the importer of the Dutch beer. In 1991 Heineken N.V. purchased the import company; for many years Heineken was the country's top beer import.[608]

By the late 1990s the Dutch brewer faced serious competition from Corona Beer. Grupo Modelo, Mexico, brews Corona; Gambrinus Company and Barton Beers Ltd import it. Anheuser-Busch has a thirty-seven per cent share in the company. Corona is currently the nation's top import beer. It sells for slightly less than Heineken, but costs more than domestic beers.[609]

In 2005 America imported 25,566,239 barrels (31 gallons/barrel) of beer; domestic production that year was 195,386,222 barrels. Imports are about fifteen percent of the American beer market. Mexico sends the most. Europe, as a region, exports about as much beer to the United States as Mexico does — close to 11 million barrels. The Netherlands are the single greatest contributors to that total. America also exports beer; in 2005 brewers shipped 3,900,597 barrels overseas. Canada, which also exports beer to the United States, was the single largest recipient of US beer.[610]

Craft brewers, most notably Jim Koch and Boston Beer, were able to market their product to the same demographic group that drank Heineken and other imported beers. Imported beer sold at a much higher rate than domestic beer; craft brewers priced their beers as if they were imports. For many craft brewers their raison d'etre, no matter how successful they become, is their determination to create a company that "subverts the definition of beer put forth by . . . Budweiser and Coors."[611]

Although craft brewers see themselves as very distinct from Anheuser-Busch and other large brewers, they still brew beer and are subject to federal control via taxation and other regulations. From 1862 on, the American brewing industry operated under the aegis of the federal government. Following the tax increase of 1951, brewers had settled back into their comfortable relationship with the Internal Revenue Service, the new name of the Bureau of Internal Revenue. The IRS collected excise and income taxes. The pursuit of illicit production and revenue fraud fell to the Alcohol and Tobacco Tax Division of the Treasury Department.

608 "Heineken," Joy P. Peterson, ed., *International Directory of Company Histories*, vol. 34 (Detroit, MI: St. James Press, 2000), 200-204.

609 Rick Wills, "The King of Imported Beers," *New York Times*, May 28, 1999, C1.

610 "Brewers Almanac 2007," Beer Institute, http://www.beerinstitute.org/ (accessed August 23, 2007).

611 Calagione, *Brewing Up a Business*, 13.

The year 1968 was a violent one in American history. The assassinations of Martin Luther King and Robert F. Kennedy prompted Congress to pass the Gun Control Act. This legislation made the Alcohol and Tobacco Tax Division responsible for limited federal gun control and insured the agency the undying enmity of the National Rifle Association.

Congressional legislation in 1972 added revenue collection to the Alcohol and Tobacco Tax Division and created an independent agency, the Bureau of Alcohol, Tobacco and Firearms. This agency became the newest partner of the brewers in their historic relationship with the federal government dating back to the Civil War. BATF authority for regulation of alcoholic beverage derives from the Federal Alcohol Administration Act of 1935.[612]

The opposition of the NRA to the BATF mission regarding the illegal gun trade prompted President Reagan to pursue dissolution of the agency in 1981. Reagan did not succeed, but the BATF remained a weak agency whose primary administrative focus was not on alcohol but firearms. Public awareness of BATF rose during the tragic events of Waco, Texas in 1993.[613] The agency's lack of interest in liquor industry issues was frustrating to neo-temperance activists but worked well for brewers.

The BATF was not just concerned with alcoholic beverages. Liquor and tobacco shared many links; the two products were the backbone of Civil War and late nineteenth century excise taxation, and movements against their use shared many participants.

Because the BATF was the regulatory agency for the liquor industry, neo-temperance activists had to confront the agency around labeling issues. The BATF is a tax collection force; the concerns and rhetoric of neo-temperance advocates revolved around consumer issues of product safety and liability. Thus, as in the anti-smoking crusade, the activists would have expected to deal with the FDA rather than a part of the Treasury Department. This administrative anomaly dated back to the revenue need during Repeal and the Depression and suited brewers admirably.

Historically brewers do not list the alcoholic content of beer on the label while wine and distilled spirits do. This also dates back to the 1930s and NRA codes. The idea, which brewers did not oppose, was that providing the alcoholic content of beer would prompt brewers to competitively increase the strength of their product. The alcohol control philosophy prevalent in Repeal legisla-

612 Amy Mittelman, "Bureau of Alcohol, Tobacco, and Firearms (BATF)" in Blocker, et. al., *Encyclopedia*, 122-124.
613 Ibid.; Fox Butterfield, "Limits on Power and Zeal Hamper Firearms Agency," *New York Times*, July 22, 1999, A1, 19.

tion promoted responsible drinking. American beers are usually around four to five percent alcohol by volume. Micro-brewers have begun to push the limits of this by producing "extreme" beer with an alcoholic content as high as nine percent.[614]

In 1987 Coors challenged the FAA labeling ban. A Federal Court knocked down the ban in 1992, and the BATF then allowed voluntary listing of alcoholic content. Most brewers have not done so. Brewers in the 1930s sought the greatest latitude in defining their product. Brewers in the 1990s were no different.[615]

Brewers also do not list their ingredients. Since 1989 all alcoholic beverage packages contain a warning label. The label informs drinkers about the risks of drinking and driving, and consuming alcohol while pregnant. Fetal alcohol syndrome (FAS) is a set of abnormalities which can occur in the infants of alcoholic mothers. The warning label was another achievement for neo-temperance and public health advocates. The focus on women drinkers was a relatively new phenomenon for the temperance movement.[616]

In the late 1990s the BATF considered allowing wine labels that would state "The proud people who made this wine encourage you to consult your family doctor about the health effects of wine consumption." Alternative language encouraged wine drinkers to get the federal government's nutritional guidelines which discussed the health benefits of wine consumption. The Center for Science in the Public Interest (CSPI), neo-temperance advocates, and Senator Strom Thurmond all opposed positive alcoholic beverage labels.[617] In 2003 Michael Jacobsen, the director of CSPI, pushed for an "alcohol facts" label that would provide alcohol content, serving sizes, calories, and ingredients.[618]

The brewing industry has had to interact with the federal government and its bureaucracy since 1862. The USBA facilitated this relationship for many

---

614 Hunter, "More Informative Beer Labels"; Wells, *Travels with Barley*, 104.

615 Eben Shapiro, "Judge Voids a Law on Beer Labeling," *New York Times*, October 30, 1992, D16.

616 Jay S. Lewis, "Gore joins assault on initial warning label regulations," *The Alcoholism Report*, vol. 18. no. 3 (Oct 1989): 7-9; Ernest L. Abel, "Fetal Alcohol Syndrome," in Blocker, et. al., *Encyclopedia*, 231-233.

617 Russ Bridenbaugh "The warning label war," *Wines & Vines*, 83.5 (May 2002): 51-55; "Wine industry may chalk up victory on health language in labeling," *Alcoholism and Drug Abuse Weekly*, November 8, 1998, 7; "U.S. Puts Wine Health Label on Hold," *Beverage Industry*, vol. 91, no. 1 (Jan 2000): 9.

618 "'Alcohol Facts' Label Proposed for Beer, Wine, and Liquor," CSPI Newsroom, December 16, 2003, http://www.cspinet.org/new/200312161.html (accessed July 28, 2006). In January 2003, the BATF split into two bureaus. The duties of tax collection and regulation of production, labeling, marketing advertising of alcoholic products went to the Alcohol and Tobacco Tax and Trade Bureau (TTB) while the law enforcement aspect of the ATF became the responsibility of the Justice Department. These changes were part of the Homeland Security Act of 2002 and were a consequence of the events of September 11, 2001. See "History of TTP," Alcohol and Tobacco Tax and Trade Bureau, http://www.ttb.gov/about/history.htm (accessed July 28, 2006).

years. Because craft brewing is a distinct segment of the larger industry the small brewers have their own trade organization, the Brewers Association (BA). This organization represents the fullest integration of the various elements of craft brewing. In 2005 the Association of Brewers, which began life in 1978 as an organization for home brewers, and the sixty-four year old Brewers' Association of America, the traditional voice of small and regional brewers, merged.[619]

The main legislative goal of the BA is to maintain the tax differential afforded to small brewers. Smaller breweries pay $7 a barrel rather than the full tax of $18 per barrel that the big companies pay. To be a full member of the BAA you must brew under two million barrels annually. Large brewers and importers can be associate members. There are also allied industry and wholesaler memberships. Anheuser-Busch doesn't belong to the BA but Boston Beer does. Malting companies, printers, and glass manufacturers are some of the allied industries involved in the BA.[620]

In 1996, the Beer Institute celebrated its tenth year of existence. John N. MacDonough would continue as chairman of the organization. MacDonough was CEO of the Miller Brewing Company, a subsidiary of Phillip Morris, the tobacco company. In the Institute's annual report, the chairman made a special point of mentioning "the exponential growth in the number of small brewers." MacDonough had been with Miller since 1992, first in the capacity as president and then as chairman and CEO. Prior to working for Miller, MacDonough had spent 15 years with Anheuser-Busch, Miller's top rival, as a marketing expert.[621]

Raymond J. McGrath was president, a professional position, of the Beer Institute. A twelve year Republican Congressmen from Long Island, McGrath became president in 1993. In the annual report for 1995-1996 McGrath highlighted the ongoing publication of the *Brewers Almanac*, first published by the United States Brewers Association in 1945. McGrath also served as president of the Alcoholic Beverage Medical Research Foundation, another institution founded by the USBA. McGrath served as president until 1999.[622]

During the ten years of the Beer Institute's existence, the number of breweries had increased fifteen times over. In 1986 the country had 63 independent breweries; by 1996 the number was close to one thousand. The Beer Institute

619 "About the Brewers Association as a Company," Beertown, http://www.beertown.org/ba/about.html (accessed September 9, 2006).

620 Ibid; "Brewers Association, Membership Roster as of 4/08/07," Brewers Associationhttp://beertown.org/ba/pdf/ba_members.pdf (accessed June 28, 2007).

621 Beer Institute, *Brewers Almanac 1996* (Washington, DC: Beer Institute, 1996), 2; Michael Janofsky, "A New Chief For Miller Brewing Company," *New York Times*, Aug 24, 1993, D5.

622 "Raymond J. McGrath," *Marquis Who's Who*, 2007, Biography Resource Center. Farmington Hills, MI.: Thomson Gale. 2007. http://galenet.galegroup.com/servlet/BioRC (accessed June 28, 2007); Beer Institute, *Almanac*, 3.

claimed this resulted in "the most competitive marketplace since Repeal of Prohibition."[623] Given that the original membership of the Beer Institute had been limited to the nation's largest brewers and that in 1996, the top three brewers, Anheuser–Busch, Miller and Coors controlled over seventy percent of the domestic market, the comment was disingenuous.

In 1997, the top three produced 154,381,000 barrels of beer while the next seven combined produced 30,914,000 barrels. Anheuser–Busch alone produced sixty-seven times as much beer as did the Boston Beer Company, producers of Sam Adams, seventh on the list and a symbol of the new brewers.[624]

Although Miller Brewing had sought the formation of the Beer Institute in 1986 as a wholly new and different national trade association, ten years down the road the Beer Institute had many similarities to the USBA. The 1996 Annual report claimed that the Institute had archives containing "650 volumes and thousands of preserved periodicals"[625] The animus towards the history of the USBA seems to have abated.

By 1996, the beer industry had been living with a doubling of the tax rate for five years. The USBA had always maintained they were active citizens willing to do their part in a crisis; once the crisis had abated it was only fair that the tax be remedied. The Beer Institute pursued a similar line of reasoning. Ever mindful of the role they played in the financial health of the nation, the Institute claimed that "rolling back the beer excise tax would not come at high price to the government. Seventy-five percent of the federal revenue lost through a beer tax rollback would be offset by payroll taxes from new jobs in the brewing industry and the overall increase in economic activity."[626]

All the other excise taxes that had been part of the 1991 legislation were on luxury items such as yachts, furs, and private airplanes. None of those taxes were still in effect. Ray McGrath, president of the Beer Institute and a former Congressman from New York, said "It just doesn't seem fair to us that beer drinkers should still be paying while wealthier Americans get the break."[627]

As part of their ongoing effort to reduce the beer tax, the Beer Institute belonged to the Coalition Against Regressive Taxation. Other members of this coalition included distillers, tobacco companies, and trucking concerns. All of these multimillion dollar industries were apparently very concerned about the effect of taxes on the average citizen. An observer described the group as "a

623 Beer Institute, *Almanac*, 4.
624 "Top 10 U.S. Brewers in 1997," http://www.beerhistory.com/library/holdings/top10.shtml. (accessed November 10, 2005).
625 Beer Institute, *Almanac*, 4.
626 "Beer Institute Supports Tax Roll-back Bills," *Modern Brewery Age*, August 19, 1996, 1-2.
627 Ibid.

gang of brewers, distillers, cigarette makers, and trucking companies all bravely fighting excise taxes in the name of Joe Six-Pack."[628] The Beer Institute saw the matter differently, describing the goal of the Coalition as "maintaining strong relationships with and monitoring the activities of the House and Senate tax writing committees."[629] Political supporters of this particular group included Don Sundquist, Republican Congressmen and Governor of Tennessee, as well as Mervyn Dymally, California Congressman and the first African-American lieutenant governor. Louis Stokes, a fifteen-term Congressman from Ohio, was another supporter. The brewing industry has many friends in Congress; in 1998 brewers contributed $1.2 million to political campaigns; two-thirds went to Republicans.[630]

All brewers, large and small, have argued for a rollback of the federal taxes. Beer is a heavily taxed commodity; it pays taxes on the federal, state, and local levels. The tax rate varies tremendously from state to state. Alaska taxes beer at a rate of $33.17, the highest in the nation. The rest of the states rates range from $3 to $30. Some states have a varying rate according to the alcoholic content of the beer; others also tax on the wholesale and retail levels.[631]

Competition in the industry continued unabated even while brewing organizations sought reductions in taxes and campaigned against various neo-temperance initiatives. In 1996, Stroh's continued its ascent into the top tier by purchasing Heileman Brewing. Heileman had made a run at achieving top tier status in the 1980s, but the Justice Department had halted its program of aggressive acquisitions. Russell Cleary, the son-in-law of Roy Kumm, and his successor, spearheaded the expansion of the company. Stalled, the company became vulnerable; in 1987 Alan Bond, an Australian investor, purchased the nation's fourth largest brewer. In 1992, Bond went to jail for fraud in connection with a deal to save an Australian bank.[632]

In the 1980s Heileman brewed many different brands of beer including Old Style, its original product, Lone Star, Schmidt, and Carling Black Label. The company was responsible for forty percent of all the new brands in the decade.[633] In

628 Bill Gifford, "The Lobbyists," *Washington Monthly*, January-February, 199, 56-59.

629 Beer Institute, *Almanac*, 9.

630 Gifford, "Lobbyists"; "Brew-ha-ha Over Beer Taxes is Brewing," *Modern Brewery Age*, August 10, 1998, 1-2; biographical information from *Biographical Directory of the United States Congress*, http://bioguide.congress.gov/biosearch/biosearch.asp (accessed June 28, 2007).

631 Alcohol and Tobacco Taxes, Informational Paper 8, Wisconsin Legislative Fiscal Bureau, January 2005, http://www.legis.state.wi.us/lfb/Informationalpapers/8.pdf (accessed April 29, 2005).

632 "Heileman's Aggressive Style," *New York Times*, August 15, 1979, D1; "Alan Bond Gets Jail in Australia," *New York Times*, May 30, 1992, 35; Bob Skilnick, "Heileman, G., Brewing Company," in Blocker, et al., *Encyclopedia*, 292-293.

633 Philip E. Ross, "Bid for Heileman Spurs Stock," *New York Times*, September 5, 1987, 31.

1991, Heileman developed yet another new product, Power Master, which was a malt liquor with 5.9 percent alcohol; most malt liquors contained 5.5 percent, regular beer 3.5 percent. African-Americans and Hispanics were the core market for malt liquors. Heileman's marketing featured a young black man. The tagline was "bold, not harsh." African-American political and community leaders objected to the beer and its marketing. Eventually BATF intervened and prohibited the company from marketing Power Master. The agency felt the name was a subtle attempt to convey the strength of the beer to the public.[634] Heileman's marketing struggles indicated how far the brewing industry had come from the self-regulation policies that they had pursued from the 1930s on.

The USBA had always stressed restraint in marketing. The Nebraska Plan that brewers developed during Repeal was the cornerstone of their approach. Increased competition in the industry and the diminished influence of the USBA led individual brewers to be bolder in their advertising. The specter of Prohibition had diminished.

In 1996, Stroh's, planning to buy Heileman, was the country's fourth largest brewer. Coors, in third place, had 10.1 percent of the market. Stroh's and Heileman's combined market share would be a little over nine percent. Stroh Brewing Company had been in existence for 149 years; in 1999 the company sold its brands to Miller and Pabst. Pabst got Schlitz. This sale marked the completion of forty years of consolidation of the brewing industry. The dismantling of Stroh, which employed 2,800 people, gave Miller and Anheuser-Busch seventy per cent of the market.[635]

At the turn of the new century the highly concentrated brewing industry was still living with the consequences of the 1991 tax increase as well as the legislative agenda of the neo-temperance movement. In 2000 the Alcohol Epidemiology Program of the University of Minnesota, School of Public Health, published a survey of alcohol polices in the states. The authors stated that their rationale for such a survey was that "Policies that affect how alcohol is produced, distributed, taxed, and used can be effective tools to diminish the persistent and costly social and health problems associated with alcohol use." Thus, at least on the state level, the public health aspects of liquor regulation appeared to be more important than the revenue concerns.

---

634 Anthony Ramirez, "U.S. is Challenging New Heileman Label," *New York Times*, June 21, 1991, D15; "The Threat of Power Master," *New York Times*, July 1, 1991, A12; "Heileman Told It Can't Use the Power Master Name," *New York Times*, July 2, 1991, D6; Kurt Eichenwald, "U.S. Rescinds Approval of a Malt Liquor," *New York Times*, July 4, 1991, D3.

635 Robyn Meredith, "Stroh to Buy Heileman in Big Brewery Deal," *New York Times*, March 1, 1996, D2; "Last Call: Detroit-Based Stroh Brewery will Sell Beer Brands to Pabst, Miller," *Minneapolis Star Tribune*, February 9, 1999, 3.

The report looked at four areas of alcohol control legislation which comprise the main agenda of the neo-temperance movement. Most states license private institutions to sell alcohol. A minority of states have direct control over the sale of alcoholic beverage. Private sales seem to increase the total number of sales; therefore activists would probably prefer state control but there was little change in this area of alcohol control policies from 1968 to 2000.[636]

Brewers maintained the tax increase had hurt the economy and was unfair to working people. Epidemiologists pointed out that once they adjusted for inflation state taxes of beer were only one third of the rate of 1968. Taxes also did not change very much and the researchers reiterated their concern that taxes have not kept pace with inflation. This was one of the major arguments used to enact the 1991 tax increase. Neo-temperance advocates feel that liquor taxes can "correct for the external costs associated with alcohol consumption."[637]

Most Americans buy alcohol in bottles and cans and then drink it at home. Some people do buy large amounts of beer in kegs to serve at parties; others drink alcoholic beverages in public settings. Very few saloons or beer gardens currently exist, yet their successors — brew pubs, bars, taverns and restaurants — are alive and well. State alcohol policies focus on controlling public drinking experiences and minimizing social disruptions from them. Two such policies are keg registration and training programs for alcohol beverage servers. Since 1968 a quarter of the states have enacted keg registration legislation and twenty-one states currently have policies mandating either mandatory of voluntary training for servers.

Drunk driving has continued to be the main focus of the neo-temperance movement; 25 percent of all alcohol control legislation in the states was on this issue. The main goal has been an increasingly lower blood alcohol level as the definition of drunken driving. In 1968, sixteen years before the passage of the Uniform Age Act, in most state the level was 0.15g/dl. By 2000, all the states were using a definition of at least .10 while nineteen states have the level as low as .08.[638]

Many, if not most, of the issues that temperance advocates promote concern the brewing industry more directly than the wine or distilled sprits industries. This reflects the historical dominance of beer in the alcoholic beverages sector. Brewers continue to focus primarily on tax relief; on public health issues they consistently portray themselves as willing participants in alcohol control poli-

---

636 Alcohol Epidemiology Program. *Alcohol Policies in the United States: Highlights from the 50 States.* Minneapolis: University of Minnesota, 2000 www.epi.umn.edu/alcohol (accessed November 10, 2006).
637 Ibid.; Chaloupka, "Economic Perspectives on Alcohol Taxation."
638 "Alcohol Policies in the United States."

cies. Recently, the brewing giant August A. Busch III, argued for returning the drinking age to eighteen.[639]

As much as taxes and alcohol control concern brewers, market share and economic growth are always the primary interests of any business. In 2000 the top three brewers were solidly entrenched with a lower tier of craft brewers but more change was on the horizon. The twenty-first century witnessed the concentration of brewing in the global market. In 2002 South African Brewing (SAB) purchased Miller from Phillip Morris. Philip Morris had recently changed its name to Altria to remove media focus on tobacco and wished to return to its core business of tobacco and food. The company still owns Kraft.[640] Miller had never achieved John Murphy's goal of overtaking Anheuser–Bush and remained in second place. John Murphy, who had played a critical role in vaulting Miller into the number two position, died in 2002.[641] SAB paid $5 million in cash and stock for a sixty-seven percent share of Miller brewing. South African Brewing began operation in 1895; it primary markets were in African, Asia, and Eastern Europe. The new company, SAB Miller, became the world's second largest brewer.[642]

In 2005, Coors merged with Molson. Coors was the third largest brewer in the United States with a distant eleven percent market share. Molson's was the second largest brewer in Canada behind Labatt, which the Belgium brewer Interbrew owned. The merger would not change either company's standing in their own country, but would create a larger international presence.[643] The battle for market share which had dominated the Untied States brewing industry for decades had now gone global.

In 2005 the list of the country's top ten brewers looked very different from 1980. The top three were Anheuser–Busch, Miller, and Coors. Only Anheuser–Busch remained a wholly American-owned brewery, a fact the company emphasized in television ads.[644] Pabst, on the strength of its ownership of many of the brands of the late twentieth century, was fourth. The remaining six were all breweries that had their origins in either the late nineteenth century or the late twentieth century. Yuengling was fifth and is the country's oldest brewery.[645]

639 "This Thud's for You," *St. Louis Post-Dispatch*, October 13, 2000, D14.

640 Stuart Elliot, "Advertising," *New York Times*, November 19, 2001, C13; Sherri Day, "Philip Morris Drops Beer to Concentrate Elsewhere," *New York Times*, May 31, 2002, C2.

641 "John A. Murphy, 72," *New York Times*, June 19, 2002, C15.

642 Suzanne Kapner, "South African Breweries Said To Be Near $5 Billion Miller Deal," *New York Times*, May 25, 2002, C2.

643 "Family Brew; Beer Mergers," *Economist (US)*, July 31, 2004.

644 Heather Timmons, "Busch Waves Red, White and Brew," *International Herald Tribune Business*, July 12, 2005.

645 Glaser, "Pre-1900 Regional Breweries."

Boston Beer is sixth, and City Brewery, which produces its beer in the original Heileman brewery in La Crosse, Wisconsin, is seventh. Employees of City Brewery, as well as former employees of Heileman, have ownership in the company. The home of Gottlieb and Johanna Heileman, the founders of Heileman Brewing, is the new company's headquarters.[646] Latrobe Brewing, brewers of Rolling Rock, was eighth. The brand is from 1939; InBev owned it until 2006 when Anheuser-Busch purchased the company. Anheuser brews the beer in New Jersey, not in Latrobe, Pennsylvania, the home of the brewery since 1893.[647] High Falls Brewing, the latest iteration of Genesee Brewing, was ninth and Sierra Nevada Brewing, one of the country's oldest craft breweries, was tenth. Paul Camussi and Ken Grossman started brewing in Chico, California in 1980.[648]

By 2006, there were over one thousand breweries in the United States. Craft brewers had experienced an economic downturn in the late 1990s but today it is the only segment of the beer industry experiencing growth. Young entrepreneurs, reaching back to the traditions of German brewers of the nineteenth century, started many of these breweries. Will the family pattern that Germans established hold true for these twenty-first century Americans? Sam Calagione, founder of Dogfish Head Brewery has examined these questions. "My son and daughter, Sammy and Grier, are five and three years old, so it will be awhile before I know if they truly want to continue in the family business."[649]

Although the family nature of brewing remains an open question what is sure is that the two features of the American brewing industry, massively large, multimillion dollar corporations at the top, and many small craft brewers at the bottom, will continue for a long time. In this way, the industry has come full circle to the point when Frederick Lauer sought to organize his fellow German brewers to promote beer as "cheap, common, wholesale and nutritious beverage for the masses of the people."[650]

---

646 City Brewery, http://www.citybrewery.com/ (accessed June 26, 2007).

647 Michael Cowden, "Latrobe says goodbye to Rolling Rock," *Associated Press*, July 28, 2006, boston.com business, http://www.boston.com/business/articles/2006/07/28/latrobe_says_goodbye_to_rolling_rock/?pl=MEWell_Pos1 (accessed June 26, 2007).

648 Erickson, *Star Spangled Beer*, 4; City Brewery, Rankings from "Top U.S. Commercial Brewers," *Modern Brewery Age*, http://www.breweryage.com/archives/winter.spring06/BreweryChart percent203-06. *pdf* (accessed June 26, 2007).

649 Calagione, *Brewing Up a Business*, 240.

650 USBA, *Proceedings Fourth Convention*, (New York), 9.

Conclusion

Can prohibition happen again? This is certainly a question that has animated the brewing industry for the nearly seventy-five years since Repeal. Brewers invariably reference the Eighteenth Amendment when they confront taxes or any of a variety of neo-temperance initiatives. Prohibition, in many ways, was the defining moment in the brewing industry's history. Federal taxation shaped the industry, and it continues to play that role. Although the brewing industry contributes relatively little to internal revenue in 2007, the economic benefits of having legal liquor production is the lynchpin of their arguments about any actual or perceived encroachments on their latitude to operate.

The history of the brewing industry's attempts to deal with both the federal government and prohibition movements links to the history of their organizations. In 1862, the United States Brewers Association provided an early and very modern way for the brewers to present a unified face to the government and American society. In turn, the story of the organizational life of the industry reflects the story of growth, competition, and consolidation that has marked the years since Repeal.

In the early twentieth-first century the battle between brewers, the federal government, and society over control and individual freedom is essentially at a stalemate. Both the federal government and the states heavily regulate the industry, yet no one questions its legitimacy. Does this mean it is not vulnerable to a more sustained attack such as the prohibition movement? The brewers only have to look to the tobacco industry for an answer. There have always been connections between the two industries, but they have not always shared the same

fate. Both tobacco and beer faced taxation in 1862 and organized their industries under the federal aegis. Through most of the nineteenth century and well
past Prohibition, tobacco did not suffer the same degree of public antipathy as
alcohol. Post-Repeal the relative fates of the two industries have switched, and
currently tobacco is under greater scrutiny and disapprobation than alcohol.
Nonetheless, despite the brewing industry's success and acceptance in the face
of tobacco misfortunes, the curtailment of smoking access can not be heartening
to the beer industry.

The tension between individual freedom to enjoy recreational behavior and
society's determination to limit the effect of such behavior appears to continue
unabated. The competitive atmosphere that has dominated the brewing industry
also appears unchanged in recent years. Although the industry is highly concentrated, the emergence of over one thousand craft brewers speaks to the ongoing
struggle over taste and market share.

For the past few years the brewing industry has lost domestic market share
to other alcoholic beverages; craft brewing is the only segment of the industry
that has experienced growth. Brewing as an economic activity in America is over
two hundred years old. What does the future hold? *Brewing Battles* presents the
story of what has happened and how we have arrived at this moment, so as to
better understand where we might be going. As a beer drinker, my hope is that
we will continue to have a rich variety of tastes and products from which to
choose. Cheers!

Acknowledgements

This book has its origins in the PhD I completed many years ago under the sponsorship of Eric Foner. Eric taught me how to be a good historian, and encouraged me to improve my writing and thinking. His own body of work set the standard for my achievements. He has always been an inspiration to me and remains so today.

Jack Blocker has been a pioneer in the field of alcohol and temperance history as well as an excellent colleague. He invited me to give my first scholarly paper, and together we, along with several other people, founded what is today the Alcohol and Drugs History Society. It has been my honor to know him for almost thirty years.

Another pioneer in the field of alcohol and temperance history is David Fahey. His unfailing energy and enthusiasm has helped the ADHS thrive for over twenty-five years. On a personal level he encouraged me to turn my research into a book for which I thank him.

The ADHS has been a wonderful presence in the field, increasing interest in scholarship about alcohol and other drugs by sponsoring conferences. The organization also publishes *The Social History of Alcohol and Drugs: An Interdisciplinary Journal*. As an independent scholar, the ability to have a forum to give papers and publish articles has been tremendously important to me.

A serious non-fiction writer cannot produce an adequate product without the help of libraries and librarians. I am very fortunate to live in Amherst, Massachusetts which has several colleges and a wonderful local library. The Jones

Library is over eighty-five years old and is everything a local library should be. The librarians have unfailing good humor and are more than willing to answer any and all questions. The library also provides excellent access to Internet databases and other libraries, which has been critically important to me since I had no institutional support in the writing of this book.

The reference librarians at the University of Massachusetts and Hampshire College have also been very helpful. In particular Ben Hood at UMASS and Dan Schnurr at Hampshire stood out.

As a writer, it is very useful to have other people read your work at every stage of the process. I was fortunate to be part of a writing group at a critical moment in my journey. My fellow members, Dan Drollette, Ruth Glasser, and Jan Whitaker all read my book proposal and gave excellent advice. Jan went the extra mile and also read several chapters. I cannot thank them enough.

Will Ryan is warm, funny, and a talented writer. It has been my privilege to have him read every chapter of this manuscript and provide me with detailed and insightful editing. I am solely responsible for the final work; his efforts have improved it tremendously.

Rosie Pearson, of Positive Proof, provided excellent copy editing and helped me to greatly improve the quality of the work.

Adding illustrations to this book turned out to be a bigger project than I anticipated. Both Norman Block, my uncle, and Carl Miller were very helpful.

Besides great libraries, my hometown is also in a state that is a center of craft brewing. My local bar, the Moan and Dove, sells many imported and craft beers; while my local package store, R&P, stocks similar products. Both these institutions make my life more enjoyable.

I have dedicated this book to the memory of my parents, Beatrice and Louis Mittelman. I know that they would share in my pride and happiness over this book. They were tremendously supportive of everything I ever did. I would not be the person I am today without their guidance and love. My family is the most important thing in the world to me. Louis has provided me with calm support and generous understanding as I labored to complete this project. He is also an excellent copy editor. Alan's critical eye and keen interest in the subject enabled me to build confidence in the work. They are both kind, intelligent people whom it is an honor to know and love.

Finally, my husband, Aaron Berman, has been my greatest ally and best friend for almost thirty years. He has always believed in every activity I have undertaken and provided me with unfailing support and encouragement at all times. I can not imagine my life without him. Thank you.

Works Cited

Government Documents

United States. Congress. *Congressional Globe.* 37th Cong., 2d sess. Washington: Blair & Rives, 1861-1862.

United States. Congress. *Congressional Record,* 56th Cong. 2d sess. Washington: Govt. Print. Off., 1901.

United States. Congress. *Congressional Record.* 51st Cong., 1st sess. Washington: Govt. Print. Off., 1890.

United States. Congress. Department of Commerce. Bureau of the Census. *Twelfth Census of the United States, 1900.* Washington: Govt. Print. Off., 1901.

United States. Congress, House, Committee on Ways and Means, *Extension of NIRA Hearings before the House Committee on Ways and Means,* 74 Cong., 1st sess. Washington: Govt. Print. Off ., 1935.

United States. Congress. House. *H. Report. 529,* Appendix C, 51st Cong., 1st sess., 1890.

United States. Congress. House. *Report of the Secretary of War,* H. Doc. 2, 56th Cong., 1st sess. Washington: Govt. Print. Off, 1899.

United States. Congress. Senate Subcommittee on the Judiciary. *Prohibiting Intoxicating Beverages.* Washington: Govt. Print. Off., 1919.

United States. Congress. Senate. Finance Committee. *Revenue Act of 1951 Hearings* 82nd Congress, Washington: Govt. Print. Off., 1951. (microfiche).

United States. Internal Revenue Service. *Annual Report of the Commissioner of Internal Revenue.* Washington: Govt. Print. Off., 1901, 1915, 1916, 1918, 1919.

United States. Office of Internal Revenue, *Decisions T.D.*, Washington: Govt. Print. Off., 1862.

United States. Senate. Committee on the Judiciary. *Brewing and Liquor Interests and German and Bolshevik Propaganda. Vol. 3 Sixty-Fifth Congress*, 3rd sess., Washington: Govt. Print. Off., 1919. (microform).

United States. Treasury Department. Records. Record Group 56. National Archives. Washington D.C.

United States. *United States Government Organization Manual, 1953-1954* Washington, D.C.: Division of the Federal Register, National Archives Establishment, 1953.

Proceedings and Reports

Anheuser-Busch Companies. *Annual Report.* St. Louis, Mo: Anheuser-Busch Companies, Inc.., 1951-1958.

Beer Institute, *Brewers Almanac 1996.* Washington D.C.: Beer Institute. 1996.

Lakins, N.E., Williams, G.D., Yi, H., and Smothers, B.A. Surveillance Report #66: *Apparent per Capita Alcohol Consumption: National, State, and Regional Trends, 1977–2002.* Bethesda, MD: National Institute on Alcohol Abuse and Alcoholism (NIAAA), 2004.

United States and David Ames Wells. Report of the United States Revenue Commission on Distilled Spirits as a Source of National Revenue. Washington: Treasury Department, 1866.

United States Brewers' Association. *Brewers' Almanac.* Washington, D.C.: United States Brewers Association, 1940, 1944, 1946, 1949-1976 (microfilm).

United States Brewers' Association. *Brewers Almanac* Washington, D.C: United States Brewers Association, 1980.

United States Brewers Association. *Proceedings of the Annual Conventions.* 1863-1900, 1909, New York.

United States Brewers Association. *Report of the Commissioners Appointed by the United States Brewers Association to the United States Revenue Commission on The Taxation and Manufacture of Malt Liquors in Great Britain and on The Continent of Europe.* Philadelphia: s.n.

United States Brewers Association. *Yearbook.* New York, 1914.

Newspapers and Periodicals

Beverage Industry, 1978-1987.

Brewer's Art, 1923-1932.

Modern Brewery 1933-1935.

Modern Brewer 1936-1940.

Modern Brewery Age 1940-2004.

New York Times. 1862-2007.

The New Voice. 1898-1900.

Poughkeepsie Eagle, Souvenir Edition, 1889.

Western Brewer. 1876-1900.

Books

Acker. David A. *Managing Brand Equity: Capitalizing on the Value of a Brand Name.* New York: Free Press, 1991.

Allen, Frederick Lewis. *Only Yesterday: An Informal History of the 1920s.* New York: Harper & Brothers, 1931.

American Industry and Manufacture in the 19th Century; a basic source collection vol. 6. Elmsford, N.Y.: Maxwell Reprint Co., 1971.

Anderson, Will. *The Breweries of Brooklyn: An Informal History of a Great Industry in a Great City.* New York: Anderson, 1976.

Arnold, John and Frank Perman. *History of the Brewing Industry and Brewing Science in America.* Chicago, 1933.

Baron, Stanley. *Brewed in America: A History of Beer and Ale in the United States.* Boston: Little, Brown and Company, 1962.

Beauchamp, Dan. *Beyond Alcoholism: Alcohol and Public Health Policy.* Philadelphia: Temple University Press, 1980.

Blocker, Jack S., David M. Fahey, and Ian R. Tyrrell. *Alcohol and Temperance in Modern History: An International Encyclopedia.* 2 vols. Santa Barbara, CA: ABC-CLIO, 2003.

Blocker, Jack S., ed., *Alcohol, Reform and Society: The Liquor Issue in Social Context,* Westport, CT: Greenwood Press, 1979.

Blocker, Jack S. *American Temperance Movements: Cycles of Reform. Social Movements Past and Present.* Boston: Twayne Publications, 1989.

Blocker, Jack S. *Retreat from Reform: The Prohibition Movement in the United States 1890 -1913.* Westport, CT: Greenwood Press, 1976.

Blum, John Morton. *V Was For Victory.* New York: Harcourt Brace Jovanovich, 1976.

Broesamle, John J. *William Gibbs McAdoo: A Passion for Change, 1863-1917.* Port Washington, NY: Kennikat Press, 1973.

Buenker, John D. *The Income Tax and the Progressive Era.* New York: Garland Pub., 1985.

Burnham, John C. *Bad Habits: Drinking, Smoking, Taking Drugs, Gambling, Sexual Misbehavior, and Swearing in American History.* New York: New York University Press, 1993.

Calagione, Sam. *Brewing Up a Business: Adventures in Entrepreneurship from the Founder of Dogfish Head Craft Brewery.* Hoboken, N.J.: John Wiley 2005.

Cherrington, Ernest, ed. *Standard Encyclopedia of the Alcohol Problem,* 6 vols. Westerville, OH: American Issue Pub. Co., 1924-1930.

Clark, Victor. *History of Manufactures in the United States.* 3 vols. New York: P. Smith, 1929.

Cochran, Thomas Childs. *The Pabst Brewing Company: The History of an American Business.* New York: New York Univ. Press, 1948.

Cosmas, Graham. *An Army for Empire: The United States Army in the Spanish American War.* Columbia, MO: University of Missouri Press, 1971.

Cross, Ira B. *A History of the Labor Movement in California.* Berkeley, CA: University of California Press, 1935.

Curry, Leonard P. *Blueprint for Modern America: Non-Military Legislation of the First Civil War Congress.* Nashville: Vanderbilt University Press, 1968.

Cyclopaedia of Temperance and Prohibition. New York, 1891.

Daniels. Bruce C. *The Connecticut Town: Growth and Development, 1635-1790.* Middletown, CT: Wesleyan University Press, 1979.

Davis, Kenneth S. *FDR, The New Deal Years 1933-193.* New York: Random House, 1986.

Dearing, Charles Lee, et al. *The ABC of the NRA.* Washington, D.C.: The Brookings Institution, 1934.

Deford, Frank. *Lite Reading: The Lite Beer From Miller Commercial Scrapbook.* New York: Penguin Books, 1984.

Dewey, Davis. *Financial History of the United States.* New York: Longmans, Green, and Co., 1903.

Donald, David ed. *Inside Lincoln's Cabinet: The Civil War Diaries of Salmon P. Chase.* New York, 1954.

Doris, Lillian *The American Way in Taxation.* Englewood Cliffs, N.J.: Prentice-Hall, 1963.

Downard, William L. *Dictionary of the History of the American Brewing and Distilling Industries.* Westport, CT: Greenwood Press, 1980.

Duis, Perry. *The Saloon: Public Drinking in Chicago and Boston, 1880-1920*. Urbana: University of Illinois Press, 1983.

Dunar, Andrew J. *The Truman Scandals and the Politics of Morality*. Columbia, MO: University of Missouri Press, 1984.

Engs, Ruth Clifford. *Clean Living Movements*. Westport, CT: Praeger, 2000.

Erickson, Jack. *Star Spangled Beer*. Reston, VA: RedBrick Press, 1987.

Estee, Charles. *The Excise Tax Law*. New York: Fitch, Estee, 1863.

Ferleger, Herbert. *David A. Wells and the Revenue System 1865-1870*. New York, 1942.

Foner, Eric. *Free Soil, Free Labor, Free Men: The Ideology of the Republican Party before the Civil War*. New York: Oxford University Press, 1995.

Foner, Eric and John A. Garraty. *The Reader's Companion to American History* Boston: Houghton Mifflin, 1991.

Foner, Jack. *The United States Soldier Between Two Wars Army Life and Reforms, 1865-1898*. New York: Humanities Press, 1970.

Forsythe, Dall W. *Taxation and Political Change in the Young Nation 1781-1833*. New York: Columbia University Press, 1977.

Gallagher, Mark and Neil Gallagher, *Baseball's Great Dynasties, The Yankees*. New York: Gallery Books, 1990.

Gates, Paul. *The Farmer's Age: Agriculture, 1815-1860*. New York: Harper & Row, 1960.

Gilbert, Charles. *American Financing of World War One*. Westport, CT: Greenwood Press, 1970.

Goodwin, Doris Kearns. *No Ordinary Time: Franklin and Eleanor Roosevelt: The Home Front in World War* II. New York: Simon and Schuster, 1994.

Grant, James. *John Adams, Party of One*. New York: Farrar, Strauss and Giroux, 2005.

Gurda, John. *Miller Time: A History of Miller Brewing Company 1855-2005*. Milwaukee, WI: Miller Brewing Company, 2005.

Hamm, Richard F. *Shaping the 18th Amendment: Temperance Reform, Legal Culture, and the Polity, 1880-1920*. Chapel Hill: University of North Carolina Press, 1995

Hammond, Bray. *Sovereignty and an Empty Purse: Banks and Politics in the Civil War*. Princeton: Princeton University Press, 1970.

Handlin, Oscar. *Al Smith and his America*. Boston: Little, Brown, 1958.

Hernon Peter and Terry Ganey. *Under The Influence: The Unauthorized Story of the Anheuser–Busch Dynasty*. New York: Simon & Schuster, 1991.

Hu, Tun-Yuan. *The Liquor Tax in the United States 1791–1947*. New York: Graduate School of Business, Columbia University, 1950.

Irwin, Benjamin H. *Samuel Adams, Son of Liberty, Father of Revolution*. New York: Oxford University Press, USA, 2002.

Jackson, Michael. *Ultimate Beer*. New York: DK Publishing, 1998.

Jellison, Charles A. *Fessenden of Maine: Civil War Senator*. Syracuse, N.Y: Syracuse University Press, 1962.

John, Tim. *The Miller Beer Barons*. Oregon, WI: Badger Books, 2005.

Kerr, K. Austin. *Organized for Prohibition, A New History of The Anti-Saloon League*. New Haven: Yale University Press, 1985.

Klein, Bob. *The Beer Lover's Rating Guide*. NewYork: Workman Publishing, 1995.

Krout, John Allen. *The Origins of Prohibition*. New York: A.A. Knopf, 1925.

Kyvig, David E. *Repealing National Prohibition*. Chicago: University of Chicago Press, 1979.

Leisy, Bruce R. *A History of the Leisy Brewing Companies*. North Newton, Kan: Mennonite Press, 1975.

Lindberg, Richard C. *To Serve and Collect: Chicago Politics and Police Corruption from the Lager Beer Riot to the Summerdale Scandal*. New York: Praeger, 1991.

Lovelace, Maud Hart. *Betsy in Spite of Herself*. New York: Crowell, 1946.

Mauldin, Bill. *Up Front*. New York: Norton, 1995.

McGowan, Richard. *Government Regulation of the Alcohol Industry: The Search for Revenue and the Common Good*. Westport, Ct., 1997.

Merrill, Dennis ed., *Documentary History of the Truman Presidency*, University Publishers of America, 2000, vol. 28.

Miller, Wilbur. R. *Revenuers and Moonshiners, Enforcing Federal Liquor Law in the Mountain South, 1865-1900*. Chapel Hill: University of North Carolina Press, 1991.

Morris, James. *Conflict Within the AFL, A Study of Craft Versus Industrial Unionism, 1901–1938*. Ithaca, N.Y.: Cornell University Press, 1958.

Murdock, Catherine Gilbert. *Domesticating Drink: Women, Men and Alcohol in America*. Baltimore: Johns Hopkins University Press, 1998.

The National Cyclopaedia of American Biography. New York: J.T. White, 1892.

O'Connor, Richard. *The First Hurrah, A Biography of Alfred E. Smith*. New York: Putnam, 1970.

One Hundred Years Of Brewing. Chicago and New York: Rich & Co., 1903.

Papazian, Charlie. *The Complete Joy of Homebrewing.* 3rd ed. New York: Harper Collins, 2003.

Pederson, Jay P. *International Directory of Company Histories.* Vol. 34. Detroit, MI: St. James Press, 2000.

Peek, George N., and Samuel Crowther. *Why Quit Our Own.* New York: D. Van Nostrand Co, 1936.

Pegram, Thomas R. *Battling Demon Rum: The Struggle for a Dry America, 1800-1933.* Chicago: Ivan R. Dee, 1998.

Pemberton, William. *Bureaucratic Politics: Executive Reorganization during the Truman Administration.* Columbia, MO: University of Missouri Press, 1979.

Perkins, Van L. *Crisis in Agriculture: The Agricultural Adjustment Administration and the New Deal, 1993.* Berkeley: University of California Press, 1969.

Polenberg, Richard. *War and Society: The United States, 1941-1945.* New York: J.B. Lippincott Company, 1972.

Porter, Glenn. *The Rise of Big Business, 1860-1910.* Arlington Heights, IL: AHM Pub. Corp., 1973.

Powers, Madelon. *Faces Along the Bar: Lore and Order in the Workingman's Saloon, 1870-1920. Historical studies of urban America.* Chicago: The University of Chicago Press, 1998.

Root, Waverly and Richard de Rochemont. *Eating in America, A History.* New York: William Morrow and Company, 1976.

Rorabaugh, William J. *The Alcoholic Republic.* New York: Oxford University Press, USA, 1979.

Rosenzweig, Roy. *Eight Hours for What We Will: Workers and Leisure in an Industrial City, 1870-1920.* Cambridge: Cambridge University Press, 1983

Rumbarger, John J. *Profits, Power, and Prohibition, Alcohol Reform and the Industrializing of America, 1880-1930.* Albany, 1989.

Salinger, Sharon V. *Taverns and Drinking in Early America.* Baltimore: Johns Hopkins University Press, 2002.

Samuel, Child, *Every man his own brewer, a small treatise, explaining the art and mystery of brewing porter, ale, and table-beer; recommending and proving the ease and possibility of every man's brewing his own porter, ale, and beer, in any quantity. From one peck to an hundred bushels of malt. : Calculated to reduce the expence of a family, and lessen the destructive practice of public-house tippling, by exposing the deception in brewing.* Philadelphia: T. Condie, 1796, microform, Early American Imprints, 1st series, no. 30189.

Scheter, Barnet. *The Devil's Own Work The Civil War Riots and the Fight to Reconstruct America.* New York: Walker & Co., 2005.

Schlereth, Thomas J. *Victorian America: transformations in Everyday Life 1876-1915*. New York: Harper Collins, 1991.

Schlesinger, Arthur M. Jr., ed. *The Almanac of American History.* (New York: G. Putnam's Sons, 1983.

Schlesinger, Arthur M. Jr. *The Age of Roosevelt: The Coming of the New Deal.* Boston: Houghton Mifflin, 1965.

Schlüter, Hermann. *The Brewing Industry and the Brewery Workers' Movement in America.* New York: B. Franklin, 1970.

Schmeckbier, Laurence F. and Francis X. A. Eble, *The Bureau of Internal Revenue; its history, activities and organization*. Baltimore: The Johns Hopkins Press, 1923.

Skilnik, Bob. *Beer: A History of Brewing in Chicago.* Fort Lee, N.J.: Barricade Books, 2006.

Skowronek, Stephen. *Building A New American State, The Expansion of National Administrative Capacities, 1877 1920*. New York: Cambridge University Press, 1982.

Smith, Frederick H. *Caribbean Rum, A Social and Economic History.* Gainesville, FL: University Press of Florida, 2005.

Smith, Gregg. *Beer in America The Early Years 1587–1840.* Boulder, Colorado, 1998.

Syrett, Harold C., ed., The *Papers of Alexander Hamilton.* vol. 7. New York, Columbia University Press, 1961-1987.

Thomann, Gallus. *Documentary History of the United States Brewing Association.* New York: United States Brewers Association. 2 vols. 1896-1898.

Thompson, Peter. *Rum, Punch and Revolution Taverngoing and Public Life in Eighteenth-Century Philadelphia.* Philadelphia: University of Pennsylvania Press, 1999.

Timberlake, James H. *Prohibition and the Progressive Movement.* Cambridge: Harvard University Press, 1963.

Tremblay Victor J. and Carol Horton Tremblay. *The United States Brewing Industry.* Cambridge, MA: MIT Press, 2005.

Tyrrell, Ian R. *Sobering Up: From Temperance to Prohibition in Antebellum America, 1800–1860.* Westport, CT: Greenwood Press, 1979.

U.S. Department, Internal Revenue Service, *History of the Internal Revenue Service 1791-1929, prepared under the direction of the Commissioner of Internal Revenue,* Washington, D.C.: U. S. Government Printing Office, 1930.

United States Brewers Association, *Report of the Commissioners Appointed by the United States Brewers Association to the United States Revenue Commission on the Taxation and Manufacture of Malt Liquors in Great Britain and on The Continent of Europe.* Philadelphia, 1866.

United States Internal Revenue Service. *History of the Internal Revenue Service.* Washington, 1930.

United States Treasury Department. *The United States Treasury.* Washington, D.C: Treasury Department, Office of Information, 1961.

Van Munching, Philip. *Beer Blast: The Inside Story of the Brewing Industry's Bizarre Battles For Your Money.* New York: Times Business, 1997.

Wells, Ken. *Travels with Barley: A Journey Through Beer Culture in America.* New York: Free Press, 2004.

Witte, John F. *The Politics and Development of the Federal Income Tax.* Madison, WI: University of Wisconsin Press. 1985.

Wittner, Lawrence S. *Cold War America; From Hiroshima to Watergate.* New York: Praeger, 1974.

Yenne, Bill. *The American Brewery.* St. Paul, MN: MBI, 2003.

Articles

DeJong, William, Charles K. Atkin, and Lawrence Wallack. "A Critical Analysis of 'Moderation': Advertising Sponsored by the Beer Industry: Are "Responsible Drinking" Commercials Done Responsibly?" *The Milbank Quarterly* 70, no. 4. (1992): 661-678.

Fox, Hugh F. "The Prosperity of the Brewing Industry." *The Annals of the American Academy of Political and Social Science* 34,(November, 1909): 61-68.

Fox, "The Saloon Problem." *The Annals of the American Academy of Political and Social Science* 32, no. 3 (November 1908):61-68.

Grant, Ernest A. "The Liquor Traffic before the Eighteenth Amendment." *Annals of the American Academy of Political and Social Science,* 163, (September, 1932): 1-9.

Gordon, Michael A. "The Labor Boycott in New York City, 1880-1886." *Labor History* 16 (Spring 1975): 194-213.

Hugh, Jack and Clayton A. Coppin. "Wiley and the Whiskey Industry: Strategic Behavior in the Passage of the Pure Food Act." *Business History Review* 62 (Summer 1988): 286-309.

Kingsdale, Jon. "The Poor Men's Club: Social Functions of the Urban Working-Class Saloon." *American* Quarterly vol. 25, no. 4 (October 1973): 472-489.

Littlefield, Nathan. "Holiday cheer: the world's most bibulous countries," *The Atlantic Monthly* 294.5 (Dec 2004): 57.

Meacham, Sarah Hand. "They Will Be Adjudged by Their Drink, What Kinde of Housewives They Are: Gender, Technology, and Household Cidering in England and the Chesapeake, 1690 to 1760." *Virginia Magazine of History & Biography* 111, no. 2.(2003): 171-151.

McGahan, A. M. "The Emergence of the National Brewing Oligopoly: Competition in the American Market, 1933-1958." *The Business History Review*, vol. 65, No. 2 (Summer 1991): 229-284.

McWilliams, James. "Brewing Beer in Massachusetts Bay, 1640-1690." *The New England Quarterly* 71, no. 4 (December 1998): 543-564.

Melendy, Royal L. "The Saloon in Chicago." The *American Journal of Sociology*, 6, no. 3 (November, 1900): 289-306.

Mittelman, Amy. "Who Will Pay the Tax." *Social History of Alcohol Review* no. 25 (Spring 1992): 28-38.

Mittelman, Amy. "'A Conflict of Interest': The United Brewery Workmen in the Nineteenth Century." *Contemporary Drug Problems* (Winter 1985): 511-541.

Rothbart, Ron. "The Ethnic Saloon as a Function of the Immigrant Experience." *Internal Migration Review* 27, no. 2 (Summer 1993): 332-358.

Stack Martin. "Local and Regional Breweries in America's Brewing Industry, 1865 to 1920." *The Business History Review* vol. 74, no. 3. (Autumn 2000): 435-463.

Wilkes Paul. "Harry John Was Not Your Average American Catholic." *National Catholic Reporter* 17 (September 1993): 13-21.

Pamphlets, Dissertations, and Unpublished Materials

Alcohol Epidemiology Program. *Alcohol policies in the United States: Highlights from the 50 states.* Minneapolis: University of Minnesota, 2000.

Benson, Ronald Morris. "American Workers and Temperance Reform, 1866-1933" Ph.D. diss., Notre Dame, 1974).

Brown, Thomas H. "George Sewall Boutwell: Public Servant 1818-1905" Ph.D. diss., New York University, 1979.

Brundage, David. "The Producing Classes and the Saloon: Denver in the 1880s." Unpublished manuscript, 1979.

Chaloupka, Frank. "Economic Perspectives on Alcohol Taxation." NIAAA-MADD Alcohol Research Symposium, Sept. 15, 1999, Albuquerque, New Mexico.

Drescher, Nuala McGann. "The Opposition to Prohibition, 1900-1919: A Social and Institutional Study." Ph.D. diss., University of Delaware, 1964.

Engels to H Schülter In New York, London, January 11, 1890, Engels to Schülter (Ex-cerpt), London, May 15, 1885, "Letters of Marx and Engels." Marx & Engels Internet Archive.

Herrewig, Dave. "Fred C. Miller," unpub. manuscript in author's possession.

Holland, Lee W. "The Evolution of the Brewers Association of America." Colorado: Brewers Association of America, 1994.

International Union of United Brewery, Flour, Cereal, Soft Drink, and Distillery Workers of America. *Union with a Heart: 75 Years of a Great Union, 1886-1961.* Cincinnati, Ohio: The Union, 1961.

LaForge, Robert. "Misplaced Priorities: A History of Federal Alcohol Regulation and Public Health Policy." Sc. D. diss., Johns Hopkins University, 1987.

Madd: Mothers Against Drunk Driving, VHS. Directed by William A. Graham. Universal Studios, 1983.

McCook, James Papers., (microfilm). "Extracts from SemiAnnual Reports of Post Commanders of the Canteen System, Dec. 31, 1890,." roll 9, Series IX, Folder B. Hartford, CT: Antiquarian and Landmarks Society, Inc.

Mittelman, Amy. "The Politics of Alcohol Production: The Liquor Industry and the Federal Government, 1862–1900." Ph.D. diss., Columbia University, 1986.

Pennock, Pamela. "Public Health Morality and Commercial Free Expression: Efforts to Control Cigarette and Alcohol Marketing 1950s–1980s." Ph.D. diss., Ohio State University, 2002.

Schaefer, F. & M. Brewing Company, "To commemorate our 100th year: the F. & M. Schaefer brewing co.: America's oldest lager beer." Brooklyn, N.Y., The Company, 1942.

Schlüter, Hermann Papers, International Institute of Social History, Online.

Shea, Donald. Interview by author, Washington D.C., September 13, 2005.

Walding, Lynn. "Alcohol Marketing 2005." (powerpoint presentation) Iowa Alcohol Beverages Division.

INDEX